The Reinhold
Book of Needlecraft

Jutta Lammèr

The Reinhold Book of Needlecraft

Embroidery, crochet,
knitting, weaving, macramé,
appliqué, patchwork and
many other handicraft
techniques, old and new

289 drawings by Ellen-Ingrid Baumanns and others

418 photographs in black-and-white and colour
by Manfred Bauer and Barbara Schulten

VNR VAN NOSTRAND REINHOLD COMPANY
NEW YORK CINCINNATI TORONTO LONDON MELBOURNE

Published in 1973 by Van Nostrand Reinhold
Company, a division of Litton Educational Pub-
lishing Inc., 450 West 33rd Street, New York,
N.Y. 10001

© Otto Maier Verlag, Ravensburg 1971
This translation © Ward Lock Limited, London
1973

Library of Congress Catalog Card Number
73 — 1630
ISBN 0 442-24671-4

Text filmset in England by Servis Filmsetting
Limited, Manchester
Printed in the United States of America

16   15   14   13   12   11   10   9   8   7   6   5   4   3

Contents

Embroidery

For American threads equivalent to those specified in this chapter, see the table on page 292

The three types of embroidery described in this book are: embroidery based on counted fabric threads, embroidery based on the fabric pattern and Free-style embroidery.

Counted Thread embroidery is the classical embroidery worked by counting the threads of the fabric and working each stitch over an exact number of threads. Evenweave fabric or canvas must be used.

Embroidery based on the fabric pattern is worked by following the existing woven or printed pattern on the fabric (e.g. squares, stripes or dots) which is complemented by decorative stitches.

Free-style embroidery is worked following the design which is tranferred or traced on to the fabric.

Almost all fabrics can be embroidered if the thread, needle and fabric are correctly matched. The table on page 53 gives a list of suitable embroidery materials as well as the needle sizes for different embroidery fabrics.

Counted Thread embroidery is worked with a tapestry needle with a rounded point which passes easily through the holes of the fabric without forcing the threads apart. A sharp, pointed crewel needle is used for Free-style embroidery. It is advisable to use embroidery rings when working with lightweight fabric in order to keep the fabric taut and enable the stitches to be worked at an even tension.

Commencing embroidery: terminal knots should not be used on embroidery thread as they would show through on the right side when the article is pressed. Where fabric is completely covered with stitches (filling embroidery) a short length of thread is darned through the threads of the fabric and smoothly stitched over, thus becoming invisible. To commence a design which consists of motifs or outlines push the needle through the fabric on the right side about 1 in. (2·5 cm) from starting point, leaving a short end of thread on the right side. When the embroidery has been completed, draw loose ends through to the wrong side of the fabric and darn neatly into the embroidery.

Counted Thread embroidery

Counted Thread embroidery is worked on the crossing of the fabric threads (a square woven weft and warp pattern). The different colours of the design are identified by different signs. The meaning of these signs is explained in each counted design. Should one wish to design one's own counted design, squared or graph paper is used. Even though one is bound to follow the rectangular form of the fabric weave it is possible to embroider

9

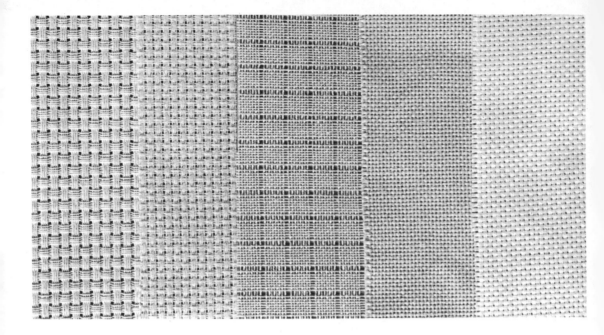

motifs with any outline, as shown by the photographs in this chapter. The stitches used for embroidery governed by the fabric weave are: Cross stitch, Canvas stitch (in many variations), Kelim stitch, Florentine stitch, Satin stitch, Hardanger embroidery,

Suitable fabrics for Counted Thread embroidery. Canvas fabrics for Cross stitch and canvas work on page 19

Hemstitch, Drawn Thread embroidery, as well as Filet and Tulle embroidery. The above photograph shows a selection of fabrics suitable for Counted Thread embroidery.

Cross stitch

Bring the needle out at the lower left-hand side, insert three threads up and three threads to the right, bring out three threads down thus forming a half cross; continue in this way to the end of the row – Diagram *a* (1). Working from left to right complete the other half of the cross – Diagram *a* (2). Cross stitch may be worked from left to right as shown or from right to left. It is important that the upper half of all the stitches lie in

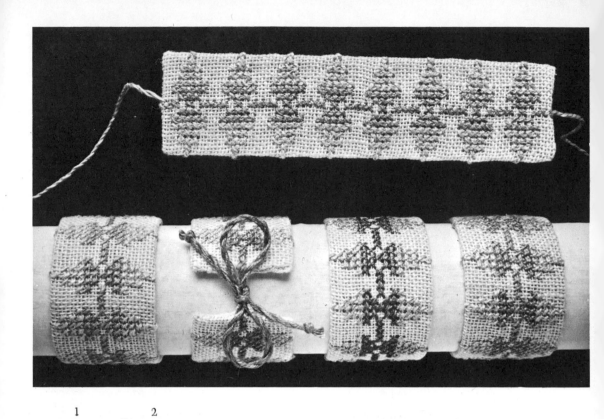

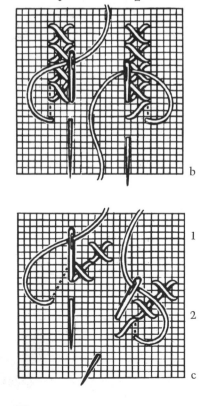

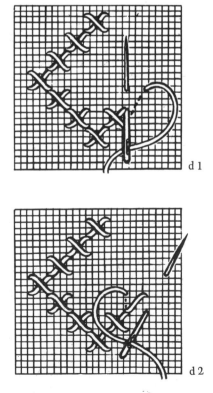

the same direction. Cross stitch may be worked in horizontal rows – Diagram *a* (3); vertically, Diagram *b* or diagonally, Diagrams *c* and *d*. When the counted design has a border which must be continued around a

Those not familiar with Counted Thread embroidery will find pre-printed canvas (below) easy to use. This canvas is sold in handicraft shops. The simple counted pattern of the napkin ring (on the left) is easier to follow than the peasant motif (below right)

corner (e.g. on a tablecloth) a frameless pocket mirror can be used to follow the design in its proper sequence. The mirror is placed at an angle on the border (Diagram *e*) so that a right-angle is reflected. The mirror is then pushed slowly along the border until a neat join is formed. This position is marked with pins along the lower edge of the mirror, then the embroidery is continued until the border becomes straight and follows the counted pattern. The mirror can also be placed on the design and a diagonal line drawn. Anyone who does not feel confident enough can draw the corner on squared paper and use in the same way as a diagram.

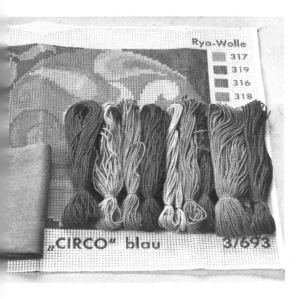

Diagram for embroidering the rug (above).
On the right: motif enlarged (Coats Anchor
Tapisserie Wool on canvas)

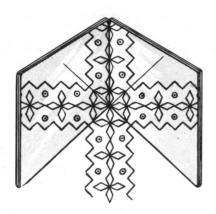

f

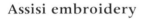

left unworked and the surrounding areas filled with Cross stitch. The illustration at the foot of the page shows a Cross stitch design (Diagram *a*) and the same design in Assisi embroidery (Diagram *b*).

Cross stitch cushion using Assisi technique: the motif appears light, the background dark. Petit point work on silk gauze: 52 stitches to 1 in. (2·5 cm) (photographs, page 17, above and below)

To widen the border the mirror is placed on one of the lengthwise sides; to form a motif, two pocket mirrors are set up as shown in Diagram *f*. Those who are not familiar with Cross stitch work can work at first on pre-printed canvas (photograph, page 13) in order to concentrate completely on the embroidery technique. This canvas is sold in handicraft shops.

Assisi embroidery

A simple and attractive Italian embroidery worked mainly in Cross stitch. Unlike ordinary Cross stitch embroidery, the design is

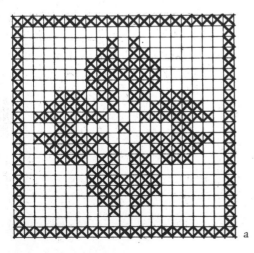

a

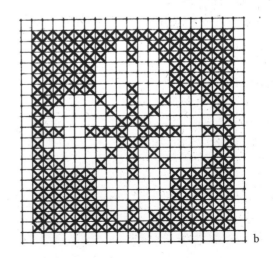

b

Canvas embroidery

Colour-printed canvas is recommended for the beginner as this allows complete concentration on the stitch techniques. The more advanced embroiderer can use either a trammé design or the classical counted design. The trammé design is a canvas on which long threads of the appropriate colours fill in the design. These will be covered by the stitches. Trammé designs are expensive since the pre-working of the threads, which can also be done by the embroiderer, is very time-consuming. Working to a trammé design is, however, easier than to a counted design.

In a counted design the various colours of the embroidery are identified by different signs which correspond to the sign key. The large group of canvas stitches includes: Tent stitch (*petit point* and *gros point*), Half Cross stitch, vertical stitch and ribbing stitch. The Tent stitch and the Half Cross stitch are most widely used. The Tent stitch

17

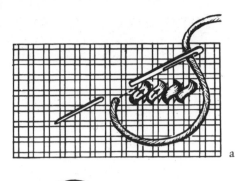

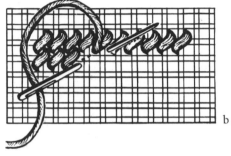

a

b

is worked over one crossing of canvas threads (in the case of double thread canvas, over one double crossing) horizontally in forward and return rows (Diagrams *a* and *b*). In Half Cross stitch commence at the right-hand edge of a coloured area; the thread is laid on the decorative side to the left, and this thread is covered from left to right so that each stitch encloses the laid thread and one crossing of canvas threads (or one double crossing in the case of double thread canvas). At the end of the row the thread is again laid over the fabric and stitched over from left to right (Diagrams *c* and *d*, page 20). All threads can be laid first and worked as for Tent stitch in forward and return rows.

Tent stitch embroidery is flatter then embroidery in Half Cross stitch which appears more solid owing to the laid threads. The straight (vertical) Gobelin stitch, like the Half Cross stitch, is worked over a laid thread; however, two stitches side by side must be made for each sign in the chart.

Canvas embroideries are worked on several types and weights of canvas, e.g. single

Tent stitch embroidery (above left); Half Cross stitch work (right); above: small pictures; below: spectacle case

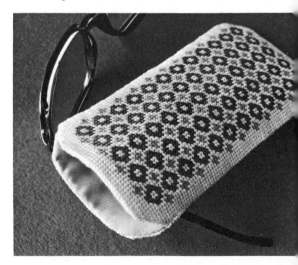

18

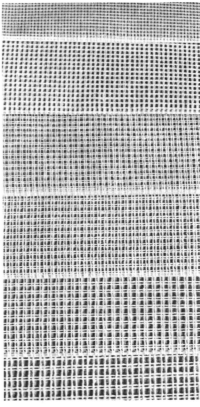

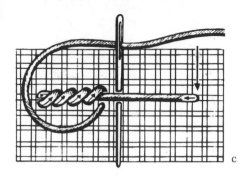

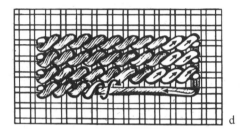

c

d

number of threads to 1 in. (2·5 cm) determines the size of the stitch; Kelim embroidery can also be worked on a jute fabric, depending on the purpose for which the embroidered item will be used (wall tapestry, table runner, foot or chair cushion, small mat cover). The work is carried out with tapisserie wool to a counted pattern with different signs identifying the individual colours. Regretfully there are no longer many counted patterns available for Kelim work since this technique is somewhat overshadowed by canvas and Cross stitch work. If no special counted pattern is available it is then possible to work to a canvas, Cross stitch or carpet knotting pattern. For each square of the counted pattern two stitches must be made in opposite directions (together they form a V). Kelim stitches are made in horizontal as well as in vertical and diagonal rows. The herringbone pattern stitches contact each other so that the completed surface has a zig-zag pattern (see below). One stitch spans two squares of the fabric in length and one fabric square in width. The gaps in the lower and upper edge resulting from the zig-zag pattern are filled by Half Cross stitches in the direction of the openings.

thread, double thread, coarse and fine. *Petit point* is worked with Clark's Anchor Stranded Cotton. Chair covers, cushions and bags are made on a stronger canvas. The embroidery is worked in Coats Anchor Tapisserie wool. For comparable U.S. embroidery and other yarns see pages 291–2. The photograph on page 17 shows an example of *petit point* embroidery worked on bolting silk with approximately 52 threads to 1 in. (2·5 cm). This particular fabric is very difficult to obtain outside Austria; however, *petit point* can be worked on other fine evenweave fabrics. Note: the number of threads to 1 in. (2·5 cm) governs the size of the design, therefore the greater the number of threads the smaller the design. Heavy canvas embroidery is worked on Sudan canvas (photograph on page 201), which is sold with woven-in squared pattern. Sudan canvas – obtainable from 26 in. to 50 in. (65 to 130 cm) wide – is embroidered with Sudan wool.

Kelim

Kelim embroidery can be stitched, like canvas embroidery, on canvas in which the

c   d

In Kelim work the outlines are stitched first, especially in the case of patterns with large areas. Diagram *a* shows the embroidery with the diagonal stitches pointing to the right and to the left. The change from the horizontal to vertical rows is shown in Diagram *b*; Diagrams *c* and *d* show the embroidery work in ascending and descending rows.

Florentine (Bargello) embroidery

Florentine embroidery or Bargello – like canvas and Kelim – is a Counted Thread embroidery which fills an area. It is worked vertically on canvas over a varying number of canvas threads; the stitches can be long or short depending on the design or may be a mixture of both. These stitches or groups of stitches are not arranged in rows but are staggered and always meet, which, in addition to the colouring of the pattern, gives a very pleasing effect. The point of exit or insertion of a completed stitch is also the point of insertion of the stitch above or below. Florentine embroidery is worked to a simple line pattern (see drawing, page 22 and the photograph below) as in the case of Satin stitch embroidery (page 23). This involves a limitation in the formation of the pattern which at the same time is the very essence of this embroidery technique; only ornamental patterns are possible, and no figures. The work is carried out with Coats Anchor Tapisserie wool on canvas. The correct relationship between the embroidery

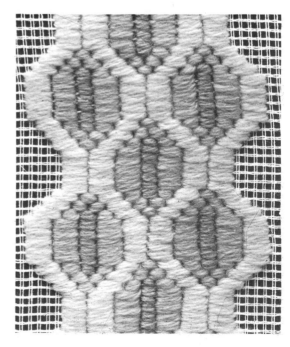

Florentine embroidery – also called Bargello – a surface-filling embroidery worked with wool on a canvas background (photographs, page 22 centre, left and right)

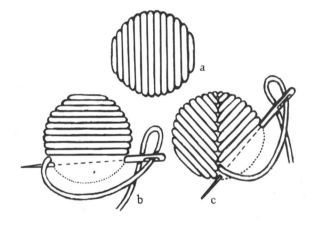

canvas and the embroidery thread is important (lower photographs, page 22). If a thread is used which is too thin, the canvas will not be completely covered; if the thread is too thick the stitches will be crowded, giving an untidy impression. It is recommended to use Coats Anchor Tapisserie wool, on single thread canvas, 18 threads to 1 in. (2·5 cm), or double thread canvas, 10 holes to 1 in. (2·5 cm).

Satin stitch and Laid stitch

Satin stitch is a decorative stitch which can be used for a motif as well as for filling areas. In Satin stitch work the embroidery needle runs once on the front and once on the back of the embroidery fabric with the result that the work has almost the same appearance on both sides. Satin stitch can be worked vertically, horizontally, straight or at an

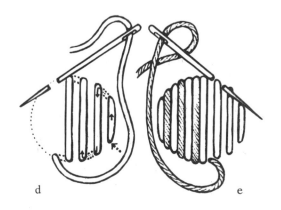

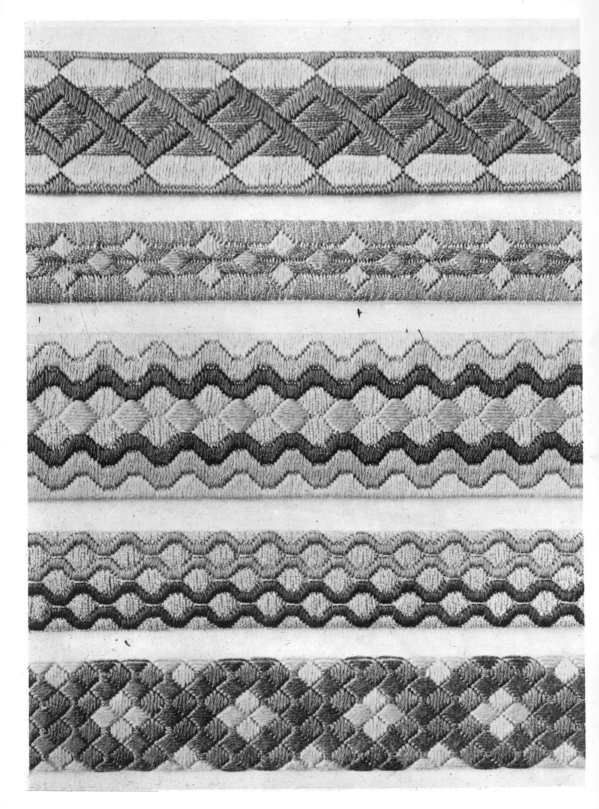

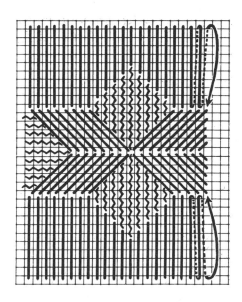

angle (Diagrams *a, b, c,* page 23) and it can be used for Counted Thread work as well as for free-style embroidery (without considering the threads of the fabric). It is seen from this that Satin stitch can be used for almost all materials. Satin stitch in Counted Thread embroidery will give a neater pattern than when freely worked. It is worked to line patterns as shown in the diagrams on pages 25 to 27. The patterned trimmings and samples were worked with Clark's Anchor

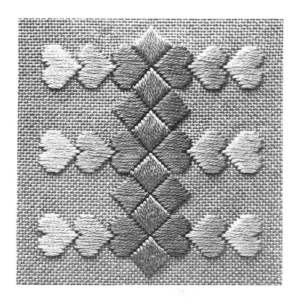

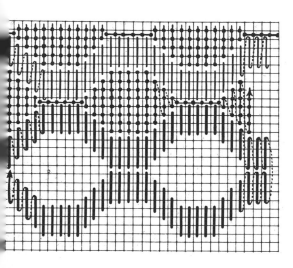

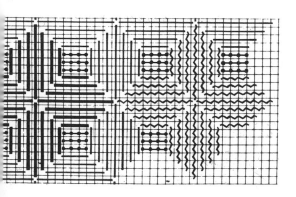

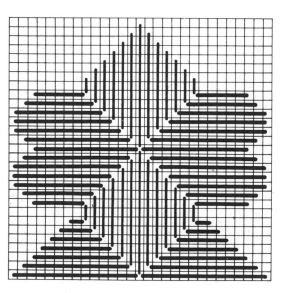

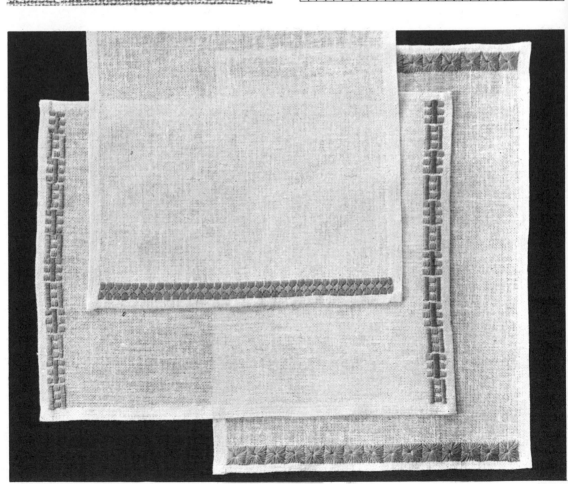

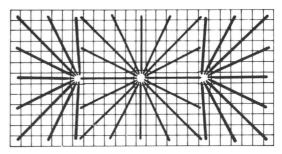

Stranded Cotton on evenweave linen, 21 threads to 1 in. (2·5 cm).

Laid stitch is related to Satin stitch owing to the similar effect. This stitch is worked forward and backward. On forward working the thread is taken from one outline to another. At each outline the needle covers two fabric threads (Diagram *d*). On return exactly the same method is used except that the gaps between the earlier stitches (Diagram *e*) are now covered. This is illustrated in the diagrams on page 23. The Laid stitches can also be worked by spacing as shown in the photograph, below left.

Hardanger embroidery

The characteristic feature of Hardanger embroidery is the combination of the Satin stitch blocks and open work patterns. The work is carried out on evenweave linen with 29 fabric threads to 1 in. (2·5 cm). The embroidery is worked with Clark's Anchor Pearl Cotton, No. 5 for the blocks, No. 8 for the remainder of the embroidery. Originally the Hardanger embroidery was white on white, but contrasting colours of fabric and embroidery thread are now widely used and give a pleasing effect. The line patterns below show three classical Satin stitch blocks. The Satin stitch blocks are worked before the fabric threads are cut. The fabric threads within the blocks are then cut and withdrawn. The remaining loose threads – in some cases four threads – are overcast alternately from each side. The work is carried out at right-angles until all the loose threads

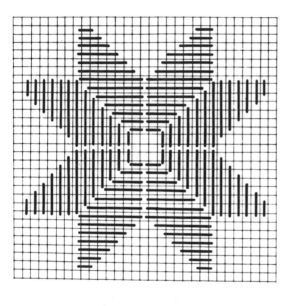

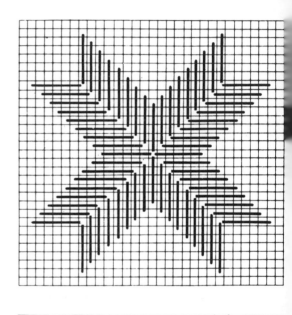

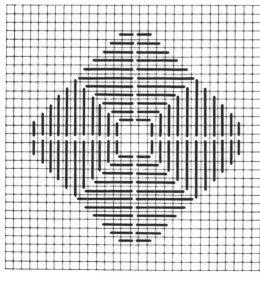

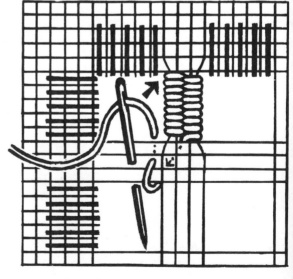

arc enclosed by needleweaving. The openings between the bars can be worked with additional filling stitches if desired.

Hemstitching

Hemstitch has many uses in addition to forming a neat finish to a hem. It can be used as a decorative stitch over the loose threads which are left after some of the warp and weft threads have been withdrawn from the fabric. Any fabric which is not too fine, such as evenweave linen, that is, fabrics in which the warp and weft threads have the same spacing, can be used for hemstitching.

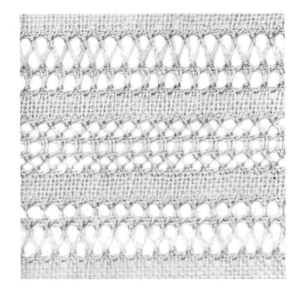

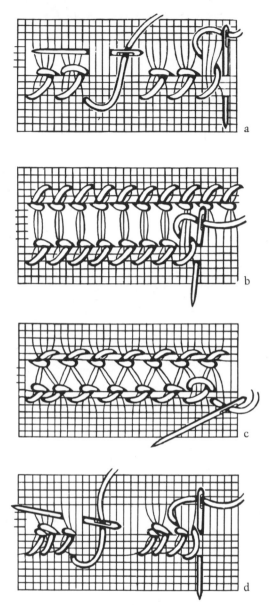

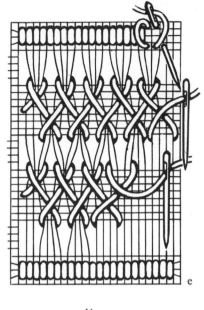

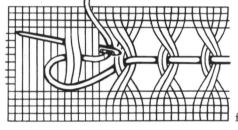

threads can be darned in to the wrong side of the fabric. The diagrams on page 30 show the method of working different variations of Hemstitch.

Diagram *a* – Hemstitch. Bring the working thread out four threads down from the space of drawn threads, pass the needle behind four loose threads, insert needle four threads to the right and bring out four threads down in readiness for the next stitch.

Diagram *b* – Ladder Hemstitch. This stitch is worked in the same way as Hemstitch, the stitches in this case being worked along both edges of the space of drawn threads.

Diagram *c* – Zig-zag Hemstitch. This stitch is worked in the same way as Ladder Hemstitch but in the second row the groups of fabric threads are divided in half so that each group is composed of half the number

The work is carried out with Clark's Anchor Stranded Cotton, the number of strands depending on the weight and type of fabric used. Where Hemstitch is used as a decorative stitch within a design, mark the length of the threads to be withdrawn. Cut the threads at the centre and withdraw gradually outwards on each side for the desired length. Fasten the threads neatly with small stitches on the wrong side and cut away loose ends. On coarse or thick fabric the withdrawn

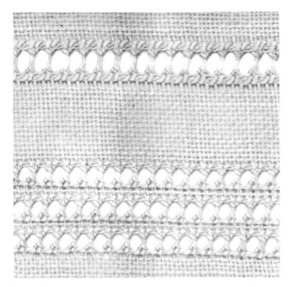
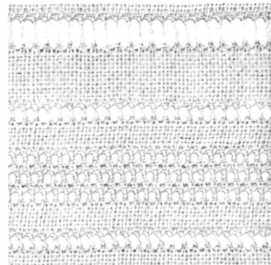
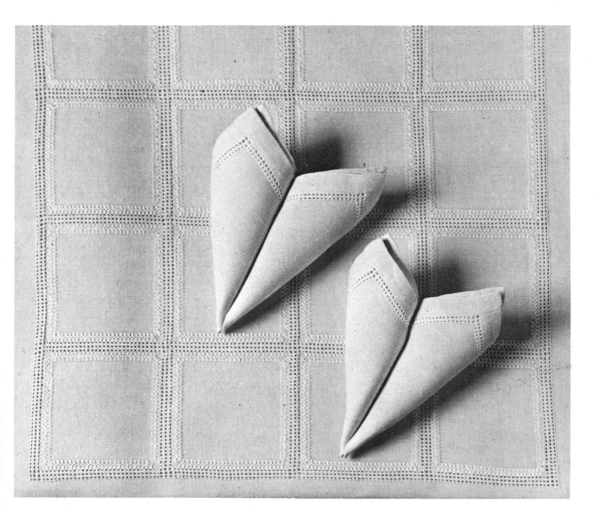

Tablecloths with Hemstitching and Counted Thread embroidery. Material: pure linen, in white (below) and pink (on the right), embroidered with Clark's Anchor Stranded Cotton, white, using two strands

of threads from one group and half from the adjacent group.

Diagram *d* shows another variation: in this case two similar stitches are made around each group of threads over each other or side by side. What is known as pierced work (Diagram *e*) is not genuine Hemstitch. In this case the fabric threads are whipped with large Herringbone stitches in alternate pairs (see page 64).

Diagram *f* – Interlaced Hemstitch. Draw threads as usual, then fasten a long thread at right-hand side centrally at the loose fabric threads and interlace groups of threads as shown.

Hemstitched trimmings and hems with their many kinds of stitches and arrangement of thread groups, together with other open-work, offer a number of possible variations which can be complemented further by Satin and Herringbone stitch embroidery.

Threaded Backstitch embroidery

Threaded Backstitch embroidery is little known even though it is easily carried out. In this technique one is dealing with what is known as 'White Work' in which the fabric and the embroidery thread should be of the same colour or at least agree in shade. Even-weave fabric is best suited for this work, but other materials with a similar structure

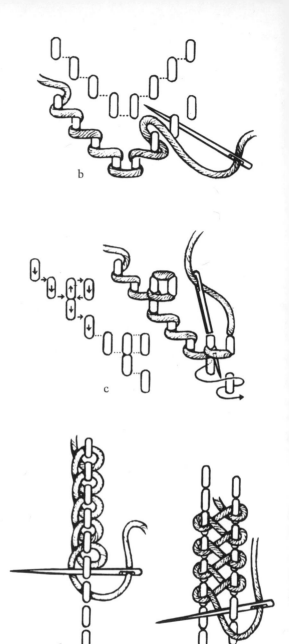

b

c

d

e

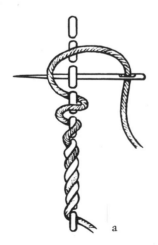

a

can also be used. In Threaded Backstitch embroidery a pattern is used in which the stitches are marked by lines on squared paper (i.e. a counted thread pattern in which the stitches are not shown by crosses or points, but by horizontal and vertical lines which correspond to the lie of the embroidery thread). The work is carried out in two phases. In the first phase small running stitches (simple up and down stitches) are made. The gaps between the running stitches must cover the same number of fabric threads as the stitches – i.e. the stitches are worked up and down over the same number of threads. In the second phase the gaps are bridged with embroidery thread, which, however, is not stitched through the fabric. The needle is guided from right to left under each of the stitches visible on the decorative side (Diagrams *a–c*). The embroidery thread can also be guided in loops (Diagram *d*) or between two parallel rows of running stitches alternately in zig-zag pattern (Diagram *e*); however, this is not the classical

method. The Threaded Backstitch gives a raised impression.

À *jour* **embroidery (drawn fabric)**

À *jour* embroidery, also called pulled work, can only be worked on an evenweave linen or similar fabric with approximately 21 threads to 1 in. (2·5 cm). Its charm lies in its open pattern which is similar in appearance to Drawn Thread or Cutwork embroidery.

Drawn Fabric embroidery on fine evenweave fabric: the holes are made by pulling each stitch tightly

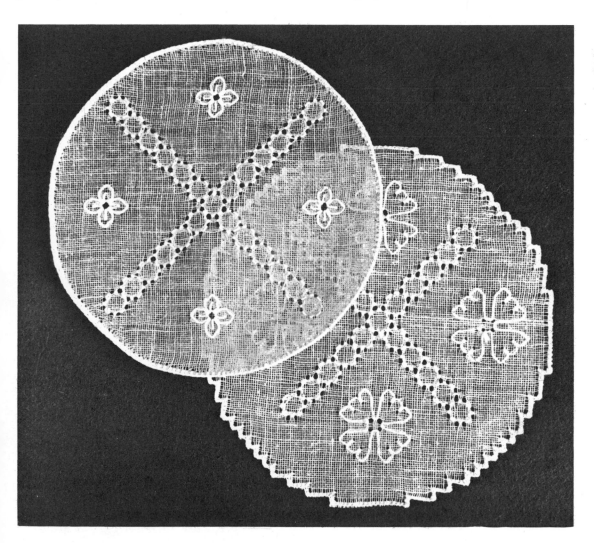

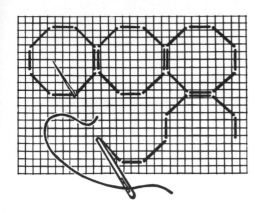

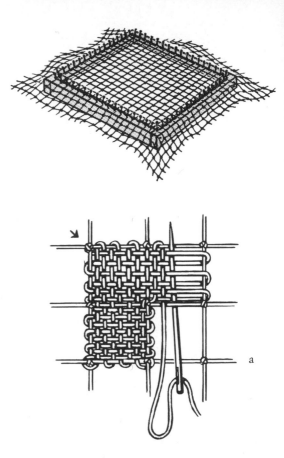

This, however, is achieved without withdrawing or cutting fabric threads. The lacy effect is obtained by pulling the working thread firmly with each needle movement so that the spaces are formed between the threads. An embroidery frame is essential for this work in order to keep the fabric threads taut and straight. The most widely used stitch is the Octagonal Honeycomb stitch, which can also be worked as a hexagon. It is worked forward and backward as shown on the drawing above. In general the work is carried out with embroidery thread which matches the shade of the fabric; however, it can be worked with threads which have been withdrawn from the edge of the fabric.

Filet and Tulle embroidery

Filet and Tulle work must have the same thread tension as the embroidery fabric and for this reason it must not be worked without an embroidery frame. It is important that the fabric is mounted on the frame with the fabric threads straight.

The Filet embroidery is worked on large mesh knotted net, or linen scrim with Clark's Anchor Stranded Cotton or Coats Mercer Crochet Cotton. The fabric is placed over a small wooden frame (picture frame). The fabric must be mounted tightly over the frame and fastened round the edges with

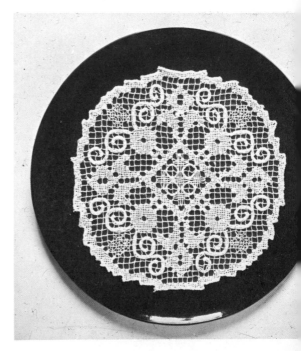

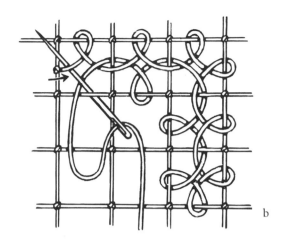

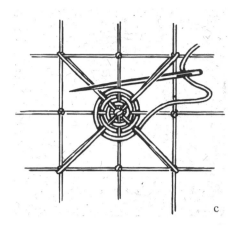

b

c

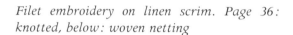

Filet embroidery on linen scrim. Page 36: knotted, below: woven netting

drawing pins spaced to coincide with the mesh of the fabric (drawing above). The gaps between the fabric threads are now filled with darning stitches. The most widely used stitches are the weaving stitch (Diagram *a*), the spiral or diagonal stitch

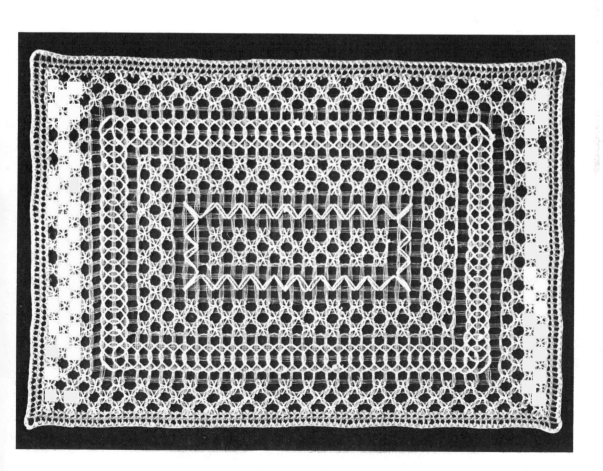

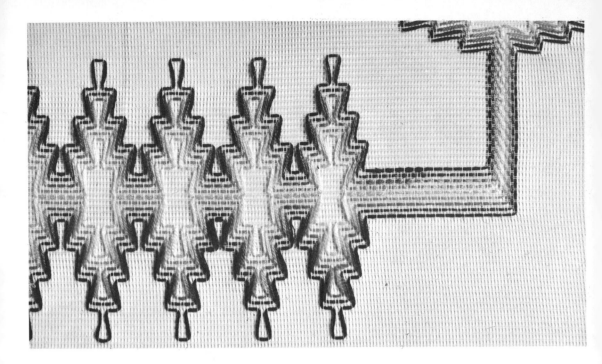

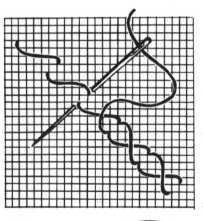

a

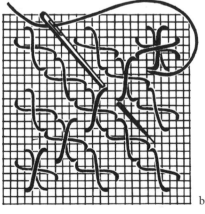

b

(Diagram *b*) and the Spider's Web filling (Diagram *c*). In Filet work the edge is worked with weaving stitch before cutting out and edged with blanket stitch (page 51). Only then is the surplus fabric on the outer edge carefully cut away.

Linen scrim was used for the mat on page 37. In this case, after completion of the edges in simple Hemstitching, four threads at a time were withdrawn from the open weave in both directions so that the fabric has an openwork weave. The embroidered star pattern appears when the crossings of the fabric threads are darned in forward and backward rows over the diagonals as shown in Diagrams *a* and *b*. The honeycombs are worked between two starred trimmings (see *À jour* embroidery, page 36).

The Tulle embroidery is in principle worked in the same way as the Filet embroidery: here, too, the fabric threads are pulled through, whipped or darned with the embroidery thread. The fabric, however, is finer. The section of pattern, seen above, was embroidered with Clark's Anchor Stranded Cotton in five colour gradations from

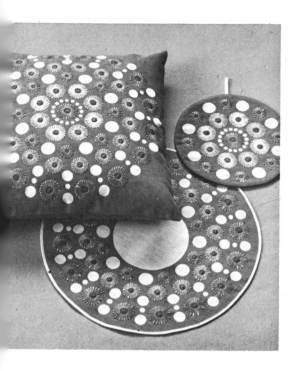

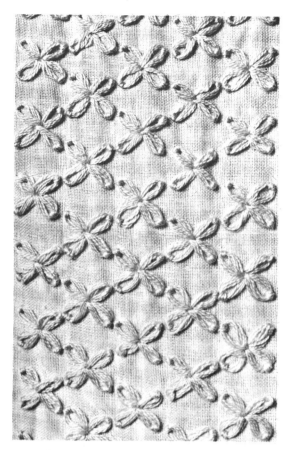

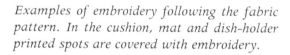

Examples of embroidery following the fabric pattern. In the cushion, mat and dish-holder printed spots are covered with embroidery.

yellow to brown on Trevira curtain material, without a frame.

Embroidery following the fabric pattern

Embroidery following the fabric pattern is the simplest to work; it is therefore very useful for beginners who are not skilled in free embroidery. In embroidery following the fabric pattern it is not necessary to count threads or to transfer a design on to the fabric. The process consists of embroidering over the existing printed (photograph, above) or woven (photograph, on the right) motifs or to complement them by embroidery. Cushions, dishcloths and coverlets were embroidered with large lazy-daisy stitches on white dots. The centre was worked in

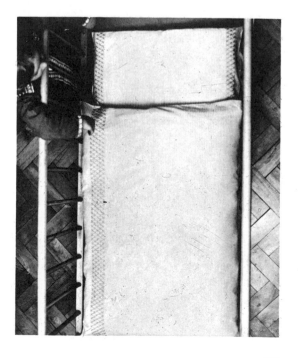

Satin stitches with a stem stitch edging. A cot layette in pink and white was diagonally stitched over nine squares with lazy-daisy stitches (Clark's Anchor Stranded Cotton) in staggered rows. For further embroidery stitches see pages 51–56.

A large number of fabric designs exist which are suitable for embroidery following the fabric pattern. However, there are limits to the scope, but even so this method is more satisfying than the soulless working along printed or traced patterns in embroidery which do not follow the fabric weave, i.e. Free-style embroidery.

Free-style embroidery

An embroidery frame (page 7) should be used in Free-style embroidery. Only very strong materials do not distort in the hand. A sharp pointed crewel needle which matches the

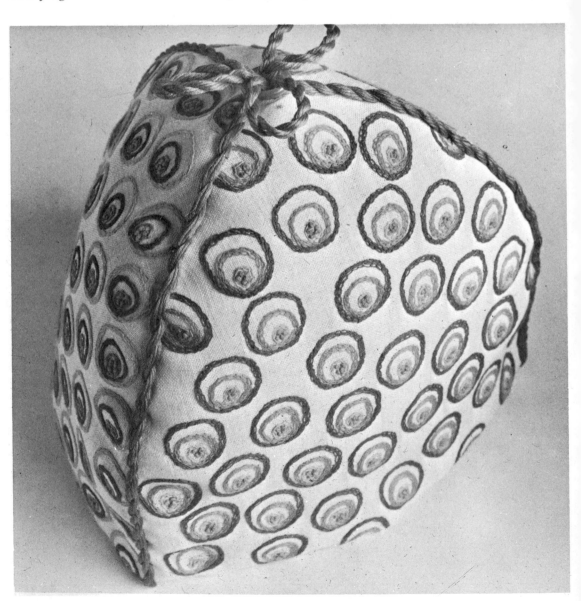

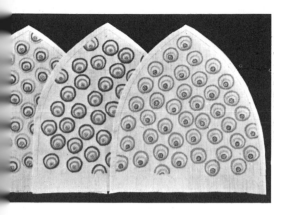

thickness of the thread is used for stitching (table on page 53). In Free-style embroidery the motif to be embroidered is transferred on to the fabric. The embroidery is then worked over the transferred design.

First a tracing on transparent paper is made from the design or from the embroidery pattern with an accurate drawing of the whole design or of the motif which is to be repeated. Only then is the drawing transferred on to the fabric. Several methods can be used, for example:

1. In the case of thin fabrics (batiste, organza, voile) the tracing can be placed under the fabric and the design drawn directly on to the fabric with a sharp pencil.

2. Transferring of the drawing with copying paper (*not* carbon paper) is suitable for linen, cotton fabrics and silk. The copying paper comes in white, yellow, orange, red and black. Select the colour which will stand out most distinctly on the fabric. The fabric is spread out with its threads straight, the copying paper is placed on top with the coated face downwards, and the tracing with the design is placed on top of the copying paper. The upper edge of this assembly is held down with a heavy object (such as an iron) in order to prevent movement. The design is then traced with a ballpoint pen.

3. For larger motifs which are often repeated it pays to prepare perforated tracings. The motif can then be copied without much trouble as often as required. Place the trans-

The sections (above left) for the tea cosy (page 40) were embroidered with Clark's Anchor Stranded Cotton in yellow, orange and red on embroidery linen. Initials worked in Chain, Stem and Lazy Daisy stitches are simple to embroider. The letters can be modelled on large poster or newspaper letters

43

The embroidery alphabet on pages 42–45
The method of transferring a design on to the embroidery fabric is described on pages 41–51. The letters are worked in Satin stitch, the vines in Stem stitch. If a whole monogram is to be embroidered in this manner instead of a single letter, then the vines must be divided, as shown, for example, for the letter I. The spacing between the letters can be filled as for the letter H. Both letters of the monogram can be moved together and one vine embroidered, as for L

parent paper drawing on a soft underlay and pierce (perforate) on the wrong side with a medium-size needle. Do not pierce the holes too closely, otherwise the drawing will become detached. Then smooth the perforations with emery paper. After this a rubber is made from a strip of felt by rolling the strip tightly and tying with string. The perforated tracing is placed with the correct side uppermost on the previously marked position of the fabric, the outer edges are held in position by weights, then powdered

Fine Thread embroideries (Clark's Anchor Stranded Cotton using two strands) appear especially delicate on dark fabric.
Right: cushion worked to a pre-printed motif. Page 46: rosette based on a folded paper pattern. Circles are drawn with pencil and string (page 290)

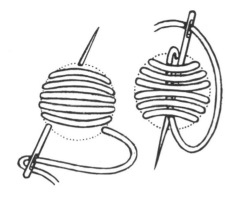

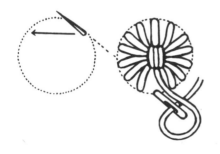

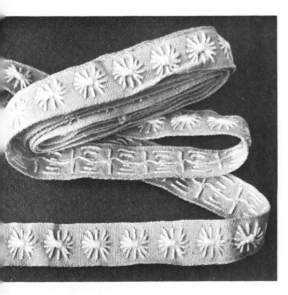

Wool embroidery on heavy linen. The Stem stitch circles are drawn with pencil and string (page 290). The flowers are drawn only as circles and embroidered freely

Photograph, lower left: hearts embroidered with Satin stitch. Outlines are edged with simple Stem stitch

Colour photograph on pages 48 and 49: These border motifs, here reproduced full size, are easily embroidered without a pattern. The motifs can be embroidered separately on serviettes, placemats, egg cosies or bags. The borders can be embroidered on tablecloths, sets of mats, cushions or curtains

charcoal (for light fabrics) or chalk (for dark fabrics) is dusted on to the tracing. This charcoal or chalk is rubbed with the straight face of the rubber through the perforations on to the fabric. A colourless fixative is sprayed on to the traced drawing in order to make it permanent. The next motif can be traced in the same manner. This method of transferring is also suitable for felt and woollen fabrics with surface pile which does not readily take on the imprint of copying paper.

4. The drawing cannot be transferred directly on to terry towelling or similar fabrics. The motif is drawn with pencil on organdie and this is fastened to the fabric. After the outlines have been embroidered, the organdie is cut away or, as far as possible, picked out.

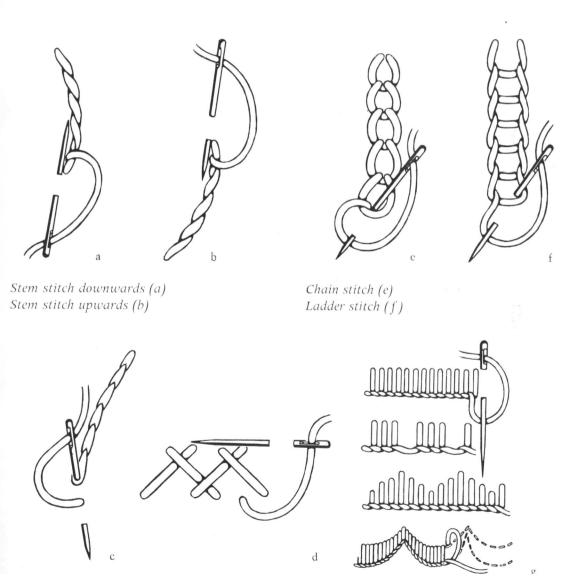

Stem stitch downwards (a)
Stem stitch upwards (b)

Chain stitch (e)
Ladder stitch (f)

Split stitch (c)
Herringbone stitch (d)

Blanket stitch and Buttonhole stitch (g)

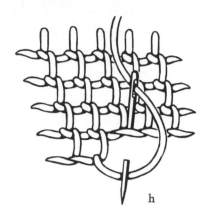

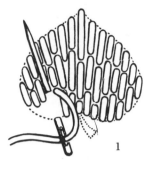

Long and Short stitch (l)

Blanket Filling stitch (h)

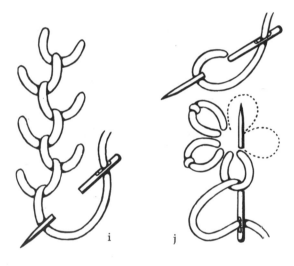

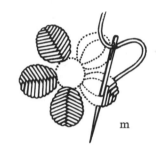

Flat stitch (m)

Feather stitch (i)
Detached Chain or Lazy Daisy stitch (j)

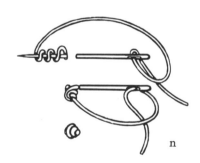

French knot (n)

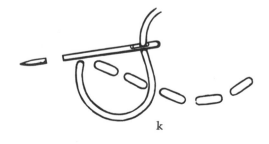

Simple Running stitch (k)

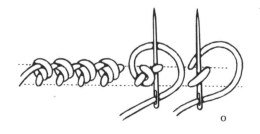

Palestrina stitch (o)

THREAD, NEEDLE AND FABRIC CHART

Fabric	Clark's Anchor embroidery threads	Thickness in strands	Milward needle sizes	Remarks
Fine linen, lawn, organdie, sheer silk or fine synthetics	Stranded Cotton Pearl Cotton No. 8 Coton à Broder No. 18	1, 2 or 3	Crewel needles (sharp points) No. Strands 8 1 and 2	These fabrics, threads and needles are for working designs traced or transferred on to the fabric
Medium weight linen, rayon, Sailcloth, satin, etc.	Stranded Cotton Pearl Cotton No. 8 Coton à Broder No. 18	2, 3 or 4	7 3 strands and Coton à Broder No. 18 6 4 Strands and Pearl Cotton No. 8 5 6 strands and Pearl Cotton No. 5	The number of strands of Stranded Cotton may be varied on any article according to the requirements of the design
Heavy linen, crash or furnishing fabric	Stranded Cotton Pearl Cotton No. 5	6		
Fine evenweave linen	Stranded Cotton Pearl Cotton No. 8, 5 Coton à Broder No. 18	1–6	Tapestry needles (rounded point) No. Strands 24 1 and 2	These threads and needles are used when working over counted threads of canvas or fabric
Medium weight evenweave linen, medium mesh canvas, etc.	Stranded Cotton Pearl Cotton No. 8, 5 Coton à Broder No. 18 or Tapisserie wool	3, 4 or 6	24 3 and Coton à Broder No. 18 24 4 and Pearl Cotton No. 8 20 6 and Pearl Cotton No. 5 18 Soft Embroidery, Tapisserie wool	
Coarse evenweave linen and fabric, heavy mesh canvas	Stranded Cotton Pearl Cotton No. 5 Soft Embroidery Tapisserie wool	4 or 6		
Medium weight square weave canvas	Stranded Cotton Pearl Cotton No. 5 Soft Embroidery Tapisserie wool	3, 4 or 6	Tapestry needles (rounded point) No. Thickness 20 6 strands and Pearl Cotton No. 5 18 Soft Embroidery, Tapisserie wool	These threads and needles are used for working over counted threads of fabric or canvas
Heavy square weave canvas	Stranded Cotton Soft Embroidery Tapisserie wool	6		
Heavy linen, crash or furnishing fabric, etc.	Soft Embroidery Tapisserie wool		Chenille needle (sharp point) No. Thickness 18 Soft Embroidery, Tapisserie wool	These threads and needle are used for traced or transferred design

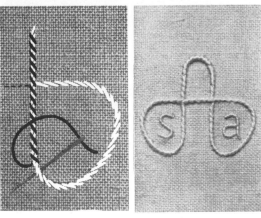

Stem stitch with whipping

Closed Herringbone or Double Back stitch

Stem stitch rows in opposite direction

Threaded backstitch

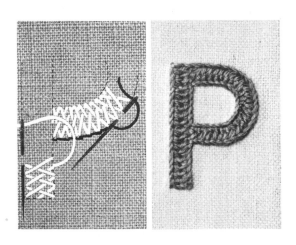
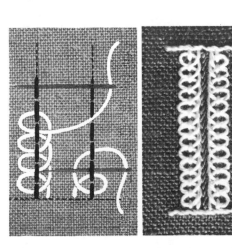

Closed Herringbone with stem stitch

Backstitch with threaded loops

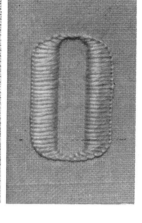
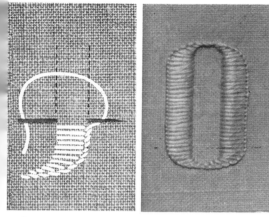

Flat Blanket stitch

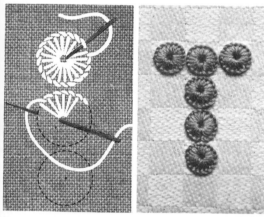

Circular Blanket stitch

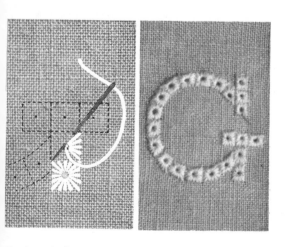

Satin stitch star

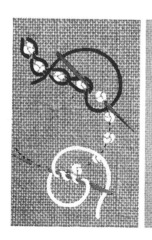

Satin stitch worked over Split stitches

Satin stitch with Stem stitch outline

Chain stitch and French knots

Feather stitch

Chain stitch, arranged as Feather stitch

Yugoslavian and Hungarian embroidery

The characteristic features of the Yugoslavian embroideries are the richly imaginative flowers which are worked in lively colours with Satin stitch. Very often the inner circles with roseate embroidery outlines have other forms of flowers or leaves. Yugoslavian embroidery is started in the centre. The work follows only separate traced circles and not complete motif drawings or complete patterns. When one flower is completed the circles of the next flower of any desired size are arranged next to it. Another circle is arranged above or below the two embroidered flowers and this is then imaginatively converted into a flower. The work is continued until the random pattern is completed. This embroidery can be carried out with Clark's Anchor Pearl Cotton or – on heavy fabrics – Coats Anchor Tapisserie wool.

Hungarian embroidery is worked to a predrawn design. Here we find flowers worked in lively colours and a variety of stitches. Different yarns (wool and artificial silk) are frequently worked together.

Yugoslavian embroidery: decoration starts in the centre (detail, above right). Hungarian embroidery: flowers, filled with other flowers (below)

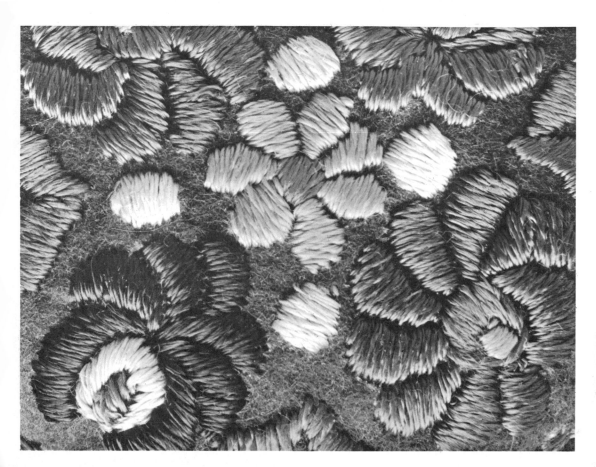

Shadow-work embroidery

Shadow-work embroidery, also called Closed Herringbone stitch, is effective only on thin fabrics as the embroidery is worked on the wrong side giving a delicate shadow effect on the right side of the fabric. The most suitable materials for this technique are voile, batiste and organdie. The embroidery is worked with two strands of Clark's Stranded Cotton. The pattern is drawn with a ball-point pen or with a felt nib pen on strong

Shadow-work embroidery: closed Herring-bone stitches are worked on the wrong side to show through the fabric

paper. Place the fabric right side down on the drawing and secure in position with drawing pins. Transfer the pattern to the fabric by drawing along the lines with a fine pencil. The embroidery is worked with closely spaced Herringbone stitches on the wrong side of the fabric (Diagram *a*) and as

small back stitches appear on the right side (decorative side) on the outlines of the pattern the motif shows delicately through the fabric. Shadow-work embroidery can be further highlighted by complementary stitches worked directly on to the right side. In shadow-work embroidery floral motifs appear especially fragile and fresh.

Broderie Anglaise

Broderie Anglaise is traditionally a white work which is usually carried out with other decorative stitches such as Satin stitch or Blanket stitch. No embroidery frame is used in this work since the fabric would stretch at

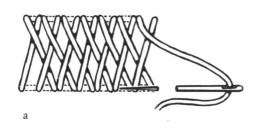

a

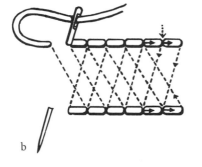

b

the cut-out sections. The holes of the design are first edged with small running stitches. The fabric is then cut with embroidery scissors crosswise along the threads to the running stitches and the four sectors are

folded over to the wrong side of the fabric. The edge of the fabric around the hole and the running stitches are then closely whipped with overcasting stitches (drawing, page 59). Surplus fabric is carefully cut away from the wrong side.

The holes in the fabric must not be too large otherwise they will not be round. They can be cut with a small punch or stiletto before the edges are whipped. Small oval forms (photograph, above, and page 61 on the left) can be made using this technique.

Cut Work

Cut work resembles Broderie Anglaise but uses a different technique and is almost exclusively used for decorative edging.

Broderie Anglaise: the hole is marked, enclosed by Running stitches, cut across and embroidered around the edge with Outline stitches

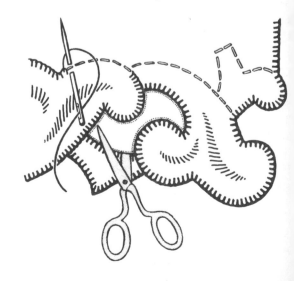

After transferring the motif on to the fabric (see Free-style embroidery, page 40) the outlines are embroidered with small closely spaced Blanket stitches (page 51). A row of Running stitch may be worked first between the double lines of the design to form a padding for the Blanket stitch (diagram, page 59). The background fabric is then cut away on the wrong side close to the Blanket stitch, taking care not to snip the stitches. To avoid mistakes it is advisable to mark with a pencil the parts to be cut. Cut Work can be decorated in exactly the same way as the Broderie Anglaise with additional Satin stitches.

Section of the Cut-work edge from the lunch mats above. Drawing on page 60

Cut-work: the outlines marked with Running stitches are embroidered over with Blanket stitches. Only then is the fabric cut out (page 60)

Place mat in Cut-work technique. Edging is embroidered with Blanket stitch and cut out

Smocking

Smocking work (decorative stitches on gathered or pleated fabric) is used most on children's clothing, lightweight blouses, dresses and lingerie. It is important to take into account the additional amount of fabric required for smocking; allow two to three times the width of the finished article. The amount of material used depends on the depth and spacing of the folds. A good safeguard for the inexperienced is to carry out the smocking work first and then cut the fabric to the required size. Smocking can be worked on all thin to medium fine fabrics; however, the stitches must not be pulled too tightly, so that the completed work retains elasticity. First, horizontal lines are drawn on the wrong side of the fabric, spacing evenly. These lines act as a guide for the running (gathering) stitches. The intervals

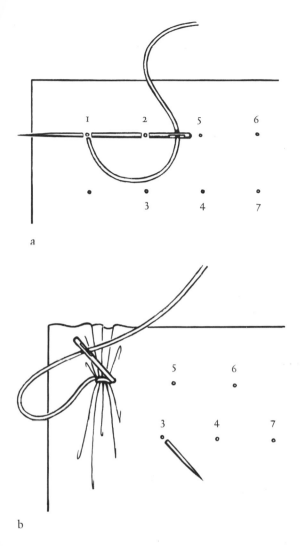

a

b

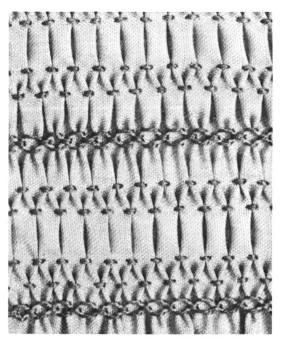

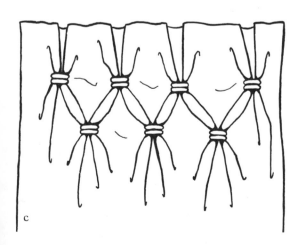

c

between the stitches will give the depth of the gathers, so it is important that all the stitches are of equal size. Subsequently the fabric is drawn together to the required width so that small standing gathers are formed. A smocking transfer may be used.

The simplest stitch is the Honeycomb stitch. Starting at the upper left-hand corner, the edges of the first and the second pleat are drawn together and stitched over with two anchoring stitches. These can run parallel or they can be worked as Flat Cross stitch. The needle is then guided into the crease of the second fold (also on the wrong side of the fabric) down to the next row; the needle emerges at the front and the second and third pleats are stitched together. Now the needle is passed upwards behind the pleat again and the third and fourth pleats stitched over. This method is continued until both rows are completed. The rows below are worked in exactly the same manner. The Honeycomb stitch with diagonal whipping is worked as described above; however, the connecting thread between the rows is carried up and down the right side of the work.

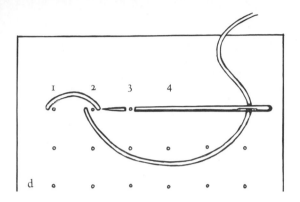

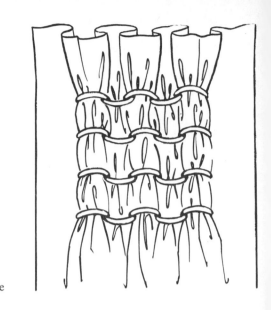

The Horizontal Gathering stitch is also worked from left to right. In this case two pleats are joined with one stitch and another stitch made on the second fold slightly below the previous stitch. The next stitch (from now on only one stitch is made) encloses the third pleat on the same level and it will be guided upwards in a slightly inclined manner. At the fourth pleat the stitch is made downwards, in a slightly inclined path, and subsequently upwards at an angle.

The drawings a, b and c on page 63 show the simple Honeycomb stitch. The Horizontal gathering stitch is shown on page 64, d and e. The photograph on page 63 shows a combination of these stitches

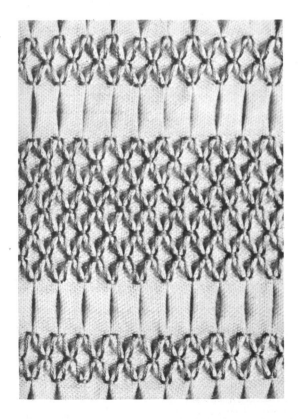

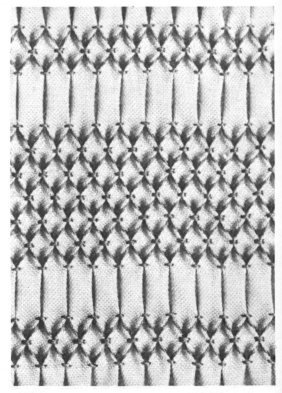

Crochet

Crochet hooks and yarns
Starting the work
Crochet stitches
Picot edgings
Shaping of crochet work
Tunisian, Irish and 'American'
   crochet

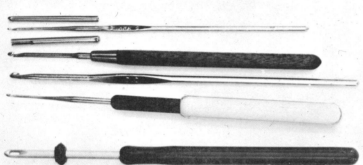

Lattice loop crochet and
   loop stitch crochet
Cluster and Shell-stitch patterns
Wave pattern
Star pattern
Peacock's eyes
Picot pattern
Crochet with beads
Hairpin crochet
Looping
Instructions for working crochet
   models

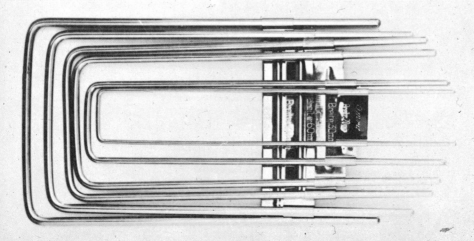

For the American equivalent hook and yarn sizes
and stitch names, see the tables on page 291

The correct relationship between hook and yarn

The size of the crochet hook to be used depends on the thickness of the wool or thread and the crochet stitch; and the type of thread should be suitable for the kind of article to be worked. A soft thread is used for baby things and a well-twisted strong thread for a handbag or a tie. As a general rule very fine threads are crocheted with steel hooks Number 0.60 (6) to 1.75 (2), thicker cotton threads and wool with aluminium hooks Number 2.00 (14) to 3.50 (9) and thick wool with hooks Number 4.00 (8) to 7.00 (2). The figures in parentheses are the present U.K. numbers and correspond to the numbers on U.K. knitting needles. The metric figures are the new international numbers. Many wool- and thread-labels carry recommended numbers for both U.K. and metric knitting needles which, therefore, also apply to the crochet hook size. For U.S. numbering and lettering see charts pages 291–2.

Start of working crochet

Most crochet starts with a loop (slip) knot. Make a loop by holding the thread between thumb and forefinger of the left hand, with the short end hanging free. Place thread coming from ball over short end and behind

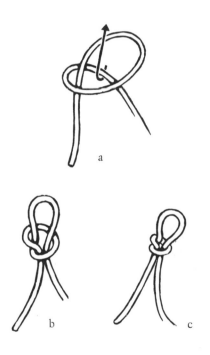

loop (a). Hold loop between thumb and forefinger. Take the thread from the ball through the loop (b) and pull both ends of thread slightly to tighten the knot (c). Place the loop around the end of the hook. Pass hook from front to back under the thread (=thread over) and draw thread through loop on hook (d) tightening stitch slightly (e). This makes the first chain stitch. Repeat last step until the required number of

67

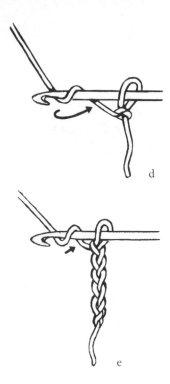

d

e

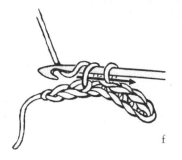

f

stitches is obtained. With practice a rhythm develops: thread over hook, draw thread through, tighten stitch slightly. Care must be taken to work all stitches of an even size so that the edges of the finished work have a neat appearance. The abbreviation for chain stitch in working instructions is: ch. If articles are to be worked without specific crochet instructions, perhaps with a dressmaker's pattern as guide, measure the width required for each part. Work the foundation chain row to the required width plus two, three or four stitches extra, depending on the thickness of the thread or wool used. This allowance will be taken up by the crochet pattern during the process of working, so that after a few rows the work will be of the required width. A tension sample should always be worked before starting on any article. If working from crochet instructions, the tension is normally stated and the number of stitches and rows for the sample given. If your tension is loose, use a size finer hook, if tight, use a size larger hook. When working without instruc-

tions, make a sample of approximately 2 by 2 in. in the chosen pattern and count the number of stitches and rows covering 1 sq. in. This is the basis for calculating the number of stitches and rows needed for any part of the article to be worked.

Slip stitch or single crochet

On a foundation row of chain stitches insert hook into second stitch from hook taking up one thread of chain stitch, draw thread through chain stitch and loop on hook. Continue in this manner into every stitch of chain-row to end (f). Make one chain stitch for turning work. When a particularly firm edge is required, a row of slip stitches should be worked before starting pattern. Abbreviation for slip stitch: ss.

Double crochet (U.S. single crochet)

On a row of chain stitches insert hook into second stitch from hook taking up two top

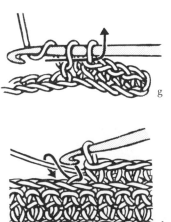

g

h

threads of chain stitch, draw thread through chain stitch, thread over hook and draw through both loops on hook (g). Insert hook into next chain stitch and work another double crochet. Continue in this manner to the end of the chain. This chain stitch is for ease of turning only and does not count as a stitch. Turn work, insert hook into first stitch (the last stitch of the previous row) taking up two top threads, draw thread through, thread over hook and draw through both loops on hook. Work one double crochet into every stitch to the end of row. For a Rib stitch, work one row of double crochet on a chain row, 1 ch, turn. Insert hook into first stitch taking up only one top thread of the double crochet in previous row (h). Abbreviation for double crochet is: dc. After the final row in crochet work has been completed the thread is fastened off. To fasten off, cut thread a few inches from last worked stitch. Draw this end through the last loop on the hook. Work one chain stitch at the end of every row for turning.

Trebles

There are four types of Trebles: the Treble, the Half Treble, the Double Treble and the Multiple Treble. For practising, work these stitches on a row of chain stitches.

The Treble: thread over hook, insert hook into 4th ch from hook and draw thread through, thread over hook, draw it through first two loops on hook, thread over hook and draw it through last two loops on hook.

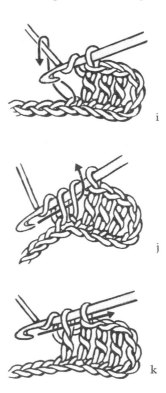

Make another treble into the next stitch and continue in this manner to the end of row (i, j, k). For the second row turn work as follows: instead of the first Treble work three chain stitches and count these as the first stitch of that row, then thead over hook, insert hook into second Treble from hook and continue as for first row. For a Rib stitch, take up only one thread of the Trebles

in previous row (see Rib stitch for double crochet). Abbreviation for Treble: tr.

The Half Treble: thread over hook, insert hook into third chain from hook, draw

thread through, thread over hook and draw it through all three loops on hook. Make another Half Treble into next stitch (1, m) and continue to end of row. Turn with 2 ch (as with double crochet, these two stitches do not count as a stitch but are worked for ease of turning). Work first Half Treble of row into first Half Treble from hook. Abbreviation for Half Treble: hlf tr.

The Double Treble: work like a Treble but take the thread twice over the hook before inserting hook into 5th ch from hook, thread over hook, draw it through first two loops on hook, thread over hook again and draw it through two loops on hook (two loops left on hook), thread over hook and draw it through last two loops. Make another Double Treble into next stitch and continue to end of row. Turn with 4 ch and count these as first stitch of that row (replacing first Double Treble). Work next Double Treble into second Double Treble from hook. Abbreviation for Double Treble: dbl tr.

The Multiple Treble: work like a Treble but take the thread over the hook several times before inserting hook into stitch of previous row: thread over hook three times for Triple Treble, insert hook into 6th ch from hook, draw thread through and crochet off two

loops at a time (see dbl tr). Turn with 5 ch
and count these as first stitch of next row,
working next Multiple Treble into second
Multiple Treble from hook. Abbreviation
for Triple Treble: trip tr. Take thread over
hook four times for Quadruple Treble, and
five times for Quintuple Treble, turning
with 6 ch and 7 ch respectively. Count
turning ch as first stitch of next row.
Abbreviation for Quadruple Treble: quad
tr; for Quintuple Treble: quin tr.
Clusters: work three or four tr or dbl tr into

*Cushion cover with Irish crochet motif –
Technique, pages 84 and 85 – in cotton*

one stitch of the previous row, leaving the
last loop of each stitch on the hook. After
the last stitch of the cluster has been made
in this way, draw thread through all loops
on hook once. Example, Double Treble
Clusters on a chain row: work 1 dbl tr into
5th ch from hook leaving last loop of dbl tr

71

on hook (two loops on hook), work another dbl tr into same ch as previous one leaving last loop on hook (three loops on hook), thread over and draw through all loops (n). One cluster of 4 ch, 2 dbl tr has been completed. Make 1 ch, miss one stitch of previous row. Work a cluster of 3 dbl tr into next stitch, leaving last loop of each on hook (four loops on hook) (o), thread over hook and

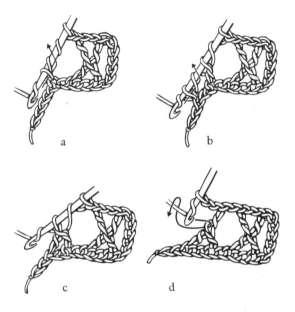

a   b

c   d

draw through all loops. Abbreviation for Cluster: cl.

Crossed Trebles: the sequence of working the four trebles forming this stitch is as follows: first treble to be worked is the lower right one (a), the second treble is the lower left one (b), the third treble is the upper right one (c), and the fourth treble the upper left one (d). On a row of ch, thread over hook twice, insert hook into 7th ch from hook and draw thread through, thread over hook and draw through first two loops on hook (three loops left), miss 2 ch, thread over hook, insert hook into next st and draw thread through, thread over hook and draw through two loops at a time until one loop remains on hook, 2 ch, 1 tr into crossing point of trebles, 1 ch. This completes the first Crossed Treble stitch. Next and following Crossed Trebles:

thread over hook twice, miss 1 ch, work the four trebles in the sequence given into the next stitch. Abbreviation for Crossed Trebles: cr tr.

Picot edgings: edges of crochet work can be decorated in several ways, and of these Picot edgings are the best known and most widely used.

Three of a great variety of picot patterns are worked as follows: No. 1: ★ 5 ch, 1 dc into 5th ch from hook; rep from ★ for desired length. No. 2: ★ 3 ch, 1 dc into 2nd ch from hook, 1 tr into next ch: rep from ★. No. 3: ★ 5 ch, 1 dc into 2nd ch from hook, 1 hlf tr into next ch, 1 tr into next ch, 1 dbl tr into next ch: rep from ★. Each repeat of these

edgings completes one picot. To crochet these edgings over the finished work instead of sewing them on, begin at the required stitch with 1 dc, now work one picot, ★ miss three (or five) stitches or appropriate space at sides of work, 1 dc into next stitch or space, one picot; rep from ★ ending with 1 dc (see photographs, page 72).

Shrimp stitch for edgings: this consists of a row of dc worked from left to right. On a row of ch or the finished article, work one row of dc. Do not turn work, but work 1 ch, insert hook into last dc of previous row and work a row of dc from left to right (see below).

Shaping of crochet work

To increase evenly at both sides of dc work, turn with 1 ch and work first dc into turning ch st (increase at beginning of row), at the end work 1 dc into turning ch of previous row (increase at end of row).

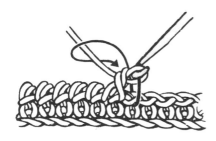

To decrease evenly at both sides of dc work, turn with 1 ch and work first dc into second dc of previous row, work dc into every stitch to last two stitches, miss 1 dc, 1 dc into last stitch of previous row.

Shaping of armhole: to decrease several stitches at the beginning of a row, work ss over the required number of stitches to be decreased, then work 1 dc, 1 hlf tr and 1 tr. Continue working trebles (or pattern made up of trebles) to the end of the first shaping row. Work the second shaping row in pattern to the last two stitches, work two stitches as follows: thread over, insert hook into first stitch, thread over and draw

through one loop, thread over and draw through two loops, insert hook into next stitch, thread over and draw through one loop, thread over and draw through two loops, thread over and draw through last three loops. Turn with a ch. Start third

shaping row with 1 ss into next stitch, 1 dc into next stitch, 1 hlf tr into next stitch, 1 tr into next stitch; then continue in pattern. The last two rows are repeated until armhole has the desired shape.

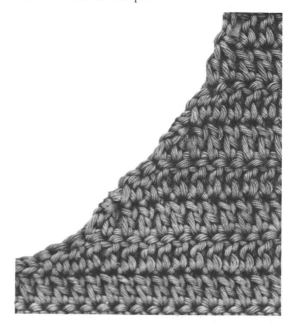

The buttonhole: for horizontal buttonholes, miss three (or required number of stitches) in previous row and replace them with the same number of chain stitches. In the next row, work the number of stitches missed in previous row into the space formed by the chain stitches, then continue in pattern. For vertical buttonholes, work in pattern to the

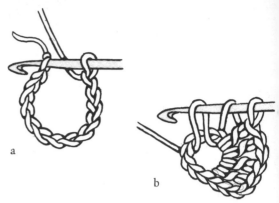

position for buttonhole, turn work and continue in pattern to the required height of buttonhole, ending at buttonhole edge. Fasten off. Rejoin thread at the base of buttonhole, work second half to same height as first half of work. In the next row, pattern across all stitches.

Circular forms in crochet

Start circular forms with a ring of chain stitches: work the required number of chain stitches and join with a ss into first ch (a) to form a ring. Depending on the pattern, work a number of dc or tr into ring (b). Each round is finished with a ss.

Round motif (for a cushion or similar article): make a chain of 8 sts and join with ss to form a ring.

1st Round: 3 ch (to replace 1st tr), 15 tr into ring, ss into 3rd ch. 16 sts.

2nd Round: 3 ch and 1 tr into same st as ss, 2 tr into each tr of previous round, ss into 3rd ch. 32 sts.

3rd Round: 3 ch and 1 tr into same st as ss, 1 tr into next st, ★ 2 tr into next st, 1 tr into next st; rep from ★ to end. 48 sts. The increases have been worked into every 2nd st.

4th Round: 3 ch and 1 tr into same st as ss, 1 tr into each of next 2 sts, ★ 2 tr into next st, 1 tr into each of next 2 sts; repeat from ★ to end. 64 sts.

The increases have been worked into every third stitch. Continue in this manner until the required size is reached. It may help to

Pot-holders in crochet – starting at centre. Using circular forms and oddments of yarn

remember that the stitch in which the increase has to be worked (i.e. 2 tr into stitch) in any particular round can be arrived at by deducting one from the round-number: in the **5th round** increase in every fourth stitch, in the **6th round** in every fifth stitch etc. This applies to normal and firm tension. Should the motif look 'wavy' and not lie flat, one round without increases may be worked and the increasing be resumed in the next round. Round motifs in double crochet are worked in a similar manner, but 1 ch at the beginning of each round does not stand for one stitch (see Irish crochet, page 84).

Tubular crochet

For children's and ladies' hats, handbags, gloves and similar articles, start work with

Loose cushion cover with rosettes in brown, green, orange and yellow wool. Instructions on page 114

a ring of chain large enough to fit easily around the head, base of bag etc. For a straight tubular shape continue in pattern and rounds without shaping. Through increases worked within the rounds, the work becomes wider, and through decreases it becomes narrower.

Crochet squares, starting at centre

Crochet squares can be worked in rows or, if preferred, started at the centre and worked in rounds as described on page 74 for the round motif.

To start a square in the centre: make 4 ch.

Tortoise in brown, kingfisher and yellow cotton thread. Instructions on page 114

1st Round: into 4th ch from hook 1 tr, 1 ch (1st corner), 3 tr, 1 ch (2nd corner), 3 tr, 1 ch (3rd corner), 3 tr, 1 ch (4th corner), 1 tr, ss into 4th ch. 12 tr and 4 ch spaces.

2nd Round: 3 ch (to replace 1 tr), (1 tr on next tr, into ch space 2 tr, 1 ch, 2 tr, 2 tr on next 2 tr) 3 times, 1 tr on next tr, into ch space 2 tr, 1 ch, 2 tr, 1 tr on next tr, ss into 3rd ch. 28 tr and 4 spaces.

3rd Round: 3 ch, (3 tr on next 3 tr, into ch space 2 tr, 1 ch, 2 tr, 4 tr on next 4 tr) 3 times, 3 tr on next 3 tr, into ch space 2 tr, 1 ch, 2 tr, 3 tr on next 3 tr, ss into 3rd ch. 44 tr and 4 spaces.

Continue in this manner until the square is of the required size. Always work 3 ch to replace 1st tr of round and 1 tr on each tr of previous round. To shape corners work 2 tr, 1 ch, 2 tr into each chain space in every

round. Each side of the square is increased by four stitches in each round.

The start of each round is in the centre of the first side of the square. Each round is closed by one slip stitch into 3rd ch.

Crochet squares, starting at one corner

Another method of working squares in double crochet is as follows: make 2 ch, and work 3 dc into 2nd ch from hook, turn with 1 ch.

1st Row: 1 dc into 1st dc from hook, 3 dc into next, 1 dc, 1 ch, turn.

2nd Row: 1 dc into each of 1st 2 dc, 3 dc

into next st, 1 dc into each of next 2 sts, 1 ch, turn.

3rd Row: 1 dc into each of 1st 3 dc, 3 dc into next st, 1 dc into each of next 3 dc, 1 ch, turn.

Continue in this manner working 1 dc into each dc of previous row, and 3 dc into centre stitch of each row.

Photograph page 78:
Pot-holders in various shapes.
Double crochet in cotton thread.
Instructions on page 115

Photographs page 79:
Nursery slippers crocheted from oddments of wool (above left).
Baby bootees and shoes: double crochet in cotton thread (below left).
Head scarf in double crochet and Chain stitches, starting at centre.
Material: mohair (above right).
All instructions on pages 116–117

Tunisian (Afghan) crochet

Tunisian crochet (also called Tricot crochet) is worked from right to left in the first row. In this row loops are picked up and left on the hook for the whole width of the work. The work is not turned as the end of the row for the second row which is, therefore, worked from left to right. In the second row the loops are crocheted off and the pattern is formed. A special long hook of uniform size in diameter with a knob at the end is used for this work. The hook should be longer, if possible, than the width of the work to allow for comfortable working. Tunisian crochet has the advantage of keeping its shape well and forming a close fabric.

Plain Tunisian stitch

1st Row: on a foundation ch row, insert hook into 2nd ch from hook, thread over hook and draw through leaving loop on hook, insert hook into next st, thread over hook and draw through leaving it too on the hook (a). Continue in this manner to the end of the ch row (b). Do not turn work.

2nd Row (from left to right): thread over hook and draw through one loop, ★ thread over hook and draw through two loops; rep from ★ to end of row (c). Pull the last st left on the hook up a little so that the edge of the work stays elastic.

3rd Row: insert hook into second upright thread of previous row, draw thread through and keep loop on hook, ★ insert hook into

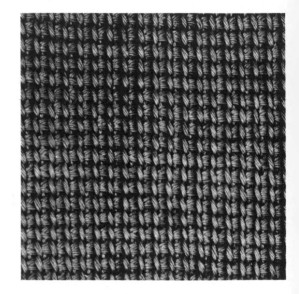

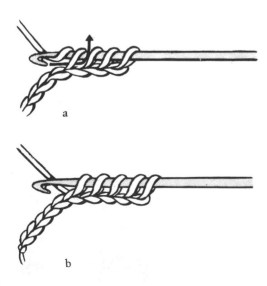

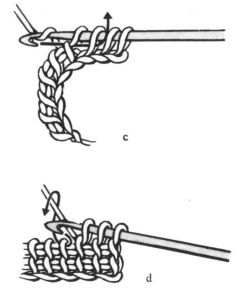

80

next upright thread, draw thread through and keep loop on hook; rep from ★ to end (d).

Work 4th row as 2nd row.

Fancy Tunisian stitch

Work two rows in Plain Tunisian stitch.

3rd Row: insert hook into first horizontal loop from hook, draw thread through and keep loop on hook, ★ insert hook into next horizontal loop between two upright loops, draw thread through and keep on hook; repeat from ★ to last horizontal loop but one (e and f).

4th Row: work as 2nd row of Plain Tunisian stitch.

5th Row: work as 3rd row but start with the second horizontal loop from hook and end row with the last horizontal loop of row.

2nd Row: work as 2nd row of Plain Tunisian stitch. In the next and following alternate rows insert hook from right to left through vertical loop of previous row and work as 1st row. 4th and following alternate rows are worked as 2nd row.

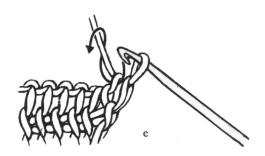

e

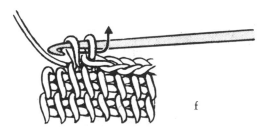

f

6th Row: as 4th row.

Rep rows 3 to 6 incl. The number of stitches in each row remains the same.

Purl or Knitted Tunisian stitch

Make a row of chain stitches.

1st Row: 1 ch ★ with thread at front of work (called Thread forward), insert hook from back into next ch, with thread under hook draw thread through; rep from ★ to end leaving all loops on hook.

Casting off of Tunisian crochet

Tunisian crochet, unlike other crochet work, has to be cast off after the last pattern row to ensure a perfect edge. The casting off row is worked from right to left. With last loop on hook, work a row of slip stitches or double crochet to end of last pattern row, working into the upright loops. Fasten off.

Increases and decreases

Tunisian crochet is shaped like ordinary

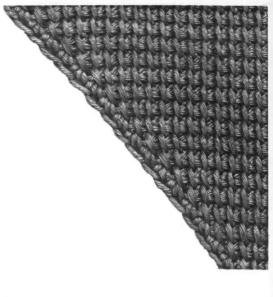

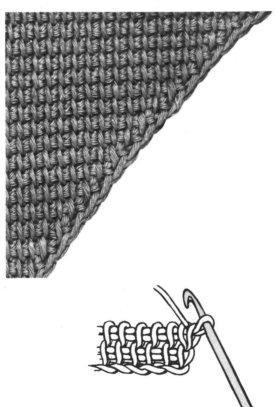

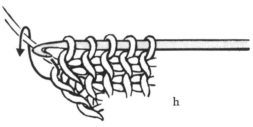

h

Increase at the end of a first row: insert hook into the upper horizontal thread before last vertical loop, draw thread through, then work last loop (h). Decrease at the beginning of a first row: miss the first upright loop of row and insert hook into second upright loop (i).

Decrease at the end of a first row: insert hook into the two last upright loops of row together and draw thread through (j).

Decrease at the end of a second row: draw

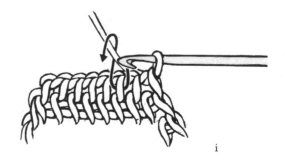

g

crochet by means of increases and decreases. Increase at the beginning of a first row: insert hook into the upper horizontal thread between the first and second stitch of previous row and draw thread through (g).

i

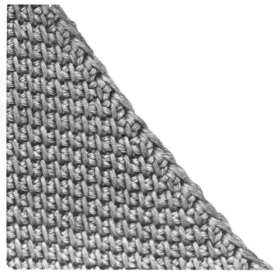

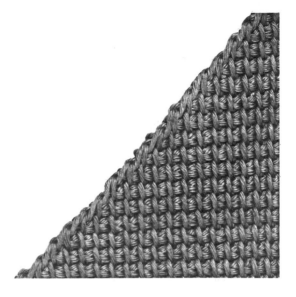

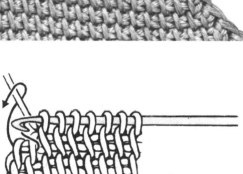

Shaping of left shoulder: Leave the required number of stitches unworked at the end of a first row. At the beginning of the second row decrease one stitch (see j).

thread through last three (instead of two) loops together (k).
Shaping of right shoulder: cast off the required number of stitches at the beginning of a first row. At the end of the second row

The Tunisian buttonhole

Buttonholes in Tunisian crochet are worked on the same principle as in ordinary crochet by missing the number of stitches required for the length of the buttonhole and replacing them with other stitches. In Tunisian crochet miss, as an example, three stitches and work thread over hook three times instead. Then continue with the usual stitches (l). In the second row the loops on hook are crocheted off in twos along with the other loops. This makes a horizontal buttonhole.

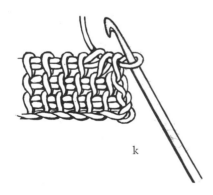

decrease one stitch (see k). In the following 1st row work 1 dc into the second upright from hook. Repeat last two rows until arm-hole has the desired shape.

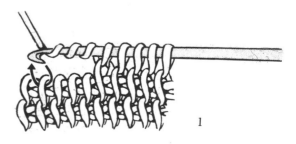

Irish crochet

Irish crochet features rosettes and motifs which – after being crocheted or sewn together – are used mainly for cushion covers, tablecloths, shoulder wraps and bedspreads. Of the many and various motifs which can be combined to form larger patterns, four basic rosette patterns are given here. From these forms many others can be created by altering stitch types or spacings.

Rosette A: make a ch of 6 sts, join with ss to form ring (page 74). Into the ring work: 3 ch, thread over, insert hook into ring and draw thread through, thread over and draw through 2 loops on hook, thread over, insert hook into ring and draw thread through, thread over and draw through 2 loops, thread over and draw through 3 loops, 3 ch, ★ (thread over, insert hook into ring and draw thread through, thread over and draw through 2 loops) three times, thread over and draw through 4 loops on hook, 3 ch; rep from ★ 6 times more, 1 ss into 3rd ch of round. Fasten off.

Rosette B: make a ch of 6 sts, 1 ss into 1st ch to form ring. Into ring work 4 ch, 5 dbl tr,

84

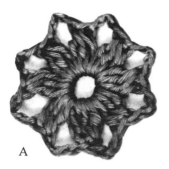

A

(5 ch, 6 dbl tr) 3 times, 5 ch, 1 ss into 4th ch of rd.

2nd Round: 1 ss into 2nd dbl tr, 3 ch, (1 tr into next dbl tr leaving last loop of tr on

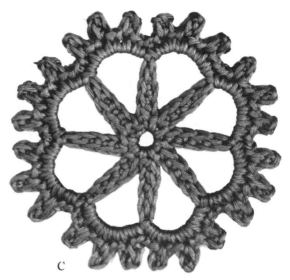

C

3rd Round: 1 ss into next 5 ch space, into each space work (2 dc, 1 picot of 3 ch and 1 dc into 3rd ch from hook) 3 times, 2 dc. Join with 1 ss into 1st ss.

Rosette D: make a ch of 5 sts, 1 ss into 1st ch to form ring.

1st Round: into ring work 6 ch, (1 tr, 3 ch) 5 times, 1 ss into 3rd ch of rd.

2nd Round: 1 ss into 1st ch space, into same

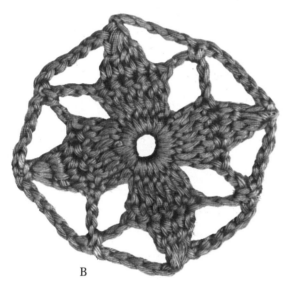

B

hook) 3 times, thread over and draw through all loops on hook, ★, 6 ch, 1 dc into ch space of previous row, 6 ch ★★, miss next dbl tr, (1 tr into next dbl tr leaving last loop of tr on hook) 4 times, thread over and draw through all loops on hook; rep from ★ 3 times more ending last rep at ★★, 1 ss into top of 1st tr group. Fasten off.

Rosette C: make a ch of 5 sts, 1 ss into 1st ch to form ring. Work (5 ch, 1 dc into 2nd, 3rd, 4th and 5th ch from hook, 1 ss into ring) 8 times. Fasten off.

2nd Round: 1 ss into turning ch of any point, ★ 5 ch, 1 ss into next point; rep from ★ to last point, 5 ch, 1 ss into 1st ss of round.

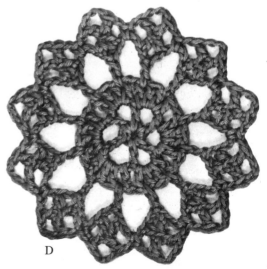

D

space 3 ch, 3 tr, 1 ch, (into next ch space 4 tr, 1 ch) 5 times, 1 ss into 3rd ch of rd.

3rd Round: 1 ss between 3 ch and 1st tr of previous rd, 10 ch, 1 tr between 3rd and 4th tr of previous rd, 7 ch, (1 tr between 1st and

2nd tr of next group of 4 tr in previous rd, 7 ch, 1 tr between 3rd and 4th tr of same group in previous rd, 7 ch) 5 times, 1 ss into 3rd ch of rd.

4th Round: 1 ss into each of next 4 ch, ★ 1 ch, 1 cr tr: right lower tr into 5th st of 7 ch to the right, the left lower tr into 2nd st of 7 ch to the left, the 2 upper tr are separated by 3 ch, 1 ch, 1 dc into next 7 ch space; rep from ★ to end, omitting last dc in last rep and working 1 ss into 4th ss of rd. Fasten off. (Crossed trebles, see page 72.)

American' crochet
(Reversed direction patches)

American' crochet – like Irish crochet – consists of single rosettes or square motifs which are joined together similar to patchwork. The difference between 'American' and Irish crochet lies merely in the method of working. 'American' crochet motifs are worked in rounds, but the work is turned after the completion of each round as follows:

Make 4 ch and join with ss into 1st ch to form a ring.

1st Round: 3 ch, into ring work 2 tr, (3 ch, 3 tr) 4 times, 3 ch, 1 ss into 3rd ch of rd. Turn and work **2nd Round** on the reverse side: 3 ch, into next ch space of previous rd 2 tr, 3 ch, 3 tr, 1 ch (into next ch space 3 tr, 3 ch, 3 tr, 1 ch) 4 times, 1 ss into 3rd ch of rd. Turn.

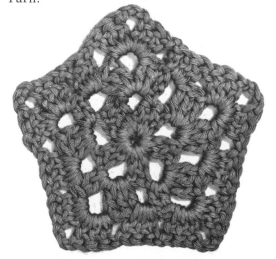

3rd Round: 3 ch, 2 tr into next 1 ch space of previous rd, 1 ch, (into 3 ch space work 3 tr, 3 ch, 3 tr, 1 ch ★★, into 1 ch space 3 tr, 1 ch) 5 times, ending last rep at ★★, 1 ss into 3rd ch of rd. Turn.

Squares can be crocheted in a similar manner (see photographs, page 88). For one of these make a ring of 4 ch.

1st Round: into ring work 3 ch, 2 tr, (3 ch, 3 tr) 3 times, 3 ch, 1 ss into 3rd ch of rd. Turn.

2nd Round: into each ch space work 3 tr, 3 ch (for corner), 3 tr, 1 ss into 3rd ch. Turn. In the 3rd and following rds work 3 tr between each group of 3 tr in previous rd and into each 3 ch space at corners work 3 tr, 3 ch, 3 tr.

500 hexagonal motifs are required to make a bedspread measuring 66 × 96 in., 20 strips with 25 motifs in each. Regular increases in the rounds change the shape of the motif from a circle in the centre to a hexagon. Instructions on page 120

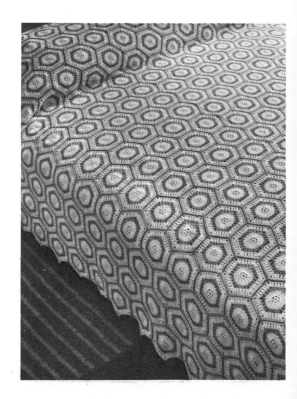

Sample squares are shown in cotton thread (left) and wool (right)

Bedspread in 'American crochet' (below and on right).

Bedspread made up of squares, triangles and zig-zag strips (left). Cushion cover or pillow slip of crocheted motifs (above and below).

Material: cotton thread. Instructions for both models on pages 118 and 119

Lattice loop crochet

For this type of crochet, which produces a lattice effect, a piece of firm smooth cardboard (or a flat ruler) is required. The height of the cardboard strip determines the height of the loop stitches which are no more than elongated double crochet stitches between rows (or a row) of double crochet of normal size.

Start with a chain row followed by a double crochet row. Pull out the chain stitch for turning until it is as long as the height of the cardboard. Place the cardboard at the

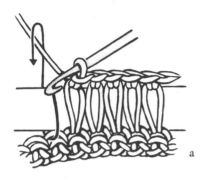

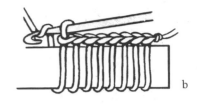

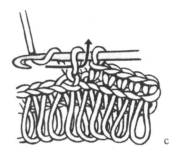

desired number of loop stitch rows and double crochet rows, finish work with a double crochet row.

Loop Stitch crochet

Loop Stitch crochet – also called Bouclé crochet – can be worked either with the aid of a cardboard strip or over one or more

back of the long stitch and the double crochet row, leaving the working thread under and behind the cardboard. Insert hook into long stitch, thread over from behind the strip and draw through, * insert hook into next stitch and under the cardboard, thread over and draw a long loop to the upper edge of the cardboard through (a), thread over and draw through both loops on hook; repeat from * to end. Pull out the cardboard after completion of row, turn with 1 ch and work one dc row (or more if desired). For the last dc in the row following loop stitch row, insert hook into top two threads of stitch as usual and also into the very last thread of loop stitch row; then crochet all loops off together. After the

fingers of the left hand. While rows of even-sized loops appear on one side (the right side of the finished article) the reverse side shows the smooth texture of double crochet rows. Loop stitch, using a cardboard strip: hold the strip between ring finger and little finger of the left hand. Hold thread and hook in the usual manner. Make 1 ch, ★ guide thread from front to back around and to the upper edge of the cardboard, thread over and make another ch (b); repeat from ★ for the required length. After completion of row pull out the cardboard, turn and work one row of double crochet without it (c). Turn, and using cardboard again ★ insert hook into dc of previous row, guide thread from front to back around and to the upper edge of the cardboard, thread over and draw through, thread over and draw through both loops; repeat from ★ to end. For smaller loops a pencil may be used instead of the cardboard strip; the resulting stitch is called Furry stitch.

Loop stitch, worked without a cardboard strip: work one row of chain stitches.

1st Row: insert hook into 2nd st from hook, ★ pass thread around middle and ring finger of left hand and draw loop through (d),

Bathroom set in Loop stitch worked in wool

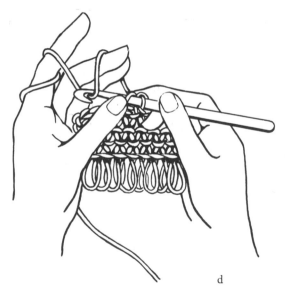

d

thread over and draw through both loops, slip loop off fingers, insert hook into next st; rep from ★ to last st, complete last st as before. These loops are formed on the back of the work. Work 1 row of double crochet, then another row of loop sts. Rep last 2 rows.

Variations of double crochet and trebles

Knit stitch (above)

This stitch is worked in forward rows only. Work from right to left without turning at the end of a row. Cut the thread at the end of each row and fasten off. Then attach thread to the beginning of the previous row with a slip stitch. Work one row of dc fasten off.

Pattern Row: ss into top of 1st st, insert hook into every st of previous row between the 2 upright threads (instead of under the 2 top threads) and draw thread through, thread over and draw through both loops. Fasten off thread at end of row. Rep pattern row.

Rose treble (below left)

Work in forward rows only without turning work. Work one row of ch and fasten off.

Pattern Row: ss into 1st st, ★ thread over insert hook into st and draw thread through st and 1st loop on hook, thread over and draw through both loops on hook, rep from ★ into every st to end of row. Fasten off. Rep pattern row.

Braid stitch (below right)

The basic stitch for this pattern is double crochet. Inserting the hook into a thread behind the two top threads gives the work a different appearance. Work in forward rows only. Work one row of dc and fasten off.

Pattern Row: ss into 1st st, ★ insert hook into the horizontal thread at the back of and below the 2 top threads and draw thread through, thread over and draw through both loops; rep from ★ into every st to end of row. Fasten off. Rep pattern row. The 2 top threads of each dc now lie at the front of work.

Pattern Row: ss into 1st st of previous row, insert hook from front to back into back thread of 1st st and from back to front into back thread of next st, thread over and draw through, thread over and draw through 2 loops, insert hook from front to back into back thread of 2nd st (already used once for previous st) and from back to front into back thread of next st, thread over and draw through, thread over and draw through 2 loops. Continue in this manner to the end of the row, making last st into back thread of last st. Fasten off. Rep pattern row.

Bosnian crochet (above)

Work one row of dc and fasten off.
Pattern Row: ss into 1st st of previous row, insert hook into the back thread on the top of each st of previous row and draw thread through and through loop on hook. At the end of the row, cut thread and fasten off. Rep pattern row.

Rumanian crochet (below)

Work in forward rows only without turning work. Work one row of dc and fasten off.

Solomon's Knot or Netting (above)

Make a row of ch sts divisible by 4 plus 2 ch.
1st Row: into 2nd ch from hook work 1 dc, ★ draw the loop on hook out to $\frac{1}{3}$ in. (longer or shorter according to closeness of fabric desired), thread over and draw through loop, insert hook into back thread of st and work 1 dc (this completes 1st half of knot), rep from ★ once (1 Solomon's Knot completed), miss 3 ch, 1 dc into next st★★. Work from ★ to ★★ to end of row. Turn with one complete and one half knot.
2nd Row: 1 dc into centre of last Knot made in previous row, ★ 1 Solomon's Knot, 1 dc into centre of next Solomon's Knot in previous row; rep from ★ to end, turn with 1 complete and 1 half knot. Rep 2nd row.

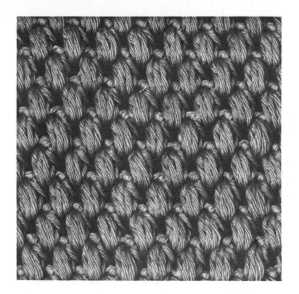

Ball stitch

Make a row of chain stitches.

1st Row: miss 3 sts, ★ thread over, insert hook into next st and draw thread through, (thread over, insert hook into same st and draw thread through) twice, thread over and draw thread through all loops on hook, 1 ch, miss 1 ch; rep from ★, omitting 1 ch, miss 1 ch at end and working 1 tr into last st, 3 ch, turn.

In the following rows work the group of three stitches into the chain spaces for a diagonal effect, or into the top of previous groups when the bobbles will lie in straight lines up and down the right side of fabric.

Ball stitch in forward rows (above)

Make a row of chain stitches divisible by 2.

1st Row: work as 1st row in previous pattern, cut thread and fasten off.

2nd Row: 1 ss into 3rd ch of previous row, into each foll ch sp work 1 group of 3 sts as before and 1 ch, 1 tr on last tr. Fasten off.

3rd Row: 1 ss into 3rd ch of previous row, 1 group of 3 sts into sp between turning ch and 1st group 1 ch, 1 group into every ch sp, 1 ch. When last group has been completed, omitting 1 ch, work 1 tr on tr of previous row. Rep 2nd and 3rd rows.

Basket weave in long trebles

On a ch row of stitches divisible by 6 plus 4, work 1 row of tr. Start pattern in **2nd Row:** 2 ch, miss 1 tr, ★ insert hook horizontally from right to left under next tr of previous row and draw through a long loop, thread over and draw through 2 loops on hook, thread over and draw through 2 remaining loops (1 long tr into front made), make 1 long tr into front of next 2 sts, insert hook from back to front under next tr of previous row and draw through a long loop, thread over and complete as previous long tr (1 long tr into back made), make 1 long tr into next 2 sts; rep from ★ ending row with 3 long tr into front of next 3 sts, 1 dc into turning ch.

3rd Row: 2 ch, work as 2nd row from ★ to end.

4th and 5th Rows: 2 ch ★ 1 long tr into back of next 3 sts of previous row, 1 long tr into front of next 3 sts; rep from ★ ending row with 1 long tr into back of next 3 sts, 1 dc in ch. Rep last 4 rows.

Section of a bedspread made up of separate motifs. The rosettes are variations of motifs C and D described on page 85

Open Work or Filet crochet

The following patterns for some of a great variety of Open Work stitches can be worked in wool or any type of yarn. They are also suitable for lace when mercerised crochet cotton and a steel hook should be used. Insertions and trimmings for bed- and table-linen, handkerchief edgings, headscarves and shawls are often crocheted in patterns of this kind and also luncheon mats, table cloths, cushion covers and bedspreads. A number of smaller motifs or sections are usually worked for bedspreads. These are joined together like patchwork (page 236). Start all Open Work patterns with a chain row.

Pattern A
1st Row: miss 7 ch, 1 ss into next ch, ★ 4 ch, miss 3 ch, 1 ss into next ch; rep from ★.
2nd Row: ★ 4 ch, 1 ss into next ch sp of previous row; rep from ★.
All following rows are worked as 2nd row.

Pattern B
1st Row: miss 5 ch, 1 tr into next st, ★ miss 2 ch, 1 tr, 2 ch, 1 tr into next st; rep from ★.
2nd and all following Rows: 5 ch, 1 tr into 1st ch sp, ★ into next ch sp 1 tr, 2 ch, 1 tr; rep from ★.

Pattern C (filet- or net-background)
1st Row: miss 5 ch, ★ 1 tr into next ch, 1 ch, miss 1 ch; rep from ★ to last st, 1 tr into last st, 4 ch, turn.
2nd and all following Rows: miss 1st tr of previous row, ★ 1 tr into next tr, 1 ch; rep from ★ to end, 1 tr into 3rd st of ch.

A

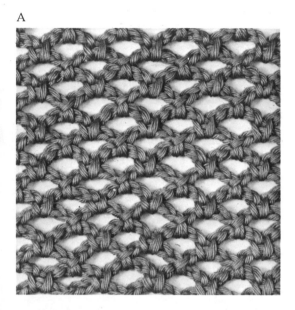

B

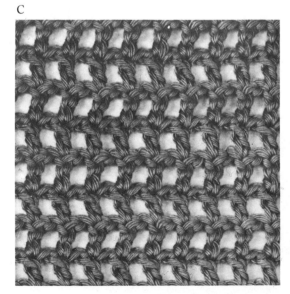

C

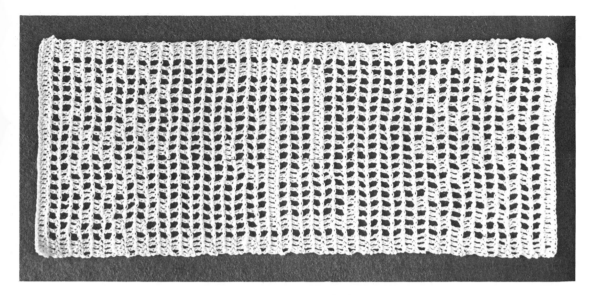

Pattern D

1st Row: miss 7 ch, 1 tr into next ch, 2 ch, ★ 1 tr into next ch, miss 2 ch, rep from ★ ending with 1 tr into last ch, 2 ch, turn.

2nd Row: ★ 3 dc into next ch sp, 1 ch; rep from ★ to last tr of previous row, 1 ss into tr, 5 ch, turn.

3rd Row: ★ 1 tr into ch sp, 2 ch; rep from ★ ending with 1 tr into turning ch of previous row, 2 ch, turn.

To continue pattern, rep 2nd and 3rd rows.

Pattern E

1st Row: miss 7 ch, 1 dc into next ch, ★ 3 ch, miss 3 sts, 1 dc into next ch; rep from ★, 4 ch, turn.

2nd Row: 1 tr into 1st ch sp, ★ 1 ch, 4 tr into next sp, 1 ch, 1 tr into next sp; rep from ★ to end, 1 ch, 1 tr into 4th turning ch, 2 ch, turn.

3rd Row: 1 dc into 1st sp, 3 ch, ★ 1 dc into next sp, 3 ch; rep from ★ ending 1 dc into into 3rd turning ch, 4 ch, turn.

D

E

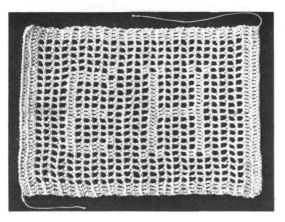

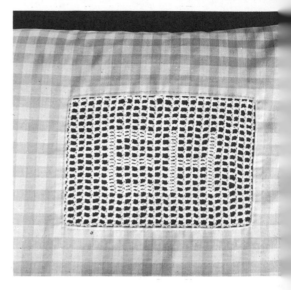

4th Row: ★ 4 tr into 1st sp, 1 ch, 1 tr into next sp, 1 ch; rep from ★ ending with 4 tr into next sp, 1 tr into turning ch, 4 ch, turn.

5th Row: 1 dc into sp after 1st 4 tr, 3 ch, ★ 1 dc into next sp, 3 ch; rep from ★ to last sp, 1 dc into last sp, 3 ch, 1 dc into 2nd ch of turning ch.

To continue pattern, rep 2nd to 5th rows inclusive.

Insertions for pillows and luncheon sets in Filet crochet are worked following simple diagrams similar to those used for Cross stitch embroidery. The filled-in squares consist of trebles replacing the Chain stitches of the Filet background pattern

Pattern F

1st Row: into 2nd ch from hook 1 dc, ★ 3 ch, miss 5 ch, into next st 5 tr, 3 ch, miss 5 sts, into next st 1 dc; rep from ★ to end.

2nd Row: 2 ch, ★ 1 tr into each of 5 tr in previous row, 1 ch, 1 dc into next dc, 1 ch;

F

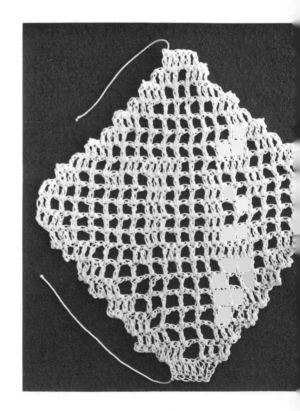

Napkin rings with initials can be crocheted following a diagram drawn on squared paper

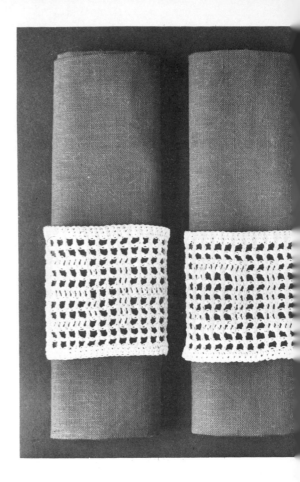

rep from ★ to end, 2 more ch, turn.

3rd Row: 2 tr into 1st dc, ★ 3 ch, into the next 3rd tr of previous row 1 dc, 3 ch, into next dc of previous row 5 tr; rep from ★ working only 3 tr into last dc, 3 ch, turn.

4th Row: 1 tr into each of next 2 tr, ★ 1 ch, 1 dc into next dc, 1 ch, 1 tr into each of next 5 tr; rep from ★ ending row with 2 tr, 1 tr into 3rd turning ch, 1 ch, turn.

5th Row: 1 dc into 1st tr, ★ 3 ch, into next dc 5 tr, 3 ch, into next 3rd tr 1 dc; rep from ★ working last dc into 3rd turning ch.

Pattern G

Make a chain of a number of stitches divisible by 5 plus 3 ch.

1st Row: miss 3 ch, 1 tr into each of next 4 sts, ★ 1 ch, miss 1 ch, 1 tr into each of next 4 sts; rep from ★ to last st, 1 tr into next st.

2nd Row: 5 ch, ★ 1 dc into next ch sp of previous row, 4 ch; rep from ★ ending with 1 dc into 3rd turning ch.

3rd Row: 3 ch, 4 tr into next ch sp, ★ 1 ch, 4 tr into next ch sp; rep from ★ to last st, 1 tr into 1st ch.

To continue pattern, rep 2nd and 3rd rows.

 G

Cluster and Shell-stitch patterns

Both types of pattern consist of a number of trebles worked into one stitch. For a cluster each treble is only half completed before the next one is worked. The required number of trebles is crocheted off together to form the typical clusters or bobbles in relief on one side of the fabric only. Trebles in Shell patterns are completed separately (sometimes combined with groups of trebles crocheted off together) and the fabric is flat, the shells appearing on both sides.

Hazelnut *(Popcorn)* stitch: on a row of ch sts work 1 row of dc, 11 ch, turn.

thread over and draw through 2 loops, (into same st: thread over and draw through, thread over and draw through 2 loops) 4 times, thread over and draw through 6 loops on hook (1 cl made), miss next st in 2nd row, 1 dc into next st; rep from *, 1 ch, turn.

4th Row: as 2nd row.

5th Row: as 3rd row but work 2 dc at beg and end of row and 1st cl into 3rd st of 3rd row.

Rep 2nd to 5th rows inclusive. (Photograph on left.)

Shell Pattern A: on a row of ch sts work:

1st Row: * 1 dc, miss 2 sts, 5 tr into next st, miss 2 sts; rep from * to last st, 1 dc.

2nd Row: 3 ch, 2 tr into 1st dc, * miss 2 tr, 1 dc into next tr, miss 2 tr, 5 tr into next dc; rep from * omitting 2 tr at end of last rep, 1 ch, turn.

Rep 1st and 2nd rows.

2nd Row: 1 dc into each dc of previous row, inserting hook into back top thread, turn with 1 ch. The 2nd row is on the right side of work.

The front top threads of stitches in 1st row lie at the front of row and will be used in next row.

3rd Row: 1 dc into 1st st of previous row, * miss 1 st of 1st row, thread over, insert hook into front top thread of next st (= 2nd st of 1st row) and draw thread through,

The two shell patterns, which are shown in the photographs below, are ideal for shawls, baby blankets or throws and can be successfully worked in either fine Shetland yarns, thicker wools or man-made fibres

A

B

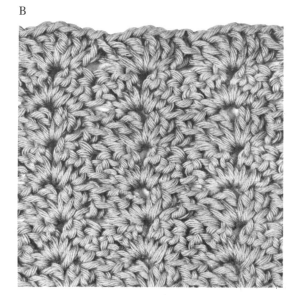

Semi-circular shoulder wrap crocheted in four colours. Instructions on page 120. The crochet must be worked very loosely and a large crochet hook is recommended

Shell Pattern B: make a row of ch sts.

1st Row: miss 3 ch, 1 tr into next st, ★ 2 tr, 1 ch, 2 tr into next st, thread over, insert hook into next st and draw thread through, thread over and draw through 2 loops, miss 3 sts, thread over, insert hook into next st and draw thread through, (thread over and draw through 2 loops) 3 times (= 2 joined tr made); rep from ★ to end.

2nd and all following Rows: 3 ch, miss 2 tr, 1 tr into next st, into ch sp 2 tr, 1 ch, 2 tr, into next and following 4th st 2 joined tr; rep from ★ making last joined tr into tr following ch sp and 3rd turning ch.

The photograph at the top of this page shows the working of the shoulder wrap in closer detail

Wave stitch

Make a row of ch sts.

1st Row: miss 3 ch, 4 tr on next 4 sts, 3 tr into next st, 5 tr on next 5 sts, ★ miss 2 sts, 5 tr on next 5 sts, 3 tr into next st, 5 tr on next 5 sts; rep from ★, 3 ch, turn.

2nd Row: miss 3 ch and 1 tr, 4 tr on next 4 tr, 3 tr into next tr, 5 tr on next 5 tr, ★ miss 2 tr, 5 tr on next 5 tr, 3 tr into next tr, 5 tr on next 5 tr; rep from ★ ending last rep with 4 tr on next 4 tr, 1 tr into last tr of previous row, 3 ch, turn.

Rep 2nd row.

Star stitch

Make a row of ch sts.

1st Row: 1 tr into 4th ch, ★ miss 1 ch, 2 tr into next ch; rep from ★, 1 tr into last ch, 2 ch, turn.

2nd Row: (insert hook into next tr and draw through a loop) 3 times, thread over and draw through 4 loops on hook, ★ 1 ch, insert hook into upright loop at back of last-made st and draw through a loop, (hook into next tr and draw through a loop) twice, thread over and draw through all loops; rep from

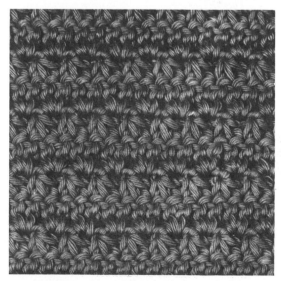

2nd Row: (thread over, insert hook into next tr and draw thread through, thread over and draw through 2 loops) 4 times, thread over and draw through 5 loops (= group of 4 tr made), ★ 4 ch, 1 dc into next tr, 3 ch, group of 9 tr into next 9 sts; rep from ★ ending with group of 5 tr into next 5 sts, 4 ch, turn.

3rd Row: 4 tr into top of 5 tr group (= centre of eye), 1 dc into next dc, ★ 9 tr into top of 9 tr group, 1 dc into next dc; rep from ★ ending with 5 tr into top of 4 tr group, 3 ch, turn.

4th Row: miss 1 tr, ★ group of 9 tr into next 9 sts, 4 ch, 1 dc into next dc, 3 ch; rep from ★ working last dc into turning ch, 1 ch, turn.

5th Row: ★ 9 tr into top of 9 tr group, 1 dc on next dc; rep from ★ working last dc into end of turning ch.

Rep 2nd to 5th rows inclusive.

Picot pattern

Picots, apart from forming a useful edging to crochet work, can also be made as a lace pattern as follows: make a chain row.

1st Row: 1 dc into 2nd ch from hook, ★ (4 ch, into 2nd ch from hook 1 dc, into 3rd ch from hook 1 tr) twice (= 2 picots made), miss 3 ch in ch row, 1 dc into next st; rep from ★, 6 ch, turn.

2nd Row: ★ 1 picot, 1 dc between 2 picots of previous row, 1 picot; rep from ★, 1 quad tr into dc of previous row, 1 ch, turn.

3rd Row: 1 dc into quad tr, ★ 2 picots, 1 dc between next 2 picots of previous row; rep from ★, 1 dc into 6th turning ch, 6 ch, turn.

Rep 2nd and 3rd rows.

★ until 1 tr of previous row remains, 1 loop from upright of last st, 1 loop from next tr, 1 loop from 3rd ch, thread over and draw through loops, 3 ch, turn.

3rd Row: 1 tr into 3rd ch from hook (= centre of star), ★ miss 1 st, 2 tr into next st; rep from ★ to end, 1 tr into 2nd turning ch. Rep 2nd and 3rd rows.

Peacock's eyes

Make a row of ch sts.

1st Row: 1 dc into 2nd ch from hook, ★ miss 3 ch, 9 tr into next st, miss 3 ch, 1 dc into next st; rep from ★, 3 ch, turn.

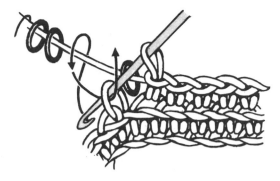

Long scarf with folded-back ends which form pockets. Rings are worked into these using the bead crochet technique (see diagram, above). For this purpose the required number of rings is threaded on one of the yarns from the two balls before beginning the work

The photograph above shows a section of picot lace pattern. Instructions for this are given on the page opposite

Crochet with beads

When beads or rings (photograph on right) are to be crocheted into the fabric, use two balls of yarn. The required number of beads or rings are threaded on to the yarn of the second ball. Work with the first ball up to the row or rounds with beads. Then use the second ball: push the bead or ring towards the hook before inserting the hook into the next stitch so that the beads or rings sit on the thread between two stitches (drawing, above right).

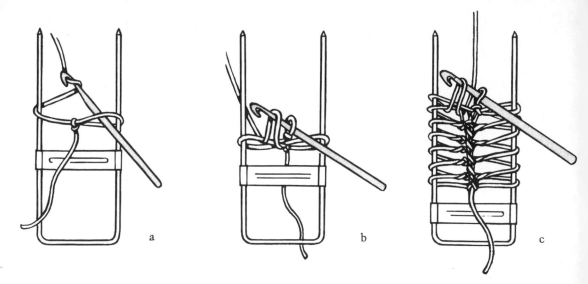

a   b   c

Hairpin or Lace crochet

Hairpin crochet is made with a crochet hook and a U-shaped metal gadget (staple) similar to a hairpin with a centre bar. Staples are obtainable in sizes ranging from $\frac{1}{4}$ in. to 3 in. wide. The width of each braid is determined by the width of the staple, while the length can be worked to any desired size. The loops of several braids are joined together with the aid of the crochet hook, and in this way articles of any size can be made. Wool or crochet cotton can be used for hairpin work, cotton threads producing a particularly clear pattern. (Samples worked in cotton thread.)

Method of working

Make a loop as for the start of a chain stitch and pull it out to half the width of the staple. Put it over the right prong with the knot in the centre. Hold the left prong with thumb and forefinger of the left hand. Take the thread in front of and round the left prong, insert crochet hook into loop and pull thread through loop (a), thread over and draw through one loop. Take hook with loop on it over and behind the right prong. Turn staple from right to left so that thread passes behind both prongs of the staple. Insert hook from below into front loop on left prong and draw thread through (b), thread over hook and draw through both loops. This makes one double crochet. Continue turning hook and working double crochet stitches as described, thus forming a braid of loops with a centre ridge on the staple (c). When the staple is filled with loops, slip work carefully off the prongs and replace on them four or five pairs of loops, the remaining braid hanging free. Do not pull this free-hanging piece too much

White Curtain in Hairpin crochet using cotton thread (below left)

as at this stage the loops are easily unravelled. Once all loops of the separate braids have been joined together the work will be strong enough to be handled easily. The joining

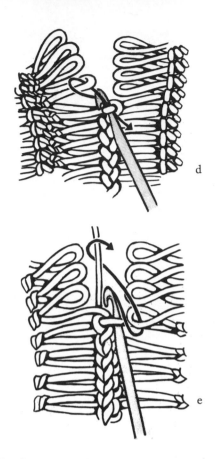

d

e

may also be used. Wool and cotton threads can be used and a variety of patterns worked. The firmness of the fabric is determined by the stitch-size which is set to be of a certain length by means of a small ring between the eye of the needle and the shaft. Looping uses more thread than crocheting or knitting. It gives, however, a considerably thicker-textured fabric with a one-way-stretch.

Method of working looping

Thread the needle with the yarn and make a loop-knot with the short end (a). Set the ring to the desired stitch size. Hold the loop-needle in the right hand similar to a knitting needle. Hold the loop with thumb and fore-finger of the left hand and push needle with yarn through this loop as far as the ring (b). Now take the thread on the left side of the needle with thumb and forefinger and pull needle back again, the distance depending on the ring-setting. Hold this loop with the fingers of the left hand as before (c) and continue making a row of chain stitches. Care must be taken not to turn the needle. The thread on the left side of the needle is already part of the stitch being worked, while the thread on the right of the needle comes from the ball (d). When the chain is of the desired length hold the last loop, which is the edge of the work, and turn the chain. The chain stitch for the edge now lies to the left (e). The following rows are worked – unlike the usual crocheting – from left to right.

1st Row: push needle through the upper thread of second-last stitch and from back to front through the edge stitch (f). Hold thread to the left of the needle and pull needle back to length of ring-setting. Hold the loop and push needle through the upper thread of the next stitch and from back to front through last-made loop (g). To achieve an even tension, care must be taken always to push the needle through as far as the ring and to hold the loops firmly. Continue now: hold thread, pull back the needle, hold

can be done in various ways. One method of joining the braids requires no thread: insert hook into one, two or several loops of one braid and draw through them the same number of loops of the next braid (d). Another method, requiring the same or a contrasting thread, is to insert the hook alternately into a loop (or loops) to the left and a loop (or loops) to the right making one chain stitch between each (e). Many varia-tions of these simple methods can be achieved by twisting the loops of each braid. (Photographs, pages 108 and 109.)

Looping

Looping is worked with a special tool which resembles a very large darning needle with a shaft. It is obtainable in two sizes under the name K-TEL knitter or Betty-Ann knitter. Susan Bates yarn needle or yarn end weaver (U.S.) or Boye Stole-Weaving needle (U.S.)

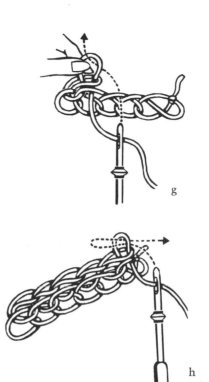

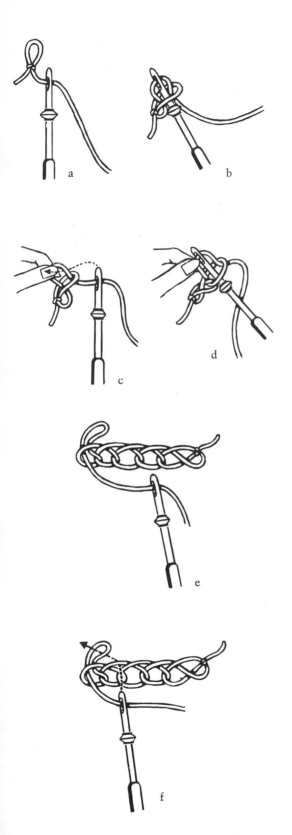

loop, push needle into next stitch and so on to the end of the row. The loop for the edge is worked as follows: push needle from the back through last-made loop, make next loop in the usual way, hold it and turn work (h). After the first row push the ring a little towards the shaft and continue as described for as many rows as required. Always push the needle into the front top thread of the stitches in previous rows – not through both top threads. As the tension is not regulated by the fingers of the left or right hand holding the working thread – as it is in crochet and knitting – it is advisable to unwind a little thread at a time from the ball and leave it lying near the work. In this way there will be no pulling of the working thread between work and ball, and the stitches will be even. Care should also be taken always to pull the needle back sufficiently far after pushing it through a loop as far as the ring and before forming the next loop. This also will avoid uneven loops. Ring-settings for different yarns are roughly as follows: thin yarn $=\frac{1}{2}$ to $\frac{3}{4}$ in.; medium yarn $=\frac{3}{4}$ to 1 in.; thick

111

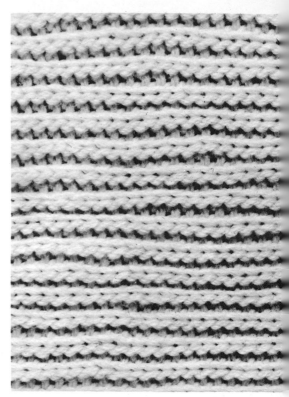

yarn = 1 to $1\frac{1}{3}$ in. This is the distance between tip of needle and ring.

Horizontal rib pattern

Work one row of chain stitches as described on page 67.

1st Row: hold last loop of chain row between thumb and forefinger and turn work, miss next chain stitch, pull needle back about $\frac{2}{5}$ in. and push from front to back through next chain stitch (a). Hold thread on left of needle, pull needle back about $\frac{2}{5}$ in. push it into next loop to the left from front to back and then into first loop (edge-loop) from back to front (b). Hold thread on left of needle, pull needle back about $\frac{2}{5}$ in. and push it through the next loop to the left (c), pull needle back thus forming loop. Continue as described, missing every second stitch of chain row (d), form loop, take two loops

The technique of Looping offers fewer possibilities for variety in patterns than crochet. However, the basic Looping stitches (above and on right) can be varied in many ways

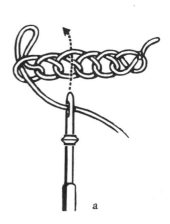

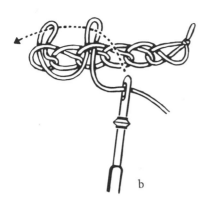

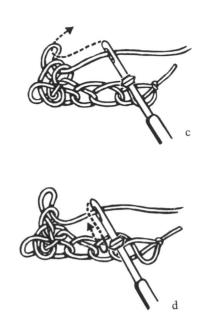

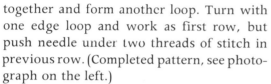

together and form another loop. Turn with one edge loop and work as first row, but push needle under two threads of stitch in previous row. (Completed pattern, see photograph on the left.)

Looping-work needs no casting off. After last loop has been made cut thread and pull end through loop. Sew in end.

Instructions for crochet models

Abbreviations:

Col: colour; rd: round; st(s): stitch(es); sp: space; inc: increase(s); dec: decrease(s); rep: repeat; beg: beginning; cont: continue; ch: chain; ss: slip stitch; dc: double crochet; tr: treble; hlf tr: half treble; dbl tr: double treble; trip tr: triple treble; quad tr: quadruple treble; quin tr: quintuple treble; cr tr: crossed treble; cl: cluster.

Loose cover for cushion, page 76

Size: 13 by 17 in. Tension: 8 tr and 4 rows = 2 sq. in. Materials: Patons Double Knitting Wool in 50-g balls. 2 balls Loam Brown (5), 1 ball each Spruce (6628), Burnt Orange (5020) and Primrose (2455). Crochet Hook No. 5.00 (6). The cover consists of 12 squares in spruce with brown surrounds. One orange and one primrose rosette are sewn to the centre of each square. Square: starting at centre with spruce work three rounds as given on pages 76 and 77.

4th Round: brown, 15 tr each side. Pin out each of the 12 squares to measure 4 by 4 in. and press gently under damp cloth. Make 3 strips of 4 squares each. To join 2 squares: oversew not too tightly through back top threads of 15 tr each on 2 adjoining sides. Join 3 strips in similar manner to form an oblong. Join brown to a corner of oblong and work 3 ch, 1 tr, 1 ch, 2 tr into corner ch sp, 15 tr on 15 tr, ★ 1 tr into ch sp of square, 1 tr into ch sp of next square, 15 tr on 15 tr; rep from ★ to end of side ★★, 2 tr, 1 ch, 2 tr into corner ch sp; rep from ★ all round ending last side at ★★, ss into 3rd ch. This completes the front of the cover. Work 2 more rds of tr without increases, i.e. one tr into each corner.

Next Round: 1 tr into every 2nd tr of previous rd. Fasten off. Make a chain about 75 in. long of brown, used double, fasten off. Large rosette: make a ring of 5 ch.

1st Round: 3 ch, 11 tr into ring, ss into 3rd ch.

2nd Round: 3 ch, 2 tr into same sp as ss, 1 ch (miss 1 st, 3 tr into next st, 1 ch) 5 times, ss into 3rd tr.

3rd Round: with No. 3.00 hook work picots, (1 dc into next st, 3 ch, 1 dc into 3rd ch from hook) 24 times, ss into 1st dc. Fasten off. Small rosette: with No. 3.00 hook make ring of 4 ch.

1st Round: 9 dc into ring, ss into 1st dc.

2nd Round: as 3rd rd of large rosette making 9 picots. Fasten off.

To make up: sew 1 large rosette to the centre of each square and 1 small rosette on top of each large one. Slot chain through last rd of cover and fold last 3 rds to the back of cushion pad. Tie chain.

Tortoise, page 77

Materials: Twilley's Stalite No. 3 Cotton, 1 ball each Chocolate (37), Spun Gold (27), Kingfisher (23). Crochet Hook No. 3.00 (10/11). Abbreviations: Chocolate: C; Spun Gold: S; Kingfisher: K.

Back: with C make 15 ch sts.

1st Round: into 3rd ch from hook 1 dc, 11 dc on next 11 ch, 3 dc into next ch (= 1st ch), on opposite side 12 dc into next 12 loops, 2 dc into next turning ch.

2nd Round: 2 dc into next turning ch, 12 dc on 12 dc, (2 dc into next dc) 3 times, 12 dc on 12 dc, (2 dc into next dc) twice.

3rd Round: work 36 dc.

4th Round: (2 dc into next dc) twice, 12 dc on 12 dc, (2 dc into next dc) 6 times, 12 dc on 12 dc, (2 dc into next dc) 4 times.

5th and 6th Rounds: work 48 dc.

7th Round: (2 dc into next dc, 1 dc into next dc) twice, 12 dc on 12 dc, (2 dc into next dc, 1 dc into next dc) 6 times, 12 dc on 12 dc, (2 dc into next dc, 1 dc into next dc) 4 times.

8th and 9th Rounds: work 60 dc.

10th Round: (2 dc into next dc, 1 dc into next dc) 3 times, 12 dc on 12 dc, (2 dc into next dc, 1 dc into next dc) 9 times, 12 dc on 12 dc, (2 dc into next dc, 1 dc into next dc) 6 times. Fasten off.

114

11th Round: with K work 78 dc into back top threads.

12th to 15th Rounds: work 78 dc through both top threads.

16th Round: with S into back top threads: (1 hlf tr into next st, 1 tr into next st, 2 dbl tr into next st, 2 dbl tr into next st, 1 tr into next st, 1 hlf tr into next st) 13 times. Fasten off.

Underside: with K work as back until 5th round has been completed. 48 sts.

6th Round: (2 dc into next dc) 4 times, 12 dc on 12 dc, (2 dc into next st) 12 times, 12 dc on 12 dc, (2 dc into next dc) 8 times.

7th and 8th Rounds: work 72 dc.

9th Round: (2 dc into next dc, 1 dc into next dc) 4 times, 12 dc on 12 dc, (2 dc into next dc, 1 dc into next dc) 12 times, 12 dc on 12 dc, (2 dc into next dc, 1 dc into next dc) 8 times.

10th Round: work 96 dc. Fasten off.

Leg (make 4): with K make 5 ch.

1st Round: into 3rd and 4th ch 1 dc each, into next ch 3 dc, on opposite side 2 dc on 2 ch, 2 dc into 1st turning ch.

2nd Round: 2 dc into turning ch, 2 dc on 2 dc, (2 dc into next dc) 3 times, 2 dc on 2 dc, (2 dc into next dc) twice. 16 dc.

3rd to 11th Rounds: work 16 dc. Fasten off and leave 10 in. of thread hanging.

Head: with K make 4 ch.

1st Round: into 3rd ch 1 dc, into 4th ch 3 dc. on opposite side 1 dc into ch, 2 dc into next ch.

2nd Round: 2 dc into next ch (2 dc into next dc) 7 times.

3rd and 4th Rounds: work 16 dc.

5th Round: (2 dc into next dc, 1 dc into next dc) 8 times.

6th to 9th Rounds: work 24 dc.

10th Round: (2 dc into next dc, miss 1 dc, 1 dc into next dc, miss 1 dc) 8 times.

11th to 16th Rounds: work 18 dc. Fasten off and leave 10 in. of thread hanging.

Tail: with K make 2 ch.

1st Round: 5 dc into 2nd ch.

2nd Round: 2 dc into each of 5 dc.

3rd and 4th Rounds: work 10 dc.

5th Round: (2 dc into next dc, 1 dc into next dc) 5 times.

6th and 7th Rounds: work 15 dc. Fasten off and leave 10 in. of thread hanging.

Circles for back: with S 3 rounds as for tail.

4th Round: 2 dc into each of next 10 dc, ss into next dc. Fasten off and leave thread hanging about 4 in.

Make 21 circles in all.

To make up: sew circles to back as in the photograph, stuffing each with the ends of thread. Sew back at last dc-round and underside together leaving opening for head. Stuff body and head with cotton wool and sew head to body. Stuff legs and tail and stitch tops of each together, then sew to body.

Pot-holders, page 78

Materials: Twilley's Knitcot, Crochet Hook No. 3.00 (11).

Heart: 1 ball White (78), 1 ball Scarlet (88). With white make 2 ch.

1st Row: into 2nd ch from hook work 3 dc, 1 ch, turn.

2nd Row: 3 dc on 3 dc 1 dc into ch.

3rd Row: 4 dc on 4 dc, 1 dc into ch. Cont inc in this manner at the end of every row until there are 28 dc.

Next Row: 14 dc, 1 ch, turn. Dec 1 st at the beg of next and every following row by missing 1st dc until 3 sts remain. Fasten off. Rejoin thread at centre to remaining sts, dc 14 sts to end. Complete to correspond to 1st side, dec at end of every row. Edging: with Scarlet work 2 rounds of dc around the outer edge, starting at 1st row of division. At end of last rd make a loop of 14 ch and work 24 dc into loop. Fasten off. Make 2.

Triangle: 1 ball Scarlet (88), 1 ball White (78). Work as for Heart, but cont inc until there are 32 dc. Fasten off. With contrasting colour make a small triangle (see photograph) and sew to larger one. Using the 'Bobinette' make a chain long enough to fit around larger triangle plus 6 in. Sew chain around triangle, make loops at each corner. Make 2.

Woven Strips: 1 ball White (78), 1 ball Gentian Blue (92). Strip: make a chain of 28 sts. Work 5 rows of 27 dc in each row. Fasten off. Make 5 strips in blue and 5 strips in white. Weave them together to form a square and sew them at the crossing points. Starting at a corner, work 2 rds of dc around the square. At end of last rd make a loop of chain and dc as for heart. Fasten off. Make 2. Ribbed Square: Twilley's Stalite No. 3 Cotton, 1 ball. Crochet Hook No. 3.00 (11). Make a ring of 20 ch, then work 1 rd of dc into back top thread of each ch.

1st Row: 4 dc into back top thread of 4 dc, 3 dc in to next st, 4 dc into next 4 dc, 1 ch, turn.

2nd Row: 5 dc on 5 dc, 3 dc into next dc, 5 dc on 5 ch, 1 ch, turn. Cont in this manner inc in the centre st of every row until there are 61 sts. Fasten off. Work 1 row of picots as given on page 72, No. 1.

Nursery slippers, page 79

Materials: oddments of 4-ply wool. Crochet Hook No. 3.00 (11). Size: approximately 4½ in. Top: make a ring of 5 ch.

1st Round: 5 dc into ring.

2nd Round: 2 dc into every st.

3rd Round: (2 dc into next st, 1 dc into next st) 5 times. 15 sts.

4th Round: (2 dc on 2 dc, 2 dc into next st) 5 times. 20 sts.

5th Round: (3 dc on 3 dc, 2 dc into next st) 5 times. 25 sts.

6th Round: inc in every 5th st. 30 sts.

7th Round: inc in every 6th st. 35 sts.

8th Round: 5 dc on 5 dc, (2 dc in next st, 6 dc on 6 dc) 5 times, 2 dc in next st, 5 dc on 5 dc, 28 ch to be joined to 1st dc of rd.

9th Round: inc in every 6th st 4 times, dc to end.

10th to 15th Rounds: work 60 dc. Fasten off. Work 1 rd of 1 dc, 1 ch into 3rd rd as decoration. With right side of work facing 10 dc into free 10 dc of circle, 1 dc into side of rd, 28 dc on opposite side of ch, 1 dc into side of rd. Work 11 rds of 40 dc. Make 1 rd of picots (page 72, No. 1).

Sole: use back of tortoise as guide, from 15 ch to 5th rd inclusive as back.

6th Round as 7th rd of back. 60 sts. Fasten off.

With wrong sides facing each other crochet sole and top together with 1 rd of dc.

Baby bootees, page 79

Materials: Twilley's Stalite No. 3 Cotton, 1 ball. Crochet Hook No. 3.00 (11). Size: 4 in. Make a ch of 15 sts. Starting at 3rd ch from hook, 7 dc into next 7 ch, 1 hlf tr into next ch, 5 tr into next 5 ch, 3 tr into next ch (= 1st ch), on opposite side working into loops of ch 5 tr, 1 hlf tr, 7 dc and 3 dc into turning ch. 32 sts. Mark last st of this and following rounds.

2nd Round: (13 dc on 13 dc, 2 dc into next 3 sts) twice. 38 sts.

3rd Round: (13 dc on 13 dc, 2 dc into next 6 sts) twice. 50 sts.

4th Round: 13 dc on 13 dc, (2 dc into next st, 1 dc into next st) 3 times, (1 dc into next st, 2 dc into next st) 3 times, 25 dc to end. 56 sts.

5th and 6th Rounds: 56 dc.

This completes the sole. From 7th to 11th rd inclusive work dc into top back loop.

7th and 8th Rounds: 56 dc.

9th Round: 14 dc on 14 dc, (miss 1, 2 dc on next 2 dc) 6 times, 26 dc to end.

10th Round: 13 dc on 13 dc, (miss 1, 1 dc on next dc) 6 times, 25 dc to end.

11th Round: 13 dc on 13 dc, (miss 1, 1 dc on next dc) 3 times, 25 dc to end. ** Work 14 dc, 1 ch, turn, work 36 dc, 1 ch, turn. On 36 sts work 9 rows of dc, dec 1 st at beg of next 8 rows. 28 sts. Work 1 rd of picots around the opening (page 72, No. 1). With top facing, work 1 rd of dc through sts of 6th rd to mark sole. Slot ribbon through sts between 7th and 8th rds.

Baby shoes: Twilley's Stalite No. 3 Cotton, 1 ball. Crochet Hook No. 3.00 (11). 2 small buttons. Size: 4 in. Work like bootees as far as **.

Next Row: 8 dc, 1 ch, turn.

Next Row: 30 dc, 1 ch turn. On 30 dc work 5 rows, make a ch of 12 sts at the end of last row for tab of left shoe. For right shoe fasten off at end of 4th row. Make 12 ch and then work 5th row. Cont in dc over all sts. Make a buttonhole over 2 sts in 7th row (see page 74). After completion of 8th row fasten off. Mark sole with 1 rd of dc as given for bootees.

If liked, work 1 rd of dc in embroidery cotton all round opening, and embroider three rosebuds on front. Sew on buttons.

Mohair scarf, page 79

Materials: Twilley's Mohair in 20-g (200 yd) balls, 2 balls. Crochet Hook No. 5.00 (6).

Start the square scarf in the centre: make 4 ch, ss into 1st ch to form ring.

1st Round: into same ch as ss work 1 dc, 3 ch, 1 dc, (into next ch 1 dc, 3 ch, 1 dc) 3 times, ss into 1st dc.

2nd Round: ss into 1st ch of last rd, into 2nd ch work 1 dc, 3 ch, 1 dc, (into next 2nd ch 1 dc, 3 ch, 1 dc) 3 times, ss into 1st dc. Work all following rounds loosely.

3rd Round: ss into 1st ch, 1 dc, 3 ch, 1 dc into 2nd ch, (1st corner), 3 ch, 1 dc into 2nd ch of following 3 ch, 3 ch, 1 dc, 3 ch, 1 dc into next 2nd ch (2nd corner), 3 ch, 1 dc into 2nd ch of following 3 ch, 3 ch, 1 dc, 3 ch, 1 dc into next 2nd ch (3rd corner), 3 ch, 1 dc into 2nd of following 3 ch, 3 ch, 1 dc, 3 ch, 1 dc into next 2nd ch (4th corner), 3 ch, 1 dc into 2nd of following 3 ch, 3 ch, ss into 1st dc. Cont in this manner, inc in 4 corners by working 1 dc, 3 ch, 1 dc into 2nd of 3 corner-ch in every rd and 1 dc, separated by 3 ch from previous and next dc into all other 2nd ch of 3 ch. End each rd with a ss into 1st dc of rd. Finish scarf at the end of a round.

Pot-holder with rosette, page 84

Materials: Twilley's Knitcot, 2 balls White. Twilley's Stalite No. 3 Cotton 1 ball each Fire (63) and Almond Green (32). This quantity makes 2 pot-holders. Crochet Hook No. 3.00 (11).

For this pot-holder two squares are made which are then crocheted together with one round of dc and edged with one round of picots (page 72, No. 1).

With white make a square of tr (see page 77) in 7 rounds. Fasten off.

Rosette: with red, make a ring of 6 ch.

1st Round: 16 dc into ring.

2nd Round: (1 dc into next dc, 1 picot of 3 ch, 1 dc into 3rd ch from hook, miss 1 dc) 8 times, ss into 1st dc.

3rd Round: (4 ch, 1 dc round next dc = taking hook from back to front and out at back) 8 times.

4th Round: (into ch sp 1 hlf tr, 4 tr, 1 hlf tr) 8 times, ss into 1st dc of 3rd rd.

5th Round: as 3rd Rd.

6th Round: (into ch sp 1 hlf tr, 5 tr, 1 hlf tr) 8 times, ss into last dc of 5th Rd.

7th Round: as 3rd, working 5 ch each time.

8th Round: (into ch sp 1 hlf tr, 2 tr, 2 dbl tr, 2 tr, 1 hlf tr) 8 times, ss into last dc of 7th rd. Fasten off.

9th Round: with white (7 dc on 7 sts, miss 1) 8 times. Fasten off.

10th Round: with green: attach thread to 2nd dc of previous rd, 8 ch, starting at 4th ch 5 tr into ch, ss to back of 3rd dc, 10 ch, starting at 4th ch 7 tr into ch, ss to back of 5th dc, 8 ch, 5 tr as 1st leaf ss into back of 6th dc. Fasten off. Make 3 more sets of leaves into every foll 2nd petal. Fasten off.

11th Round: with White * ss into a 2nd leaf (corner), 5 ch, ss into 3rd leaf, 4 ch, 2 tr into top back thread of 3rd and 4th dc on petal, 4 ch, ss into next 1st leaf, 5 ch; rep from * all round.

12th Round: (1 tr into ss, 5 tr into ch sp, 5 tr into next ch sp, 1 tr between 2 tr of last rd, 5 tr into next ch sp, 5 tr into next ch sp, 1 tr into ss) 4 times.

13th Round: as 7th rd of square. Fasten off. Place wrong sides of both squares together and work 1 rd of dc with green all round, taking 2 tr together (=1 from each square) for each dc. Finish off with picot edging and a loop of 14 ch in a corner. Work 18 dc round loop and fasten off.

Bedspread in zig-zag pattern,
page 90

Materials: Patons Doublet in 50-g balls, 22 balls Terra Cotta (292), 21 balls Snow Cream (6603), 42 balls Bright Olive (6068), 12 balls County Brown (6605), 13 balls Musk (5509). Crochet Hook No. 7.00 (2). Tension: 12 sts and 8 rows in pattern = 5 sq. in., (very slightly stretched). The bedspread consists of 12 squares, 4 zig-zag strips and 12 triangles. Abbreviations: hlf tr – half tr worked as follows – wool over hook, insert hook into stitch and draw loop through to $\frac{3}{4}$ in., wool over and draw through all loops. Colours: Terra Cotta – TC; Snow Cream – SC; Bright Olive – BO; County Brown – CB; Musk – M. Approx size (excluding fringes): 65 by 109 in. Square: work in rounds. With TC make 4 ch, ss into 1st ch to form ring. At end of this and all following rds draw ss-loop to $\frac{1}{2}$ in.

1st Round: into ring (2 hlf tr, 1 ch) 4 times. At end of this and all following rounds, ss into 1st hlf tr.

2nd Round: start this and all following rounds in 4th ch sp of previous rd: (into ch sp 2 hlf tr, 1 hlf tr between next 2 sts, into ch sp 2 hlf tr, 1 ch) 4 times. 20 hlf tr.

3rd Round: (into ch sp 2 hlf tr, 4 hlf tr between 5 sts, into ch sp 2 hlf tr, 1 ch) 4 times. 32 hlf tr.

4th Round: (into ch sp 2 hlf tr, 7 hlf tr between 8 sts, into ch sp 2 hlf tr, 1 ch) 4 times. 44 hlf tr.

5th Round: (into ch sp 2 hlf tr, 10 hlf tr between 11 sts, into ch sp 2 hlf tr, 1 ch) 4 times. 56 hlf tr.

6th Round: (into ch sp 2 hlf tr, 13 hlf tr between 14 sts, into ch sp 2 hlf, tr, 1 ch) 4 times. 68 hlf tr.

7th Round: (into ch sp 2 hlf tr, 16 hlf tr between 17 sts, into ch sp 2 hlf tr, 1 ch) 4 times. 80 hlf tr.

8th Round: (into ch sp 2 hlf tr, 19 hlf tr between 20 sts, into ch sp 2 hlf tr, 1 ch) 4 times. 92 hlf tr.

9th Round: with SC (into ch sp 2 hlf tr,

22 hlf tr between 23 sts, into ch sp 2 hlf tr, 1 ch) 4 times. 104 hlf tr.

10th Round: (into ch sp 2 hlf tr, 25 hlf tr between 26 sts, into ch sp 2 hlf tr, 1 ch) 4 times. 116 hlf tr.

11th Round: (into ch sp 2 hlf tr, 28 hlf tr into 29 sts, into ch sp 2 hlf tr, 1 ch) 4 times. 128 hlf tr.

12th Round: (into ch sp 2 hlf tr, 31 hlf tr between 32 sts, into ch sp 2 hlf tr, 1 ch) 4 times. 140 hlf tr. Fasten off. Make 11 more squares.

Zig-zag strip: work in rows in the following colours: rows 1, 2, 3 and 4 – BO; row 5 – TC; row 6 – M; rows 7 and 8 – CB; row 9 – M; rows 10, 11, 12 and 13 – BO. Make a chain loosely of 213 sts.

1st Row: 1 hlf tr into 4th ch, miss 1 ch * 32 hlf tr on next 32 ch, into next ch 2 hlf tr, 1 ch, into next ch 2 hlf tr, 32 hlf tr on next 32 ch **, (miss 1 ch, 1 hlf tr into next ch) twice, miss 1 ch; rep from * 3 times ending last rep at **, miss 1 ch, 1 hlf tr into next ch, 3 ch, turn.

2nd and following 11 Rows: miss 1 st 1 hlf tr in next st miss 1 st, * 32 hlf tr on next 32 sts, into ch sp 2 hlf tr, 1 ch, 2 hlf tr, 32 hlf tr on next 32 sts **, (miss 1 st, 1 hlf tr into next st miss 1 st) twice, rep from * 3 times ending last rep at **, miss 1 st 1 hlf tr into next st, 3 ch, turn. 212 hlf tr. At end of 13th row fasten off. Make 3 more strips.

Triangle: work in rows. With M make 6 ch, ss into 1st ch to form ring.

1st Row: into ring 2 hlf tr, 1 ch, 2 hlf tr, 3 ch, turn.

2nd Row: 2 hlf tr into 1st hlf tr of previous row, 1 hlf tr into next st, into ch sp 2 hlf tr, 1 ch, 2 hlf tr, 1 hlf tr into next st, 2 hlf tr into next st, 3 ch, turn. 10 hlf tr.

3rd Row: 1 hlf tr into 1st hlf tr, 2 hlf tr into next st, 3 hlf tr on 3 sts, into ch sp 2 hlf tr, 1 ch, 2 hlf tr, 3 hlf tr on 3 sts, 2 hlf tr into next st, 1 hlf tr into next st, 3 ch, turn. 16 hlf tr.

4th Row: 1 hlf tr into 1st hlf tr, 2 hlf tr into next st, 6 hlf tr on 6 sts, into ch sp 2 hlf tr,

118

1 ch, 2 hlf tr, 6 hlf tr on 6 sts, 2 hlf tr into next st, 1 hlf tr into next st, 3 ch, turn. 22 hlf tr.

5th Row: 1 hlf tr into 1st hlf tr, 2 hlf tr into next st, 9 hlf tr on 9 sts, into ch sp 2 hlf tr, 1 ch, 2 hlf tr, 9 hlf tr on 9 sts, 2 hlf tr into next st, 1 hlf tr into next st, 3 ch, turn. 28 hlf tr.

6th Row: with CB, 1 hlf tr into 1st st, 2 hlf tr into next st, 12 hlf tr on 12 sts, into ch sp 2 hlf tr, 1 ch, 2 hlf tr, 12 hlf tr on 12 sts, 2 hlf tr into next st, 1 hlf tr into next st, 3 ch, turn. 34 hlf tr.

7th Row: 1 hlf tr into 1st hlf tr, 2 hlf tr into next st, 15 hlf tr on 15 sts, into ch sp 2 hlf tr, 1 ch, 2 hlf tr, 15 hlf tr on 15 sts, 2 hlf tr into next st, 1 hlf tr into next st, 3 ch, turn. 40 hlf tr.

8th Row: with M, 1 hlf tr into 1st hlf tr, 2 hlf tr into next st, 18 hlf tr on 18 sts, into ch sp 2 hlf tr, 1 ch, 2 hlf tr, 18 hlf tr on 18 sts, 2 hlf tr into next st, 1 hlf tr into next st, 3 ch, turn. 46 hlf tr.

9th Row: with BO, 1 hlf tr into 1st hlf tr, 2 hlf tr into next st, 21 hlf tr into next 21 sts, into ch sp 2 hlf tr, 1 ch, 2 hlf tr, 21 hlf tr on next 21 sts, 2 hlf tr into next st, 1 hlf tr into next st, 3 ch, turn. 52 hlf tr.

10th Row: 1 hlf tr into 1 st hlf tr, 2 hlf tr into next st, 24 hlf tr into next 24 sts into ch sp 2 hlf tr, 1 ch, 2 hlf tr, 24 hlf tr into next 24 sts, 2 hlf tr into next st, 1 hlf tr into next st, 3 ch, turn. 58 hlf tr.

11th Row: 1 hlf tr into 1st hlf tr, 2 hlf tr into next st, 27 hlf tr into next 27 sts, into ch sp 2 hlf tr, 1 ch, 2 hlf tr, 27 hlf tr into next 27 sts, 2 hlf tr into next st, 1 hlf tr into next st, 3 ch, turn. 64 hlf tr.

12th Row: 1 hlf tr into 1st hlf tr, 2 hlf tr into next st, 30 hlf tr into next 30 sts, into ch sp 2 hlf tr, 1 ch, 2 hlf tr, 30 hlf tr on next 30 sts, 2 hlf tr into next st, 1 hlf tr into next st. Fasten off. 70 hlf tr. Make 5 more triangles A. Triangle B: as Triangle A, but in the following colours: rows 1 to 8 – col 1; rows 9 to 12 – col 2. Make 6 Triangles B.

To Make Up

With wrong side facing block pieces and press using a warm iron and damp cloth.
Strip 1 : Join corners of 2 squares. Join top corners of each of 2 triangles B to outermost 2 corners of the 2 joined squares.
Strip 2 : Join corners of 3 squares.
Strips 3 and 4 : as strips 1 and 2.
Strip 5 : as strip 1.
Slip-stitch 1 zig-zag strip to long edge of strip 1. Slip-stitch strip 2 to other edge of zig-zag strip. Continue in this way until all strips are joined. Slip-stitch 3 triangles A each in position to short sides of bedspread. Work two rows of double crochet all around the bedspread working 3 sts in each corner. The fringes are optional and may be attached to either the long sides or to one or both narrow sides. Allow extra quantity of wool for fringes. To slip stitch together: insert hook into the back thread at top of first st of one edge and into the back top thread of the corresponding st on the other edge and draw wool through. Do not work too tightly.
Alternative colours: Kingfisher (6610), Blue (7286), Braemar Green (6629), Jack Tar (6613), Snow White (504).

Cushion cover, page 91

Materials: Twilley's Lysbet Super Cotton, 3 balls. Crochet Hook No. 3.50 (9). Tension: 1 motif = $2\frac{1}{2}$ by $2\frac{1}{2}$ in. Size of rectangle: $16\frac{1}{2}$ by 13 in. from side to side.
Make 32 motifs as follows: ring of 6 ch.

1st Round: into ring work 4 ch, 5 dbl tr, 5 ch, (6 dbl tr, 5 ch) 3 times, ss into 4th ch.

2nd Round: ss into same st as ss work 3 ch, cl of 2 tr, cl of 3 tr into next 4 dbl tr, 3 ch, 1 dc into ch sp, 3 ch, (cl of 3 tr into next 5 dbl tr, 3 ch, 1 dc into ch sp, 3 ch) 3 times, ss into 3rd ch. Fasten off.

Pin out each motif to size and press on wrong side. Arrange motifs to form a rectangle as shown in the photograph and sew them together with sewing thread along the ch st corners. Pin, tack and sew the joined motifs to fabric. When sewing back and front of fabric together, allow $\frac{1}{2}$ in. all round between edges of crochet work and seam.

Irish crochet motif bedspread,
pages 86 and 87

The bedspread, consisting of hexagonal motifs, may be worked in any desired size by making more or fewer motifs (or strips) than in the instructions. Materials: Coats Chain Mercer Crochet Cotton in 20-g balls, 97 balls light shade (L), 57 balls contrasting shade (C). Steel Crochet Hook No. 1.50 ($2\frac{1}{2}$). Tension: 1 motif $4\frac{1}{4}$ in. from point to point. Size: 66 by 96 in.

With L work 8 ch, ss into 1st ch to form ring.

1st Round: 1 ch, 17 dc into ring, ss into 1st ch, 18 sts.

2nd Round: 6 ch (miss 2 dc, 1 dc into next dc, 5 ch) 5 times, ss into 1st ch.

3rd Round: ss into 1st sp, 5 ch, 7 trip tr into same sp, (8 trip tr into next sp) 5 times, ss into 5th ch.

4th Round: 1 ch, 1 dc into every trip tr, ss into 1st ch. Fasten off. 48 sts.

5th Round: attach C to dc after ss in previous rd, cl of 4 ch and 2 dbl tr into same dc, (3 ch, miss 2 dc, cl of 3 dbl tr into next dc, 3 ch, miss 2 dc, 3 dbl tr cl, 6 ch, 3 dbl tr cl into next dc, 3 ch **, miss 1 dc, 3 dbl tr cl into next dc) 6 times, ending last rep at **, ss into top of 1st cl. Fasten off.

6th Round: with L work 6 dc into each 6 ch sp, 3 dc into each 3 ch sp, ss into 1st dc. 90 sts.

7th Round: into same dc as ss work 1 cl of 4 ch and 2 dbl tr, * 3 ch, miss 1 dc, 3 dbl tr cl, 6 ch, 3 dbl tr cl into next dc, 3 ch, miss 1 dc, 3 dbl tr cl into next dc, 3 ch, (miss 2 dc, 3 dbl tr cl into next dc, 3 ch) 3 times **, miss 1 dc, 3 dbl tr cl into next dc; rep from * 5 times, ending last rep as **, ss into top of 1st cl.

8th Round: as 6th round. 144 sts. Fasten off.

9th Round: with C work 144 dc. Fasten off. Work 25 motifs for one strip and 20 strips for the size given. Join two motifs by placing them with wrong sides together and working one row of 24 dc between centres of two points, crocheting together 1 dc from each side. Join strips in similar way.

Semi-circular shoulder wrap,
page 104

Materials: Jaeger's Celtic Spun Shetland, 1 oz balls: 2 balls Cornelian (46), 1 ball each Oriental Gold (50), Jasmine (43), Snowcap (13), or one 50-g ball of each colour. Crochet hooks No. 7.00 (2) and 6.00 (4).

Tension: 5 pattern repeats and 9 rows = 4 sq. in.

With No. 7 hook and Cornelian, work loosely: make a chain of 30 sts.

1st Row: into 5th ch from hook 1 dc, 1 dc into next ch, * 1 ch, 2 dc into next 2 ch; rep from * to end, 4 ch, turn. 2nd and all following rows: 1 dc into 1st dc, * 1 ch, into next ch sp 2 dc; rep from * to end, 4 ch, turn. At end of 31st pattern row omit 4 ch at end. Cont with 1 row of dc around 3 sides, worked into spaces at beg and end of rows as follows: 59 dc down 1st side into spaces of 30th to 1st row, 3 dc into each of 9 ch spaces below 1st pattern row, 59 dc along other side from 1st to 31st row. Fasten off. Scallop-edging: with No. 6 hook and Oriental Gold, work **1st Row:** 5 ch, 3 trip tr into 1st dc of last dc row, (miss 2 dc, 1 dc, 3 ch, 1 dc into next dc, miss 2 dc, 7 trip tr into next dc) 24 times, ending last rep with 4 trip tr instead of 7. Fasten off.

2nd Row: with Jasmine: 1 dc into 5th ch of last row, * 9 trip tr into 3 ch ring, 1 dc into 4th trip tr of previous row; rep from * to end. Fasten off.

3rd Row: with white: 1 dc on 1st dc, * 1 dc on next 4 trip tr, 2 dc into next trip tr, 1 dc on next 5 sts; rep from * to end. Fasten off. Pin out centre of scarf (not the scallop-edging) to measure approximately 14 in. from 1st to 31st pattern row and 32–33 in. at widest part. Press gently under a damp cloth. A mini-jacket may be made by sewing together the 3rd and 8th scallop on each side. Alternative colours: Tuscany (22), Gorse (7), Oatmeal (1), Snowcap (13).

Knitting

*This cushion can be made up from four dia-
gonally knitted sections or it can be knitted in
one piece starting from the centre. Techniques
are described on pages 145, 158 and 165*

For the American yarns equivalent to those
specified in this chapter, see the table on page 292

Basic methods

In knitting there are two basic methods:
knitting forwards and backwards with two
needles, and circular knitting in which the
work is carried out in tubular fashion in
rounds, so no turning is involved and there
is no seam. In circular knitting the work can
be carried out either with four needles (one
set of double-pointed needles) or with a
single round needle. The first method is the
one most used for the main parts of a garment, with the circular needle recommended
for yokes, crew, polo and turtle necks

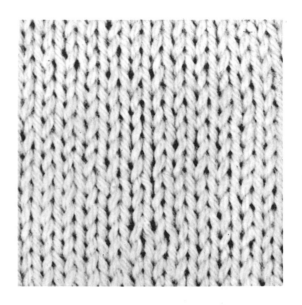

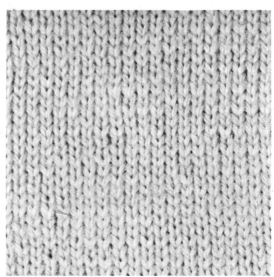

Choosing the needles and yarn

A wide range of knitting needles is available. The size you use is of great importance as it affects the tension and therefore the measurements of the work. For best results, choose rigid knitting needles with perfectly formed tapered points, made in a lightweight metal alloy. Select the appropriate length of needles for the work you are undertaking. All well-known branded makes are produced in a variety of lengths. Choose needles which are long enough to hold the number of stitches without bunching. All instruction leaflets give the size of the needles required for the pattern and the tension that will be achieved when using the recommended yarn. Tension should always be checked before the main work is started. This is extremely important and should never be neglected. The tension check states how many stitches and rows will produce a small square of specified size. But this is only a guide to the *average* tension. Do not be surprised if your tension sample differs (that is, that the stated number of stitches and rows gives you a larger or smaller sample) since people vary enormously in the way they knit – loosely, normally, or extremely tightly, as shown in the three samples photographed on page 123. Those who knit loosely will need to use needles a size smaller than specified; those who knit tightly should use needles a size larger than specified. In any case, it is essential to produce a tension sample of the correct dimensions before proceeding with the main work and you must work on different size needles until you achieve this. The following guidelines should help you: fine wools – 3-ply yarns – are usually knitted with needles size 12; medium yarns – 4-ply – with size 10 and thicker yarns – double knitting – with size 8. For triple-knitting wools or yarns, needles size 4 are used. The knitting samples in this book were made with needles size 10. (See page 130 for U.S. equivalent sizes).

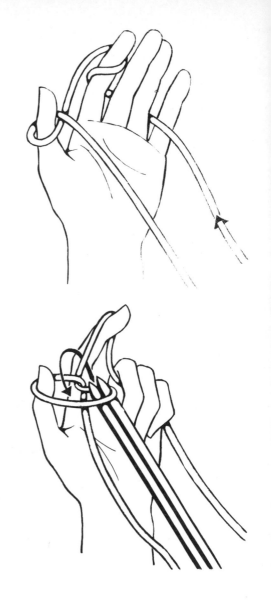

Casting on

Start by making the first stitch. Hold the wool extended between the fingers of the left hand and the needle in the right hand. Slip the point of the needle over and under the wool so that a loop is formed (Diagram *a*), wind the wool from the ball around the point of the needle (*b*) then draw the wound wool through the loop as in Diagram *c*. Finally draw the end up to form a slip knot below the first stitch on the needle (*d*).

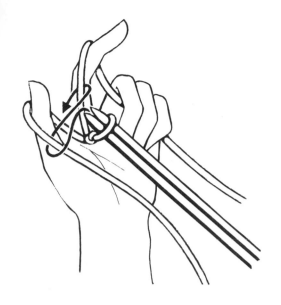

You are now ready to cast on. The first method described is casting on between the needles. Hold the needle with the stitch in the left hand, lightly holding the stitch between the thumb and forefinger. Take the second needle in the right hand and slip the point of it through the stitch to the left of the strand at the front of the needle (Diagram *e*). Push the right-hand needle through to the back of the work, wind the wool from the ball under and over the right-hand needle (*f*) then draw the wound wool through the first stitch with the point of the right-hand needle to form a loop on the needle (*g*). Now insert the point of the left-hand needle through the second stitch (*h*) then slip this stitch off the right-hand needle on to the left-hand needle to make two stitches. To make the third stitch, insert the right-hand needle between the two stitches and through

the back (*i*). Continue making stitches as you made the third stitch until you have the required number. (Diagrams p. 128).

Thumb method of casting on. This method of casting on is recommended when a firm, elastic edge is needed. Measure a length of yarn, allowing approximately 18 in. for every 40 stitches using a 3- or 4-ply yarn. You will need to allow slightly more when thicker yarns are used. Make a slip loop in the yarn at the measured distance from the end, and slip it on to a knitting needle (as shown in Diagrams *a*–*d*). Hold the measured length of yarn in your left hand, the needle and the yarn from the ball in the right hand. Twist the free end of the yarn round the left thumb from front to back (*j*). Insert the point of the needle through this loop from front to back, then take main yarn over point of right-hand

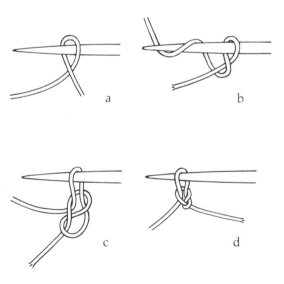

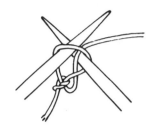

e

f

g

needle and draw it through. This makes a stitch on the needle (*k*). Slip off thumb loop and pull gently to tighten. Continue in this way, twisting the measured length round left thumb and working into it with main yarn in right hand until the required number of stitches are cast on the needle (*l*).

If you are a tight knitter, it is advisable to use two needles held parallel together, using them as one needle exactly as described above. When the required number of stitches has been made, carefully withdraw one of the needles. You will then have no difficulty in knitting the first row, and will have a firm but pliable edge. (Diagrams pages 124 and 5).

To cast on by working into each stitch. This is the third method of casting on to be described, and gives a result similar to that of the 'between the stitches' technique. Begin, as before, by making a slip loop near to the end of the yarn (not, as for the thumb method, at a measured distance away). This is shown in Diagrams *a–d*. Slip the loop on to the left-hand needle. This makes the first stitch. Take the other needle and, with the yarn supported over the forefinger of your right hand, hold it as shown in Diagram *g*, through the stitch on the left-hand needle. Using your forefinger as a guide, put the yarn under the right-hand needle and draw that needle and the yarn through the loop

of the previous stitch. The right-hand needle will now be on top of the left-hand one. Slip the loop on to the left-hand needle to form the next stitch (*h*). Continue in this way until the required number of stitches have been made. Do not pull the work too tightly.

Plain knitting. To knit the first row, transfer the needle with the stitches to your left hand, take the second needle in your right and thread the working end of the wool through the right-hand fingers.

★★ Insert the point of the right-hand needle from front to back into the front of the first loop on the left-hand needle. Feed the wool from the back to the front then round the right-hand needle (*m*) and draw this through the loop on the left-hand needle (*n*). Now let the stitch on the left-hand needle slip off. Repeat from ★★ to the end of the row.

To purl. Hold the needle with the stitches in your left hand, the second needle in your right hand and the wool threaded through your right-hand fingers. Keeping the wool in front of the needle, ★★ insert the point of the right-hand needle from the back to the front into the front of the loop of the first stitch on the left-hand needle. Take the wool round the top of the right-hand needle, anti-

Washing Hand wash all yarns unless you are sure they are machine washable. There are several machine washable yarns on the market and all are clearly marked 'Machine washable'. Hand or machine washing should be carried out in warm water only, the washing agent used should be very mild and preferably liquid, such as Stergene, but if powder or soap flakes are used, ensure that they are completely dissolved before immersing the garments in the washing solution.

Rinsing Thorough rinsing is of vital importance, insufficient care at this stage is a contributory factor to the felting and matting of garments. Rinse until water runs quite clear then rinse again adding a few drops of fabric softener to the final water. All washing agents should be used very sparingly.

Drying A light spin dry is recommended where possible, never use a wringer or hand wring as this will damage the delicate fibres. Lay garments flat and pat into shape and correct size for final drying. Never dry wool garments in direct sunlight and remember that white yarns are badly affected by strong sun. After exposure to strong light white wool garments often show cream scorch marks which are impossible to remove.

Pressing If pressing after washing is desired, use an iron on the correct setting for the fibre used. Never place the iron directly on the garment; use a damp cloth with wool yarns and a dry cloth with synthetics. Some yarns should not be ironed or pressed at all, and this is stated on the label. These are yarns finished by a heat setting process, ironing completely destroys this process and destroys the finish irreversibly. This applies to most acrylic yarns.

Trimmings Spend as much as possible on good quality buttons. Use the smallest size which is practical to ensure a neat 'quality' finish. Remove buttons before washing garments, first marking the place with a short length of bright thread to make replacement of the buttons simple and to ensure correct placement.

Storage Hand knit and crochet garments should be stored flat at all times, fold them lightly, interleave with tissue paper if desired and lay on shelves. If storage is prolonged, give the garments an occasional airing by laying them out flat on a bed for a few hours. Never store on clothes hangers as the fabric will stretch and drop out of shape. Never allow the garments to become heavily soiled.

clockwise (*o*) and draw this loop through the stitch on the left-hand needle and on to the right-hand needle (*p*). Then let the stitch on the left-hand needle slip off the needle. Repeat from ** to the end of the row. You have now 'purled' one row.

Stocking stitch. If one row is worked in plain knitting and one in purl alternately, the right side of the fabric is called stocking stitch and the wrong side, reversed stocking stitch.

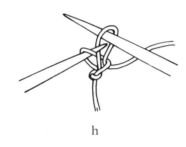

h

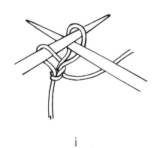

i

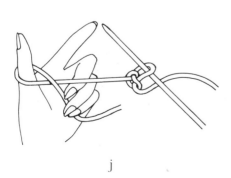

j

Joining yarn

Always start a new ball of wool or yarn at the beginning of a row. Tie the old and the new ends in a knot, then when the piece is knitted, undo the knot and darn in the ends. If a join in a row cannot be avoided, unravel the ends of the old ball for 2 in. then cut away half the strands. Do the same with the new ball. Now twist the ends together, thus making the same thickness as the original yarn.

Turning

On straight knitting the work must be turned exactly at the end of each row so that the edges will have a good appearance. Never under-estimate the importance of the edges because irregularity will result in wavy seams and spoil the shape of the finished garment.

Chain and knotted edgings (page 130)

Chain edging is used for those parts of knitting which are to have edges worked, because the stitch loops are easily picked up. Knotted edging is ideal when the parts are to be joined together.
Chain edging. 1st row (right side): slip the first and last stitch knitwise noting that the yarn will be in front between the first and

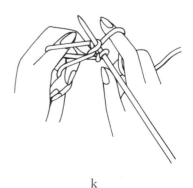

k

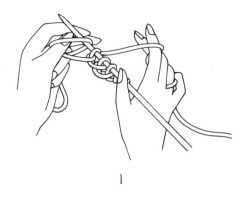

l

second stitches after work is turned. 2nd row (wrong side): purl the first and last stitches of this row.

Knotted edging. Knit the first and last stitch of every row; this gives a moss-stitch edge.

Double edging. To work this edging you need a cable needle.

1st Row: slip the 1st st on to the cable needle, the yarn being held in front of the work, slip the next 2 sts purlwise with the yarn still in front of the work, then knit the st on the cable needle, work in purl to the last 3 sts,

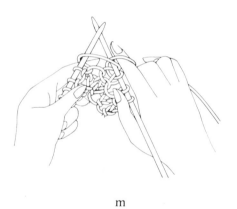

m

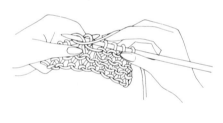

o

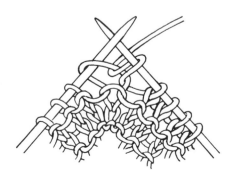

n

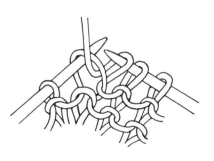

p

129

slip the next 2 sts on to the cable needle, and hold at back of work, knit the last st then slip the sts from the cable needle purlwise on to the needle and at the same time carrying the wool over in front of the work.

2nd Row: k2 sts, slip the next 2 sts as if to purl and carry the wool forward in front of the knitting, knit to the last 3 sts, slip the next st purlwise with wool in front of work, knit next 2 sts.

3rd Row: slip next 2 sts purlwise with wool at front of work, k1 st then purl to last 3 sts,

k1 st, slip next 2 sts purlwise with wool at front.

Repeat the 2nd and 3rd rows until work measures the required length.

1 × 1 rib

A simple pattern of knit and purl stitches. The best-known combination of knit and purl stitches is the ribbed pattern, which is used for the wrist and welts, and for collar and neck edgings. In other words, it is used

KNITTING NEEDLE GAUGE

American	French	English
0	2	14
1	$2\frac{1}{2}$	12
3	3	11
3	$3\frac{1}{4}$	10
4	$3\frac{1}{2}$	—
5	4	9
6	$4\frac{1}{2}$	8
7	$4\frac{3}{4}$	7
8	5	6
9	$5\frac{1}{2}$	5
10	6	4
$10\frac{1}{2}$	7	3
11	8	2
13	$9\frac{1}{4}$	1

*This doll is made up from separate parts —
pullover, pants, socks. Instructions p. 166*

whenever there is a part of the garment
which must be especially elastic. And when
a particularly close fit is required, as in a
'skinny' sweater, it can be used for the whole
garment.

When the knitting instructions are: 'Knit
one stitch and purl one stitch alternately'
then the whole row is continuously worked
in knit one, purl one stitches. The work is
then turned and continued in the same
manner. Previously knitted stitches appear
on this side as purl stitches and vice versa
(photograph, page 133, top left).

The pattern, however, will explain if you
start the row with a knit stitch, and whether
you end with a knit stitch. This depends, of
course, on whether you are working with an
even or an uneven number of stitches.

Twisted 1 × 1 rib

The work is much firmer if this method is
used. It is worked as the previous rib, but
the knit stitch is worked into the back.
Knitting or purling into the back of a stitch
is carried out in exactly the same way as

ordinary knitting and purling, except that the point of the needle, before the stitch is worked, is inserted into the back instead of the front of the stitch.

For this rib you work with a multiple of two stitches and the row will read as follows: * Knit one stitch through back of loop (usually referred to in instructions as tbl), purl one stitch *, repeat all along the row. (Photograph, page 133, below left.)

2 × 2 rib

For broader ribbed bands (photograph, page 133, top right) two knitted stitches and two purled stitches are used. For this it is necessary to cast on a number of stitches divisible by four, so that you can repeat the knit two stitches, purl two stitches pattern to the end of the row.

Varying the rib

A pattern of broad and narrow ribs will appear when four knitting and two purling stitches are used. This combination makes excellent ribbed sweaters or leggings for children. It is necessary to cast on a number of stitches divisible by six (photograph, opposite page, below right).

Child's waistcoat in plain knitting. Instructions on page 166

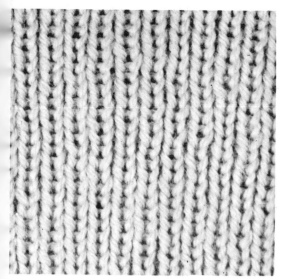
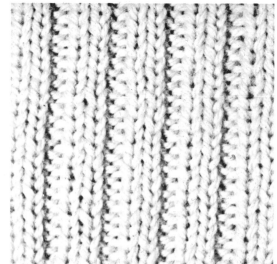

Horizontal ribs appear if the knit and purl stitches, or their groups, are not alternated within the row but if the knit and purl are alternated by rows. For example, knit four rows, purl two rows (photograph, top left, page 134).

Basket stitch is made by working knit and purl stitches alternately as for the striped rib, but changing the rhythm after a few rows. For example, work six rows in six purl and six knit stitches alternately. On the next six rows work six knit stitches and six purl stitches alternately. To obtain a squared effect the same number of rows must be worked as there are stitches in a block – that is six rows when there are six knit and six purl stitches worked. Blocks of three knit and three purl stitches must be three rows deep and so on. The cast-on number of stitches must be divisible by the number in the pattern – if the pattern is to be blocks of three then the cast-on stitches must be divisible by three (photograph, page 134).

Moss stitch (above, right)

Moss stitch is easily and quickly knitted. It produces a beautiful effect which is ideal for blankets, sweaters and children's garments. An even number of stitches are cast on and then the first row of stitches are worked as follows: knit one stitch (purl one stitch, knit one stitch). Repeat the instructions in the parentheses to the end of the row. After turning, the row is started with the same stitch with which the previous row

ended – knit one stitch, purl one stitch to the end of the row. In this method of knitting, the knit and purl stitches of the two rows are staggered on top of each other.

Brioche

The ordinary Brioche (opposite page, top left) produces a thicker fabric than ordinary knitting. The basic principle is the travelling thread which is worked in with the knitted stitch. The travelling thread is always worked on the 'wool forward' principle and the wool forward is always followed by a slipped stitch.

On the following row, the slipped stitch is always knitted together with the wool forward.

An even number of stitches are cast on in the usual way, but it is advisable to use a larger needle for casting on than for the knitting.

Work as follows: knit one stitch, put wool forward, slip one stitch purlwise, knit one stitch, repeat to the last stitch, knit this stitch. This row is not repeated. It is a foundation row for the fabric to be produced. The row that is repeated is as follows: knit one stitch ⋆, bring the wool to the front of the needle, slip one stitch purlwise, place the wool over the needle then knit two

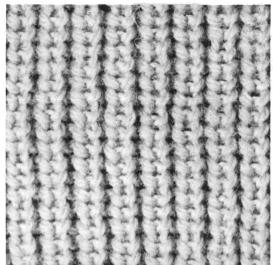

stitches together, repeat from the ★ to the last stitch, knit this stitch.

Before casting off, the stitches should be reduced to the number cast on by working as follows: knit one stitch ★ knit one stitch, knit two stitches together, repeat from ★ to the last stitch, knit this.

Half brioche
An even number of stitches must be cast on.

A Dachshund draught-excluder: knitted as a long stocking from scraps; pompon feet

After casting on, begin the pattern as follows: Knit the first stitch, put the wool over the needle once, slip the next stitch on to the left-hand needle purlwise, repeat to the end of the row. Turn and knit the second row thus: the slipped stitch of the previous row is knitted with the loop over the needle, the next stitch is purled, then the slipped stitch is knitted with the loop over needle and so on until the end of the row. Work next row as the first and the fourth row as the second.

Buttonholes

Horizontal and vertical buttonholes. The horizontal buttonhole is the most common one used for jackets, children's outfits and coats. To work to the position of a buttonhole, cast off the number of stitches stated on the pattern, then work to the end of the row. On the second row, work to the cast-off stitches of the previous row, then turn and cast on the number of stitches cast off in the previous row. Turn and work to the end of row.

Vertical buttonholes. The work must be divided at the required position. Two balls of wool are used from this point, the first ball being for the first group of stitches, the second ball for the second group. The number of rows given in the pattern should now be knitted. This is the number of rows required to give the correct depth of the buttonhole to correspond with the size of buttons being used. When the buttonhole has been completed, break off the second ball of wool, leaving a length to darn in for a secure finish. Continue working with the first ball as before. When making up the complete garment, buttonholes may be worked around as in fabric garments.

Picot edging and row of holes

This edging forms an attractive finish to necks of lacy matinée jackets, sweaters, bed jackets etc. The row of holes is used for threading ribbon or cord through a neckline, waistline or at the wrist. For a row of holes on a stocking stitch surface (one row knit, one row purl) cast on an odd number of stitches and work 4 rows in stocking stitch. **Next row** (the row that introduces the row of holes): knit one stitch, ★ bring the wool forward to make a stitch, then knit the next two stitches together, repeat from the ★ to the end of the row. Work three more rows in stocking stitch, beginning with a purl row. Now 'knit up a hem' (as explained on the following page) and this action will fold the work over at the centre of the row of holes forming a picot as shown in the photograph.

For a row of holes on a stocking stitch surface the method is the same but the 'knit up a hem' is omitted.

Knitted up hem

The cast-on stitches are first picked up with an additional needle from the wrong side.

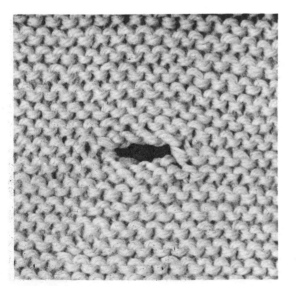

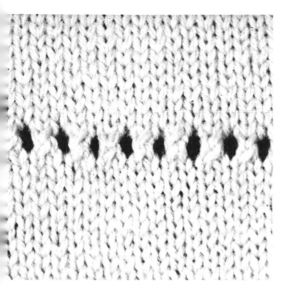

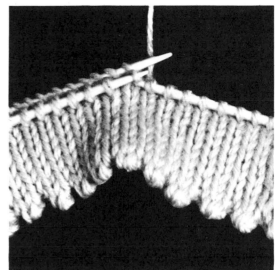

Hold the additional needles containing the picked-up stitches behind and parallel with the left needle and, using the right needle, work one stitch of the front and one stitch from the rear needle together, using a knit stitch. This may be a little difficult at first, but it is not a long job and well worth the effort involved. It is important that all the stitches are knitted up in the correct order as otherwise the hem will be distorted.

Baby's jacket with a button-on bag which could be adapted to fasten to any jacket. Instructions are given on page 166

Abbreviations:

Careful attention should be given to the following abbreviations which you are likely to come across on any knitting pattern you follow:
st(s): stitch(es); k: knit; p: purl; yrn: yarn round needle; tog: together; sl: slip; tbl: through back of loops; C2F: cable 2 sts front

These one-piece baby shoes are very easy to work. Instructions on page 167

by working across next 4 sts as follows: sl next 2 sts on to a cable needle and leave at front of work, k next 2 sts then k 2 sts from cable needle. C3F as C2F but cable 3 sts front; rep: repeat; beg: begin (beginning); st st: stocking stitch; psso: pass slipped stitch over.

Various knitting patterns

Cable pattern

A cable pattern is produced when two (or more depending on width of cable) stitches to be worked are taken on an additional needle (called a cable needle) and left at back or front of the work according to the pattern instructions (photograph, top right, this page).

From the left-hand needle work the number of stitches stated in the pattern then work the stitches from the cable needle. The cable row is always a right-side row and the cables are usually separated by purl stitches. Here is a simple cable pattern.

Cast on a multiple of 7 sts, plus 3.

1st Row: (p3, k4) to last 3 sts, p3.
2nd Row: (k3, p4) to last 3 sts, k3.
3rd Row: work as 1st row.
4th Row: work as 2nd row.
5th Row: (p3, C2F) (see abbreviations) to last 3 sts, p3.
6th Row: work as 2nd row.

Repeat these six rows for pattern. Repeat them until length required.

Cable variation

Here we have a cable separated by a vertical rib (right). For this nine stitches are used for one repeat of the pattern, so the number of cast-on stitches must be divisible by $11+5$ edging stitches.

1st Row: p2, k1 tbl, p2, k6, rep until last 5 sts, then p2, k1, p2.

2nd Row: work sts as set, k the k sts and p the p sts.
3rd and 5th Rows: work as 1st row.
4th and 6th Rows: work as 2nd row.
7th Row: p2, k1 tbl, p2, C3F, rep to last 5 sts, p2, k1, p2.
8th Row: work as 2nd row.

These eight rows form the pattern. Repeat them until length required.

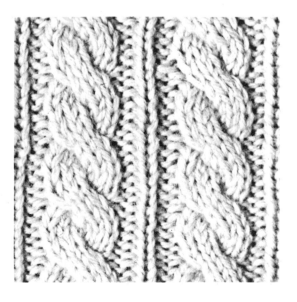

Diagonal rib pattern

You will need a number of stitches divisible by eight, plus two edging stitches.

1st Row: k1, ★ k4, p4, rep from ★ to last st, k1.

2nd Row: k2, ★ k4, p4, rep from ★ to last 8 sts, k4, p3, k1.

3rd Row: k3, ★ p4, k4, rep from ★ to last 7 sts, p4, k3.

4th Row: k1, p3, ★ k4, p4, rep from ★ to last 6 sts, k4, p1, k1.

5th Row: k1, ★ p4, k4, rep from ★ to last st, k1.

6th Row: k2, ★ p4, k4, rep from ★ to end.

7th Row: k1, p2, ★ k4, p4, rep from ★ to last

7 sts, k4, p2, k1.

8th Row: k4, ★ p4, k4, rep from ★ to last 6 sts, p4, k2.

These eight rows form the pattern. Repeat them until required length has been reached.

Lace eyelet pattern

Number of stitches divisible by four.

1st to 4th Rows: work in st st (1 row k, 1 row p), beg with a k row.

5th Row: k1, ★ yrn, k2 tog, k2, rep from ★ to last 3 sts, yrn, k2 tog, k1.

1st Row: k1, ★ p2, sl next st on to a cable needle and hold at front of work. K1, tbl, k the st from cable needle, p2, k1.

2nd Row: k1, ★ p1, k2, p2, k2, rep from ★ to last st, k1.

3rd and 4th Rows: work sts as set.

These four rows form the pattern. Repeat them until required length has been worked.

Double cable

Number of stitches divisible by 17 plus two.

1st Row: k1, ★ p1, k1 tbl, p3, k8, p3, k1 tbl,

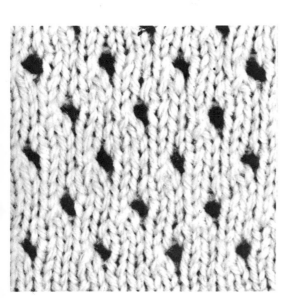

6th Row: p.

7th and 8th Rows: work in st st, beg with a k row.

9th Row: k3, ★ yrn, k2 tog, k2, rep from ★ to last st, k1.

10th Row: p.

Repeat the 3rd to the 10th row for the pattern.

Twisted cable

Number of stitches divisible by seven plus two edging stitches.

rep from ★ to last st, k1.

2nd Row: k1, ★ p1 tbl, k3, p8, k3, p1 tbl, k1 rep from ★ to last st, k1.

3rd Row: k1, ★ p1, k1 tbl, p3, sl next 2 sts on to cable needle and leave at front of work, k2, k2 sts from cable needle, sl next 2 sts on to cable needle and leave at back of work, k2, k2 sts on cable needle, p3, k1 tbl, rep from ★ to last st, k1.

4th Row: work as 2nd row.

These four rows form the pattern. Repeat them until required length is reached.

both sts drop from the needle, rep from *
ending k1. These two rows form the pattern.
Repeat to required length.

Large braided pattern

Number of stitches divisible by six plus five.
1st Row: k.
2nd Row: p.
3rd Row: k1 * sl next 3 sts on to cable needle
and leave at front of work, k the following
3 sts, then k 3 sts on the cable needle. Rep
from * to last 4 sts, k 4.
4th Row: p.
5th Row: k.
6th Row: p.
7th Row: k4 * sl next 3 sts on to a cable
needle and leave at the back of the work,
k the following 3 sts then k the 3 sts on cable
needle. Rep from * to last st, k1.
8th Row: p.
9th to 16th Rows: rep rows 1 to 8.

Plaited pattern

Number of stitches divisible by nine plus
three.
1st Row: k1, * k3, sl next 3 sts on to a cable
needle and leave at front of work, k3, then

Small braided pattern

Number of stitches divisible by three plus
two.
1st Row: k1, * cross the next 3 sts as follows:
sl 1 st on to cable needle and leave at front
of the work, k2, then, k st on cable needle.
Rep from * to last st k1.
2nd Row: k1, p1 * cross the following 2 sts
as follows: p the 2nd st then p 1st, then let

k the sts from cable needle, rep from ★ to last st, k1.

2nd Row: p.

3rd to 6th Rows: work in st st, beg with a k row.

7th Row: k1, ★ sl the next 3 sts on to a cable needle and leave at back of work, k3, k the sts from the cable needle, rep from ★ to last st, k1.

8th Row: p.

9th to 12th Rows: work in st st, beg with a k row.

These 12 rows form the pattern. Repeat them to required length.

Baby's jacket with hood: instructions on page 167

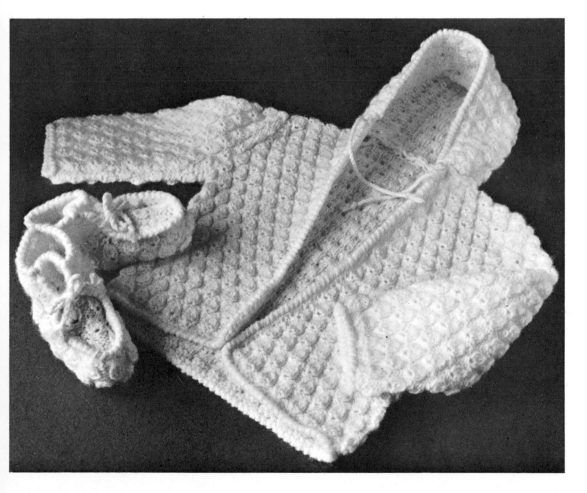

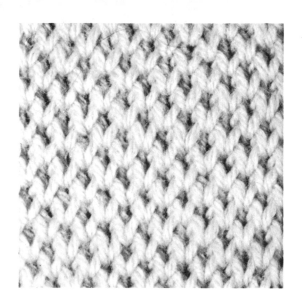

Brioche Honeycomb stitch
Even number of stitches.
1st Row: k.
2nd Row: k.
3rd Row (right side): ⋆ k1, k1b (insert the right-hand needle through the centre of the st below the next st to be knitted so that both sts are knitted at the same time) rep from ⋆ to end.
4th Row: ⋆ with the right-hand needle, k the slip thread of previous row with st above it, k1, rep from ⋆ to end.
5th Row: ⋆ k1b, k1, rep from ⋆ to end.
6th Row: ⋆ k1, k the next st with thread as on 4th row.
Repeat rows 3 to 6 inclusive for pattern.

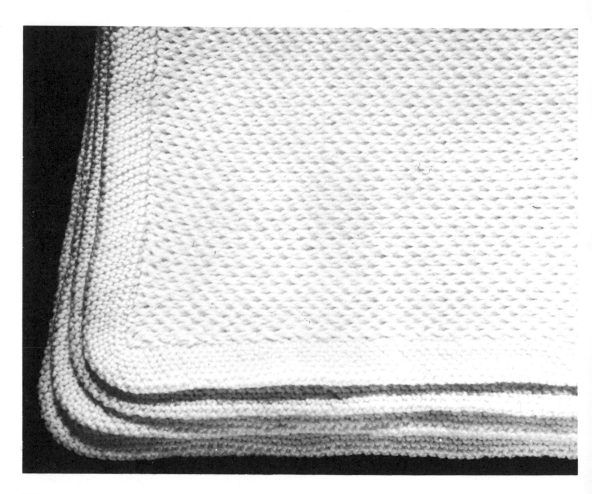

Two-colour or multi-colour knitting

In colour knitting a distinction is made between the change of colour in rows, or blocks, and the colour change within a row, the colour being worked as an actual all-over pattern or a band of colours. The general practice is to work the fabric in stocking stitch.

Change of colour in rows is simple. The colour is changed in the required order row by row and horizontal stripes are obtained. However, it must be pointed out that the colour changes should always be on the same side. This enables the yarn to be carried up the side of the work when a narrow-striped pattern is being worked. When a wider-striped pattern is required, the colours can be cut and joined in as needed. This makes knitting easier when more than two colours are being used.

In a vertical or diagonal colour change in blocks, each colour is knitted with its own ball of yarn (photograph, on the right) and the yarns are crossed at the back when colours are changed to join the knitting together. To do this the yarn of the colour just knitted will be twisted with the yarn of the new colour (drawing, below).

On changing colour with the two yarns (Jacquard, Florentine or Fair Isle knitting) the yarn of the second colour runs along on the wrong side of the work as a loose yarn. The edging stitches are usually worked with both the colours being used in the row i.e. with double yarn.

Jacquard patterns are always worked in stocking stitch. And to ensure that the stitch pattern does not pull or become tight, the yarns of the different colours must always be

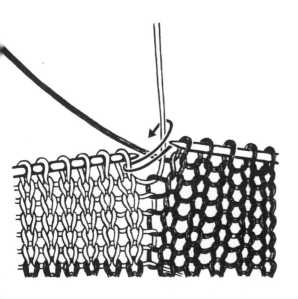

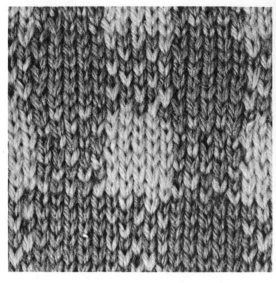

Chart a

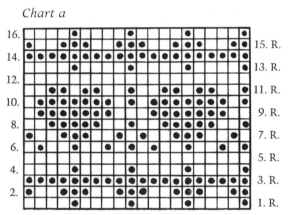

16.
14.
12.
10.
8.
6.
4.
2.

15. R.
13. R.
11. R.
9. R.
7. R.
5. R.
3. R.
1. R.

Chart b

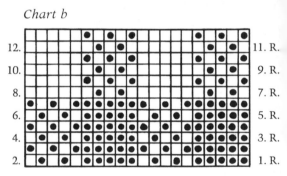

12.
10.
8.
6.
4.
2.

11. R.
9. R.
7. R.
5. R.
3. R.
1. R.

R = row

guided at the same tension around the fingers of the left hand.

It may be possible to buy a knitting 'ring' or 'thimble'. These are used on the continent of Europe, but are less common in England and America. They can be useful when knitting in two colours. The ring has small loops through which are passed the different coloured yarns, to keep them separate and untangled while working.

Jacquard and Fair Isle patterns are knitted to a counted pattern which can be drawn exactly like a cross-stitch pattern on squared paper. Each square represents one knitted stitch and one row up on the chart. Different

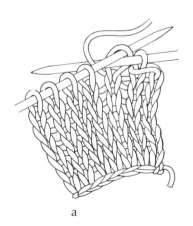

a

colours are identified by different symbols. The work is carried out in stocking stitch – the odd rows are the knit rows and are worked from right to left, the even rows are the purl rows and are read from left to right on the chart. In most charts a bracketed repeat of the pattern is given plus one odd stitch. The odd stitch is then worked only once on each row – the last stitch on a knit row and the first stitch on a purl row. On tubular knitting (page 157) each counted pattern row is read from right to left.

Heart, block and houndstooth patterns

The work is carried out according to the symbol pattern (a, b or c). The dots indicate the dark colour of the pattern given. In the first patterns mentioned, the pattern unit consists of 10 stitches, in the case of the houndstooth pattern, eight stitches.

Tweed pattern

The tweed pattern is worked in two colours in alternate stitches: the colour rhythm is staggered by the rows. The casting on is made in a single colour and with an even number of stitches.

Casting off

Knitted work can be cast off in three main ways. It can be achieved by lifting over, by

Chart c

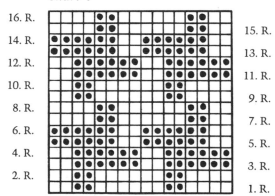

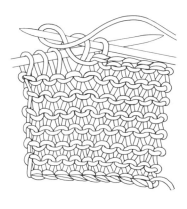

b

knitting together or by using a darning needle.

Casting off by lifting over. For all types of knitting work – except the elastic ribbed pattern – the following technique is suitable for casting off the last row of stitches. The first two stitches are worked as usual and the stitch worked first is lifted over the second worked stitch (Diagram *a*, p. 146). The third stitch is knitted and the second stitch is lifted over this. The action is repeated until all the stitches have been cast off. Then the cut-off end of the yarn is pulled through

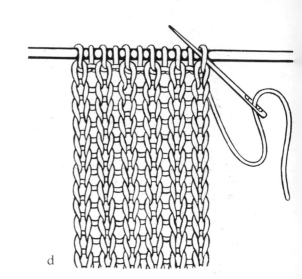

d

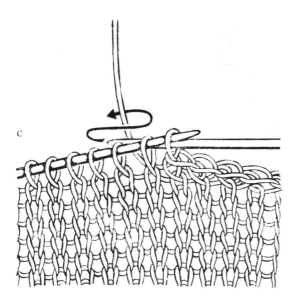

c

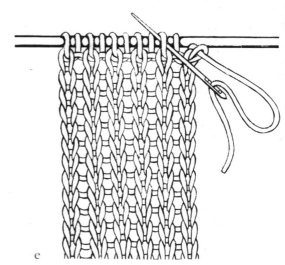

e

the last stitch, which is still on the needle. Finally the end is darned in on the wrong side of the work.

To cast off purlwise, purl the stitches instead of knitting them, and work as described above (Diagram *b*, p. 147).

Casting off by knitting together. This technique can be used equally well for all knitted work which must have a firm edge. In this case two stitches are simply knitted together by knitting into the back of the stitch (c).

The stitch formed by the knitting together is taken over on to the left-hand needle and is knitted with the next stitch again through the back of the loops. The process is repeated until all the stitches are cast off. Again the end of the yarn is pulled through the last stitch and darned in on the wrong side.

Darning for ribbed pattern. When the last row has been worked, cut the yarn, allowing the length to be twice as long as the last row. Thread this through a blunt-ended needle.

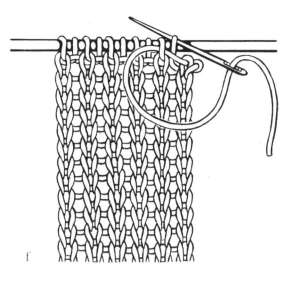

f

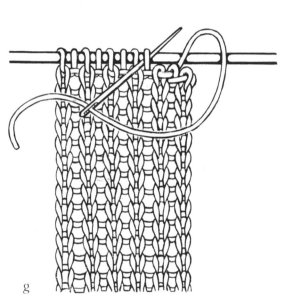

g

are taken from the knitting needle (*f*). The needle is inserted again from left to right into the next purl stitch, the yarn is pulled through but the stitch is left on the needle. Insertion is made from right to left into the knit stitch previously lifted from the needle and the yarn is pulled through (*g*). The next knit stitch is worked again as the knit stitch at the beginning. Now follow the last four working steps until there are no more stitches left on the needle; darn in the remaining end of the yarn.

Dropped stitches

A crochet hook is useful here; when possible use one of the same thickness as the knitting needle. However, if you do not have one, you can use a knitting needle. Slip the hook or needle into the dropped stitch and carefully work up the loops. The stitch pattern determines the side on which the start is made – a knit stitch is picked up on the right side of the work, a purl stitch on the reverse. In stocking stitch (one row knit, one row purl) the knit stitches are lifted as follows. Pull the horizontal yarn through the dropped stitch from back to front and in this manner the dropped stitch can be lifted row by row. In the case of purl stitches the dropped stitches lie at the back of the work with the horizontal yarn in front. The hook or needle is inserted at the back through the stitch. This is repeated until the stitch has reached the row being worked; it is then slipped on to the needle.

Increasing

If the knitted work is to be shaped by increasing the number of stitches at the edges of the work, one of the two following methods should be used.
Method 1. Loop the yarn around the thumb of the left hand and follow instructions for

Now, with the right side of the work facing, insert the needle into the first knit stitch, pull through then let the stitch drop from the knitting needle (*d*). Miss the next stitch, a purl stitch. The needle is inserted into the next knit stitch from right to left, the needle and the yarn are pulled through, but this stitch is left on the needle (*e*). The needle is now inserted from left to right into the missed purl stitch, the yarn is pulled through and both stitches (the knit and the purl stitch)

149

thumb method of casting on (see page 128) until the required number of extra stitches is obtained (Diagram *a*). Repeat at end of next row if required. This method is suitable where a mass increase of stitches is necessary. Method 2. Using a crochet hook, pick up a loop from the edge of the work and using a chain stitch, work the loop up for 2 or 3 rows to the level at which the loop can be easily slipped on to the knitting needle.

Note. If the work is to be widened by only one stitch at each edge, the edge stitch is knitted at the start of the row as a knit stitch, but the loop is left on the needle and the needle is put into the back of this loop and knitted (Diagram *b*).

At the end of the row the last stitch is knitted, the loop is not taken off the left-hand needle, but knitted into the back (Diagram *c*).

Increasing within the row

Increasing stitches within a row of stitches is carried out as follows. A new stitch is formed from the horizontal yarn lying between two stitches; it is picked up with the left needle and knitted into the back (Diagram *d*). If a number of stitches are to be increased within a row of knitting, this process is repeated at equal intervals along the row. If the pattern states a number of stitches are to be increased, but not in one row, then a coloured yarn is inserted at the place where the increase is planned.

If at each marked position only one stitch is to be increased, then the horizontal yarn is picked up on one row before and on the next

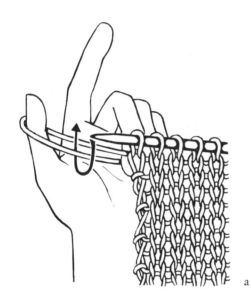

a

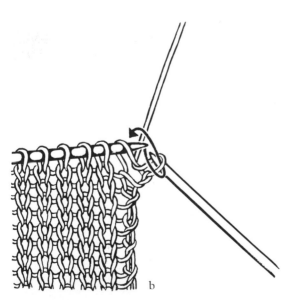

b

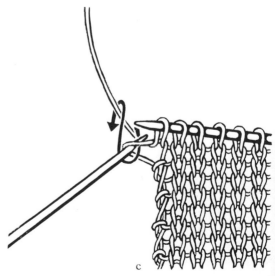

c

after the marked position. This prevents the formation of holes (knitting sample, right). If in each row two stitches are to be increased, then the horizontal yarn is picked up before and after the marked position and it is knitted into the back.

Openwork increases

It is possible to increase before and after two knit stitches so that a band of stitches is formed between the increases (photograph below). Place wool round the needle before the stitches that are to form the axis stitches, then the wool round the needle once again after knitting the axis stitches. Purl all stitches on the next row, including the two made stitches.

Decreasing within the row

In general, decreasing (reduction of the number of stitches) is carried out by simply knitting two stitches together. This can be done, either by knitting (Diagram e) or by purling, or by working into back of stitches

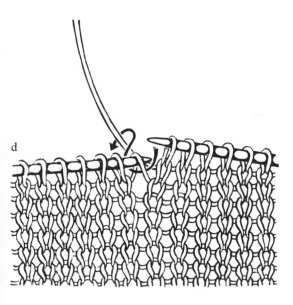

(f) depending on the pattern of the knitting. In addition the stitches can be decreased by lifting one stitch over another. If the total number is to be reduced by one stitch, then one stitch is slipped on to the right-hand needle, the next stitch is knitted, the slipped stitch on the right-hand needle is lifted over the knitted stitch. This is called psso (pass the slipped stitch over). If the number is to be reduced by two stitches, then one stitch is slipped on to the right-hand needle and

151

the next two stitches are knitted together, then the slipped stitch is lifted over the remaining knitted stitch. This is often referred to as p2s s.o.

By simply knitting two stitches together, the resulting decrease will slope to the right, but if the decreased stitches must be sloped to the left then the decreasing should be carried out by the psso method. At the other end the stitches should be knitted together for a slant to the right. If a number of stitches are to be reduced within the row, then equal spacings are counted out. If the reduction of a number of stitches within a row is to be repeated frequently in the course of the work at the same position, the position at which the decreases are made should be marked by putting a different coloured yarn through the knitted work. The work is then continued exactly as in the case of increasing by decreasing in one row before the coloured marker and in the subsequent

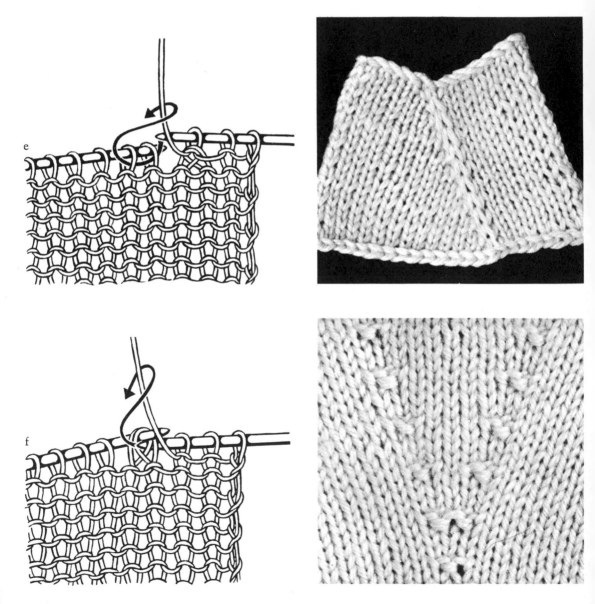

ow behind the marker. In this case, too, it is possible to allow a number of stitches to continue between two decreasing positions as a 'band' by knitting them as usual. This technique, called strip decreasing, is most often used on mittens and socks.

If at the start or at the end of a row one or two stitches are to be decreased, such as at a pointed opening or on raglan shaping, simply knit the two end stitches together. If more than one stitch is to be decreased use what is called a 'bind off' – that is, slip the first stitch to avoid a jagged edge. If at the beginning or at the end a number of stitches are to be decreased simultaneously then they are cast off at the beginning of the next two rows.

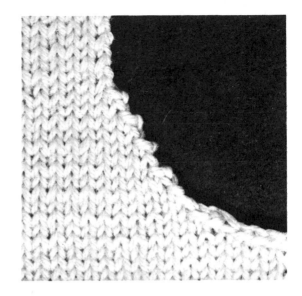

Decreasing for the armhole

The number of stitches decreased for this purpose cannot be given exactly; it depends on the thickness of the yarn and needles and on the size of armhole required, but the number of decreases is always given in the pattern and should be followed exactly. A standard armhole is worked as follows:
The photograph shows the right armhole of the back of a garment. In this case five stitches were cast off at the beginning of a right-side row. After completion of the row five stitches were cast off at the beginning of the next (wrong side) row for the left armhole. Three stitches were again cast off at the beginning of the next right-side row, the row was then knitted to the end. At the start of the new row, three were also cast off, at the beginning of the left armhole. After that once again, two or three stitches were cast off on each side, then one stitch until the number of stitches stated in the pattern remained on the needle. For a smaller armhole if using thicker wool, four stitches are cast off at each side, then three stitches at each side. After that two stitches are

decreased at each side and then one stitch at each side until the number of stitches stated in the pattern is reached.

Decreasing for necklines and shoulders

It is not possible to give exact information about the number of stitches to be decreased, since this depends on the materials used and the requirements of the pattern. These are given fully in the instructions and should be followed for correct results, but as a general rule the following methods are used:

For a 'V' neckline

Check the total number of stitches for the front part of the garment and divide into right and left shoulder sections. Each section is worked separately; the stitches for one section are slipped on to a stitch holder or spare needle while the first section is worked. One stitch is decreased for the left shoulder part at the end of the knitted row (photograph, left, page 154) while for the right

153

section, the decrease is made at the beginning of the right-side row. If the slope of the 'V' is steep, then the decreasing should be made on the second or third knitted row, but the pattern will state this and it will also state whether the first, second or third stitch should be decreased.

Shoulder shaping

In order to obtain a sloping shoulder line, four to 10 unworked stitches are left in steps on the needle. After turning the work, the

first stitch is always a slipped stitch. For example with 14 stitches, k10, turn, slip first stitch, work to end. Next row: k6 sts, turn, slip first stitch, work to end. Cast off all stitches.

Neckbands

Special attention should always be paid to neckbands since they are the most noticeable feature of a knitted garment.

Full instructions are always given in th pattern, but a few general notes will be c interest.

The ordinary ribbed neckband can b worked on a circular needle, on a set of fou needles or on two long needles. In the las case, the general rule is to pick up one stitc for every cast-off stitch and two stitches fo every row along each side of the neck. Grea care should be taken to pick up the stitche evenly, so that the fabric is not stretched o tightened and the formation of holes i avoided.

If the neckband is split for opening, wor backwards and forwards in rib. If the neck band is circular, ensure that the casting off i flexible so that the finished garment i simple to put on. A tight binding edge i uncomfortable and tends to break and un ravel. If the neckband is turned and slip stitched to form a double band, great car should be taken to ensure that the slip stitching used is loose enough to provide elasticity.

The turtle or polo neck is worked in tubular manner, either on a circular needle or on a set of four needles exactly as the ribbed band The length knitted depends on the patterr but for a neat turn-over it should not be less than 5 in. It can be knitted in single rib, k1, p1; in broad rib, k2, p2, or in a variation o k3, p1.

The V neck. The stitches of the back section are not usually cast off. The stitches of the sloping front section (decreasing of the V neck, page 154) for the ribbed pattern are picked up and knitted as for the ordinary band ribbing (page 155). Often, to get a neat join, the stitches are picked up then the first row is purled. The following rounds are worked in p1, k1, rib alternately, with the front V being formed as follows:

1st Row: sl the 2nd st knitwise before the centre st, k the following st, lift the slipped st over the knitted st, k the centre st, k the next 2 sts tog, rib to end.

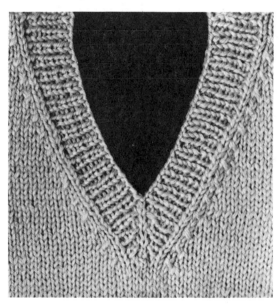

2nd Row: sl the 2nd st before the centre st knitwise, k the next st, lift over the slipped st, p the centre st, k tog the next 2 sts, rib to end.

Repeat these two rows until neckband is required depth.

Collar edgings

Collars knitted in stocking stitch (one row knit, one row purl) unless they are worked double, require an edging. This edging can be double or single.

The double edging. At the end of last return row, the stitches are picked up and knitted on the right-hand edge, with new yarn. The stitches on the needle are knitted off and the stitches are picked up and knitted from the left edge. Mark the corner stitch with a coloured thread and, in all forward rows, work twice into the stitches on either side. When the edging is the required width, one forward row is purled to denote the turning edge. After this row, knit together an equal number of stitches on each side of the corner stitch. Cast off stitches, sew the edging into place using hemming stitches (photograph, page 156, left).

Ordinary corner edging. The main part in stocking stitch is worked according to the garment pattern by starting at the collar, inner edge. The stitches are knitted up from the edge stitches of the side border and five rows are knitted on the three outer edges of the collar. In doing this three stitches must

Knitted cushion made from individual squares of ribbing sewn together

always be picked up at the corners on the wrong side of the work and these stitches are knitted up. This keeps the collar flat.

Cast off all stitches after the third rib (5th row). (Photograph, page 156, lower right.)
Curved edging. Pick up stitches as for double edging. Pick up one stitch from each stitch or rows going round the corner. After that, knit the required width of ribbed pattern and cast off stitches as they occur: by purling the purl stitches and by knitting the knit stitches (photograph below).

The knitted pocket

Knit up the pocket slot, then take as many stitches on to an additional needle as necessary for the pocket width. Increase one stitch on each side for the seam and work 10 rows of basic pattern. Then make the edge described on page 137 (row of holes) and carry on working according to the basic pattern, until double depth of pocket is reached. The stitches increased on both sides for the seam are cast off. Then the stitches are once again taken on the main needle and work is continued as before. The seams of the pocket are closed later. The open edges of the pocket edging (the 10 rows) are sewn sideways as invisibly as possible.

Diagonal knitting

In diagonal knitting, not to be confused with diagonal pattern, the work is started by casting on two stitches. At the beginning of each row, one stitch is increased by picking up the top of a loop between the first two stitches and it is worked as a stitch. The work is started at a lower corner and increased until the required width is reached. After that, one stitch is decreased at the beginning of each row, by working two stitches together, until no more stitches remain. This method of knitting will produce a square.

Tubular or circular knitting

Tubular knitting or circular knitting can be worked on a circular needle or a set of four double-pointed needles. The method of knitting dealt with up to now is called flat knitting, in contrast to circular knitting which will now be described.

The knit and purl stitches are worked in both methods in the same way, but the casting on is different. Where the work is done with a set of four double-pointed

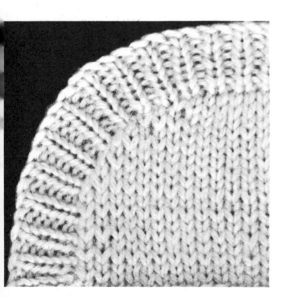
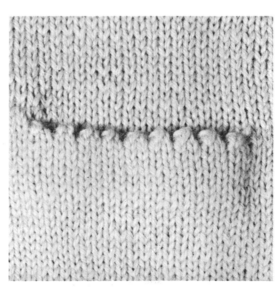

needles, difficulties can be experienced initially, particularly in maintaining an evenness in the work, but these are quickly overcome as one becomes used to the technique.

The pattern of stitches in circular knitting differs from flat work. For example: to work stocking stitch, every round is worked in a knit stitch. The right side looks the same as it does on flat knitting; the ridged side (wrong side on flat work) is inside the tube or cir-cular knitting. To work garter stitch, knit one round, purl one round alternately. Or knitting a ribbed pattern – one knit stitch

Cushion with diagonal stripes in white, red and olive: the knitting is started at one corner, increased up to the widest part, and then decreased to the opposite corner

one purl stitch, alternately – the work looks the same as that obtained by the flat knitting method. Many knitted articles can be made either by flat knitting worked on two needles, or by circular knitting using a circular needle or a set of four needles. For example, gloves and socks, at one time always knitted on four needles so that there was no seam, are now often knitted on two needles and seamed.

Making up

Very careful attention should be paid to the assembly of knitted pieces to produce a complete garment. The most frequent cause of dissatisfaction with a finished garment is incorrect assembly, lack of care when pressing and failure to block the individual parts to the correct measurements and shape.
Blocking. This is a very simple task, but one very well worth doing. Before commencing, assemble the following items:
An ordinary electric iron, regulated to 'wool' temperature as marked on the dial
A supply of long steel pins
A bowl of water
A large pressing cloth (such as an old tea towel or firm fabric)
An inch tape
An old blanket and an ironing sheet
Blocking should be done on a large square board – old table top or similar; an ironing board is not suitable. In case of necessity, use the floor.
Fold the blanket in four to form a thick pad, cover with the sheet. Wring out the pressing cloth in water.
Select the first piece to be blocked, say the back of a sweater. Lay it flat and smooth into shape with both hands. Measure at the widest part, that is just below the armhole shaping. The piece should measure 2 in. more than the size required, i.e. a man's sweater size 38-in. chest should measure

20 in. across at this point. Place a pin at each extremity, then pin into shape, inserting pins at one-inch intervals down each side, across shoulders and around armhole shapings. DO NOT PIN RIB. Using the iron at the correct temperature, gently press, do not iron, until all parts have been covered. Leave the piece to set for a few minutes, gently remove the pins and lay the pressed piece flat on a piece of paper. Repeat this with all the pieces. When they have all been pressed and are completely dry, you can begin to join them.

Socks

The work is started by casting on the stitches by one of the methods shown on pages 124 and 125. The gauge of the needles depends as always on the wool used, but this will be stated in the pattern. When enough stitches are on one needle, then the next needle is taken straight away without allowing an intermediate space and without cutting off the yarn (Diagram *a*). The casting on is completed on three needles. If this proves difficult, cast all the stitches on to one long needle of the same gauge as the set (it need not be double-pointed). The stitches can

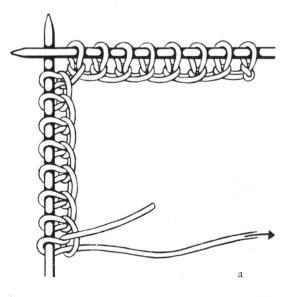

a

then be slipped off and divided between the three needles in rotation, or they can be knitted off. The second method saves time, but it is important to make sure that no stitch is twisted. The work is joined and continued with the fourth needle, always going round in a circle. In doing this the yarn between the end of one and beginning of another needle must always be pulled tight, otherwise a larger stitch gap could be formed at this point (Diagram *b*). Now you know how to knit the leg of a sock or stocking, we come to the leg, heel, heel flap, instep and toe.

Leg decreasing. A stocking becomes narrower from the calf to the heel by a quarter of its width. No complicated calculations are necessary to achieve this. If 80 stitches have been cast on, only 60 stitches will be needed at the heel. The decreasing is carried out as

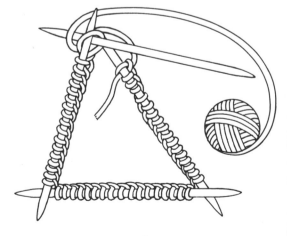

b

follows: all stitches on the third needle are worked up to the last three. Two of these last stitches are knitted together, the third and the last stitch on the needle are knitted The first stitch on the next (i.e. on the first) needle will be knitted, the subsequent two stitches are knitted together. This is the same process as at the end of the third needle, but in reverse order. In one round only two stitches are decreased, then six to 10 rounds are worked before two stitches are decreased, as described. After repeating 10 times, the stocking will have the correct width, or taper.

To divide the stitches for the heel, knit the first quarter of the total stitches on one needle, slip the last quarter of the round on to the other end of the same needle, the remainder of the stitches being left on two needles for instep.

The heel flap is worked in stocking stitch commencing with a purl row working on two needles. Always slip the first stitch knitwise on the knit row and the first stitch purlwise on the purl row, forming a chain edge down each side of the flap. Continue in stocking stitch until a square piece of fabric is completed, finishing at the end of a purl row.

To turn a French heel work a series of decs at each side of the centre portion of heel. Each dec uses 2 sts, hence the number of sts at each side of the centre portion must be a multiple of 2. To turn the heel you must work 2 or 3 sts past the centre leaving your

multiple of 2 on the end of the needle. Dec the 1st 2 sts of this multiple of 2 by sl1, k1, psso, turn the work, p1 st (the dec st of previous row), now p across the 2 or 3 sts to centre, then p the same number, 2 or 3, at the other side of centre, p the next 2 sts tog, turn the work again. K back to the dec st, k this st, sl1, k1, psso, turn the work again and p back to the p dec, p this st, then p2 tog. Continue in this manner until all the sts have been worked on to one needle.

To turn a Dutch heel the decs are continuous as the st formed by the 1st dec becomes the 1st st of the 2nd dec, thus leaving a basic number at the centre of the heel throughout. Work 3, 4 or 5 sts beyond the centre (approximately two-thirds of total number of sts on needle). Dec the next st by sl1, k1, psso, turn p the dec st, p across the centre sts, p2 tog, turn. K to dec st of previous row, sl this st, k1, psso, turn. P back to the dec of previous row, p this st tog with the following st, turn and continue in this manner until all the sts are worked on to one needle.

When you have turned the heel that must

be completed on a p row, you are now ready to k up the instep. Sl the instep sts (that is the sts that remained on the 2 needles) on to 1 needle. Using a spare needle, k other half of heel sts, then k up the sts along 1 side of

the heel flap, knitting 1 st up through both loops of the chain edge. Using a 2nd needle work across instep sts. Using a 3rd needle, k up the same number of sts along the 2nd side of heel flap then k across remaining heel sts thus completing round.

To work the instep decrease k to last 3 sts on 1st needle, k2 tog, k1, k across the instep sts on 2nd needle, k1, k2 tog tbl, at the beg of 3rd needle, k to end of round. K 1 round without shaping. Rep these 2 rounds until the combined number of sts on the 1st and 3rd needles equals the number of sts on the 2nd needle. Continue in rounds for foot for length required.

You are now ready to *shape the toe*. The sts should be divided as at completion of instep. On the 1st needle k to last 3 sts, k2 tog, k1. On the 2nd needle k1, k2 tog tbl, k to last 3 sts, k2 tog, k1. On 3rd needle, k1, k2 tog tbl, k to end. K 1 round. Rep these 2 rounds

until approximately half the total number of sts remain. Now k sts from 1st needle on to 3rd needle. Graft sts tog or cast off from 2 needles tog. Do not make any knots (photograph, above).

Mittens

The mittens are suitable for a child aged eight to 10 years. To make them, you will need a set of four double-pointed needles size 10 British (size 3 American) and about 3 oz (80 g) of 4-ply knitting yarn. The work is started by casting on, and commencing the ribbed wrist band. The band should be 42 stitches wide and 25 rounds deep. After that, work seven knit rounds. Then commence the wedge shaping, called the thumb gusset. For this gusset, increase a stitch at the beginning of the first needle by simply picking up a horizontal thread between two stitches and by knitting into the back of the stitch. Another stitch is worked after that and then another stitch is increased by picking up the loop lying between the stitches and knitting into the back of it. This is followed by two rounds worked without increasing. After that, a stitch is increased to the right and to the left of the increased stitches once again, i.e. the increasing is made straight away at the beginning of the needle, three stitches are worked and an increase is made. Two rounds must now be worked before increasing again by one stitch on the right and one on the left of the previously increased stitch. Repeat until the thumb gusset has 15 stitches.

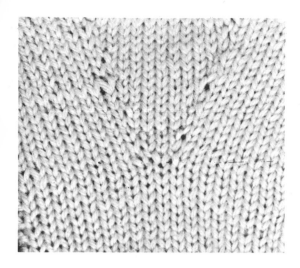

Thumb hole

The stitches of the thumb gusset are slipped on to a safety-pin and left. In their place five new stitches must be cast on so that the round for the mitten can be closed again. The collected five stitches are decreased again in the manner of a gusset by knitting the first stitch, then lifting the first stitch over the second, then the last two gusset stitches are knitted together. This is carried out again in the second round and on the next round the remaining stitch is lifted over the

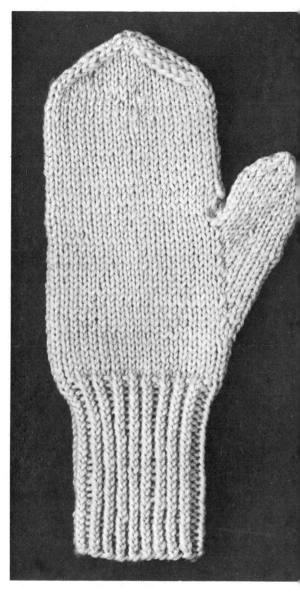

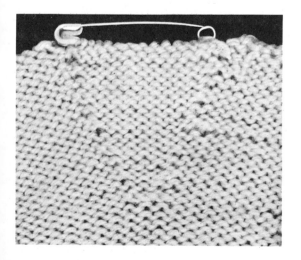

next stitch so that the work reverts to the number of stitches there were before the start of the thumb gusset. After that, knitting is continued in rounds, approximately to the tip of the small finger (about 45 rounds).

The tip of the mitten
Each round is decreased to form the tip of the mitten as follows. (Mitten photographed above.) The second and third stitch on the

first needle are knitted together; then knit 15 stitches; knit the next two stitches together, knit two more stitches, knit two stitches together, knit 15 stitches, knit two stitches together, knit remaining stitches.

Children's mittens knitted in handspun sheep's wool, without a thumb gusset

Repeat this round, but on each round two stitches less will be worked between the decrease until 10 stitches are left. Break off the yarn and thread through remaining stitches, pull tight and darn in carefully, to fasten off. Do not make a knot.

The thumb

The stitches round the thumb hole are picked up first; in doing this two stitches are decreased. After that the working is carried out around the thumb until it is long enough and then it is decreased. In the first round two stitches are always worked, decrease, work two stitches, decrease and so on. Then work two rounds straight without decreasing and finally the rhythm becomes: work one stitch, decrease one stitch, work one stitch, and so on. The existing stitches are worked in one round and finally pulled together with a yarn end, and darned in securely. Care must be taken to ensure that, if placing the

thumb gusset at the front of the mitten (photograph above) instead of the side, two similar mittens are not worked (i.e. two right- or two left-hand mittens). Mittens for babies are usually knitted without a thumb.

Knitting with a circular needle

These needles are flexible plastic or wire with a needle point at each end. Too long a needle will stretch the stitches so it is essential to choose the correct length.

The casting on is carried out exactly as for flat work. After casting on a row the first casting on stitch is worked with the end of the flexible needle; that is to say, it is not turned – but the work is closed this way and knitted in a circle. This method is used wherever a garment without a seam is required, and the work has too large a diameter for knitting on four needles, for example for pullovers, skirts, yokes etc. As already mentioned, it is sometimes used for necklines.

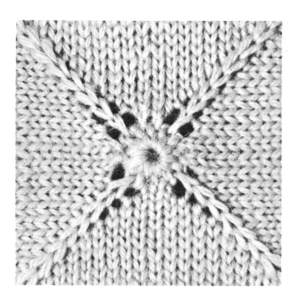

Fancy knitting

Fancy knitting is flat work which is not worked in forward and return rows but in circular spiral pattern in rounds with four needles. Circular, square, triangular, pentagon, hexagon and other shapes can be knitted, using up to eight needles.

In the beginning, a number of stitches which are divisible by the number of the corners is cast on (i.e. four in the case of a square). The casting on is carried out as follows: the end of the yarn is made into a ring and held with the index finger and the thumb of the left hand. Then the yarn is picked up alternately with the knitting needle from outside to inside through the ring and passed round the needle on the outside of the ring only (drawing, right).

Alternately, you can begin by crocheting a ring of chain stitches with the loops individually picked up to represent stitches. The picked up stitches are divided on four (or for a traingle, on three) needles. The number of stitches on each needle must be divisible by two. For example eight stitches are cast on for a square, with two stitches on each needle – the last and the first needle are taken together in the left hand and the work

is carried out with the fifth (working) needle, always working around and with firm stitches. The increase is made in the middle of each needle by two stitches in each round, so that four wedges are formed. In a triangle there are three wedges.

To knit a circular shape, one stitch is increased in each round in a staggered manner, in the first round after each stitch, in the subsequent rounds one stitch per needle twice, behind the stitch increase in the previous round.

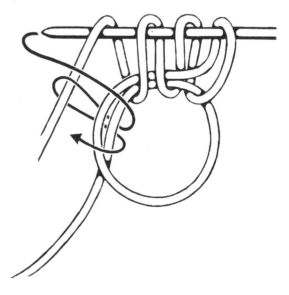

165

Knitted doll

The doll is knitted to a pattern which you make yourself, one pattern for a small pull-over and one for pants. The proportions are tested by means of the pattern. Then, the two parts are knitted separately, and the pants in diagonal ribbing. The hands are worked as the mittens' thumbs; the legs as socks. All parts are sewn together and filled with kapok. The stitches for the pullover polo neck are picked up on three needles and the work is continued by regularly increasing up to the widest part of the head – a third of the way. After that, depending on the size of the doll or the head, six to eight rounds are knitted without increasing and the head is stuffed very firmly. The work is then continued and the decreasing is made as for the toe of the mittens. The rest of the head is stuffed before the work is closed. Loops (page 93) are subsequently crocheted into the stitches of the upper part of the head to represent hair. The firmly packed filling in the lower part of the head is now loosened with a knitting needle and uniformly distributed by pushing through the stitches and pulling upwards. The face is now pressed to shape and a small nose embroidered. Then the eyes and mouth are worked. A double strand of yarn is finally pulled into the turned-over openwork edges of the polo collar and knotted under the turnover. This makes the doll's neck.

Child's waistcoat

Material: 10×25-g balls of double knitting wool. Two knitting needles size 6 British (size 8 American), a 5-mm crochet hook.
The garment is worked in garter st and the narrow welt in 2×2 rib (k2, p2).
Tension: 14 sts and 21 rows make a 4-in. square (10×10 cm).
Measurement: the waistcoat is to fit chest size 24–26 in. (60–65 cm).

Back: cast on 46 sts and k 8 rows k2, p2 rib. Then work straight in garter st for 60 rows. Dec 4 sts at the beg of the next 2 rows. K 30 more rows and then cast off all sts.
Front: cast on 24 sts, k 8 rows in rib, then k 60 rows in garter st. Dec 4 sts at the beg of the 61st row (armhole) and 3 sts at the end (button band). Then dec 1 st at the end of every alternate row for the neck shaping until 10 sts remain on the needle. Cont knitting with these sts for 20 rows. Cast off all sts. Work the 2nd front, making 5 buttonholes at intervals of 12 rows, the 1st to start at the 5th row.
Pockets: cast on 14 sts for each of the 2 large pockets and 10 sts for the small one. Work to the basic pattern, dec 1 st at each end of every alternate row; 18 rows for the large and 14 rows for the small pocket. Join seams, then crochet the edges. Lightly press seams if necessary.

Baby's jacket with button-on bag

Two knitting needles size 10 British (size 3 American). One crochet hook 3.50 mm. Eight small flat buttons.
7×50-g balls Patons Baby Quickerknit nylon.
The work is carried out in garter st, all rows k.
Bag: cast on 64 sts and k a rectangular piece $27\frac{1}{2}$ in. long.
On the 3rd row from the beg and from the bottom end, make 2 buttonholes of 3 sts (see page 136) after the 17th and 44th sts.
Lightly press the completed work using a damp cloth and warm iron. Fold the rectangle in half, buttonholes at top, and join the sides neatly. Press seams.
Jacket back: cast on 60 sts and k 40 rows. Cast off 3 sts for the armholes at the beg of the next 2 rows, 2 sts on the next 2 rows and 1 st on the next row. K 20 rows straight. Shape shoulder by casting off 5 sts at the beg of the next 4 rows and 6 sts on the

Baby shoes

The size of needles depends on the yarn used; for a Bri-nylon baby Quickerknit use No. 10 needles British (No. 3 American).
Cast on 42 sts and work 24 rows in garter st (all rows k).
Cast off 9 sts at the beg of the next 2 rows. Work 16 rows on remaining 24 sts.
17th Row: k 2 sts tog all along the row.
18th Row: p.
19th Row: k 2 sts tog all along the row.
20th Row: p.
Thread the remaining sts on to a length of double yarn and pull tight. Fasten off firmly. Sew the shoe tog by joining the centre front and back seam.

Long scarf and cap knitted in block pattern. The cap is shaped and finished at the top in the same way as a stocking toe

following 2 rows, then cast off the remaining sts for the neck opening.
Front part: cast on 45 sts and k 40 rows. Shape armhole by casting off 2 sts at the beg of the next row and 2 sts of the next alternate row. Then cast off 20 sts at the front edge, for neck. Work to end. Cast off 5 sts for the shoulder shaping on next row, then cast off 3 sts at the neck edge on the next row. Turn, cast off 5 sts at shoulder edge on next row, work 1 row, then cast off the remaining sts. Into one of the front parts work 6 horizontal buttonholes as on bag, at the following positions: after the 6th, 18th and 50th row, 5 and 30 sts from the front edge.
Sleeve: pick up and k 16 sts along the armhole edge. Next row, inc 2 sts at each end on every row until there are 32 sts on the needle. Now inc 1 st at each end until there are 46 sts. Cont straight until 46 rows have been knitted. Cast off. Press all parts of the jacket and join side and sleeve seams. Sew on buttons to correspond with buttonholes, 6 at the front and 2 at the lower edge of the back. Edge neck with double crochet.

Baby's jacket with a hood

7 × 50-g balls Patons Baby Quickerknit nylon. Two knitting needles (long) No. 9 and 8 British (5 and 6 American). One crochet hook, size 4 mm.
Basic pattern: a repeat of 4 plus 1 st.
1st Row: right side of work. P1 ★ k the following st without slipping it from the needle, yrn and k this st again so that 3 sts appear. P3. Rep from ★.
2nd and 4th Rows (wrong side of work): k3 ★ p3, k3. Rep from ★. The row ends with p3, k1.
3rd Row (right side): p1, ★ k3, p3, to end.
5th Row (right side): p1. ★ Sl the next st knitwise, k the next 2 sts tog, psso this st, p3. Rep from ★ to end.
6th Row (wrong side): k1, ★ p1, k3 alternately, rep from ★. The row ends with p1.
7th to 12th Rows: work as for 1st to 6th rows. To get a diagonal look, work in a staggered manner.
Rep 1st to 12th rows continuously.
Cast on for back and left and right front: 101 sts. K until work measures $6\frac{1}{4}$ in. then continue separately, 40 sts for the back and 26 sts each for the 2 front parts. Shape armholes by casting off 8 sts at the beg of armholes, then con until shoulder is reached.

Sleeve: cast on 37 sts for the sleeve and start at the wrist. K in pattern for $6\frac{1}{2}$ in. then dec 8 sts for the armhole shaping at the beg of the next 2 rows. Cast off the remaining 11 sts.

Hood: cast on 61 sts and k 42 rows in pattern. Finish all edges with a row of double crochet. Then work a 2nd row in shrimp st, i.e. sideways st (page 73). Join the hood by lower crocheted edge to the crochet edge of the neck opening of the jacket. Join by sewing or crochet.

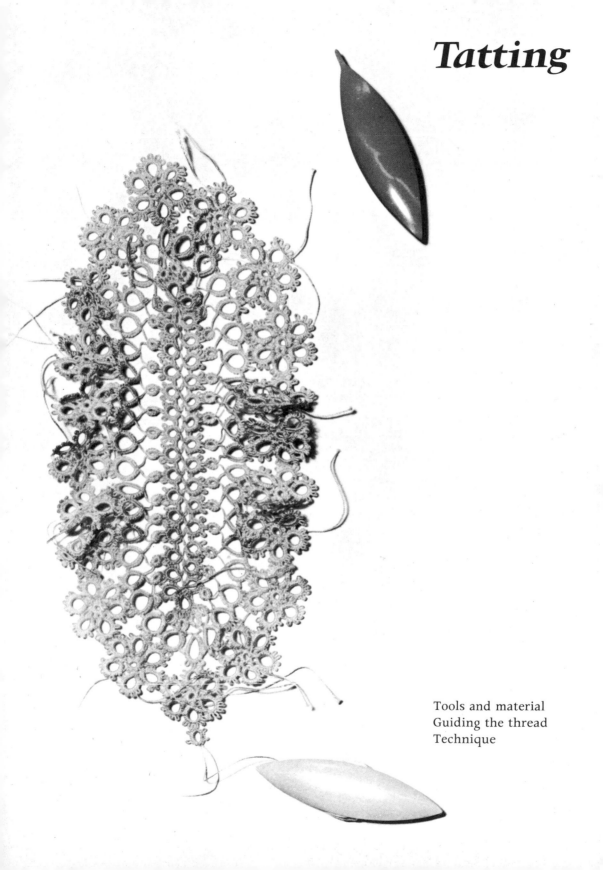

Tatting

Tools and material
Guiding the thread
Technique

As the photograph (left) shows, tatting can be made into various shapes. The classical tatting technique as shown here is carried out with fine mercerised crochet yarn; however, other yarns can be used

Tatting – also called frivolité – is a delicate handicraft technique which is used chiefly for decorative edgings on handkerchiefs, table linen, place mats or cheval sets. In tatting, stitches are worked into rings around a working thread and joined to each other to form patterns. Picots can be added.

Materials

Through the ages bone, tortoiseshell and steel have been used in the manufacture of tatting shuttles. The modern shuttle is made from plastic which is smooth, light and durable. Milward tatting shuttles, supplied in packets which contain a separate hook for joinings, and Coats Chain Mercer-Crochet Nos. 20, 40, 60 or 80 are reliable. Boye plastic shuttles are easily available in the U.S.

Winding the shuttle

Wind the thread round the bobbin in the centre of the shuttle until the space is filled, taking care not to allow the thread to project beyond the edges. When two or more shuttles are used in more complicated designs it is advisable to use shuttles of different colours or to mark shuttles with a spot of paint to avoid confusion.

Guiding the thread

The end of the thread is taken between the thumb and index finger of the left hand, then round and under the other slightly spread fingers to form a circle. The working thread, which is used for later formation of stitches, lies between the index and middle finger.
Hold the shuttle loosely between thumb and index finger of right hand. The length of thread between shuttle and ring should be about 8 in. (20 cm). Pass the shuttle thread under the fingers, then over the little finger of the right hand.
The stitches cover the length of thread between the right and left hand.

How to Tat

The basic stitch called double stitch (ds), consists of two half knots.

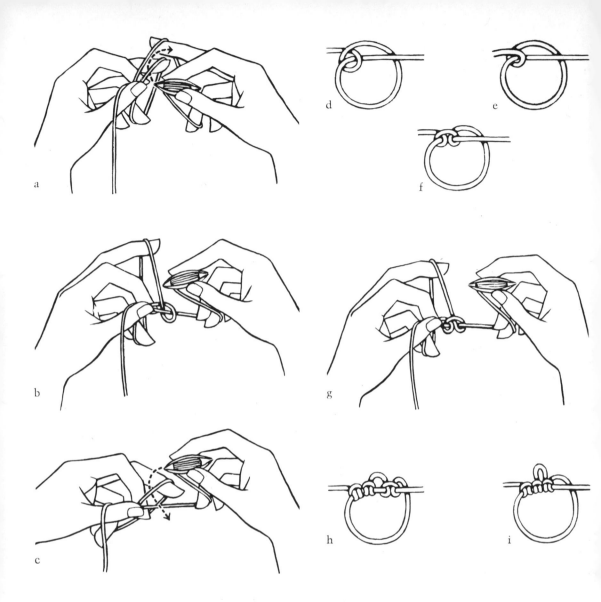

First half of double stitch

Pass the shuttle under the shuttle thread and through the circle. Guide it back over the circle thread and under the shuttle thread (a). Relax fingers of left hand, drop the thread from little finger of right hand and draw shuttle thread taut. Pass shuttle thread over little finger as before, slowly raise middle finger of left hand, slide loop into position between thumb and forefinger (b). This completes the first half of double stitch (d).

Second half of double stitch

Pass the shuttle over the circle, then back through between circle and shuttle threads (c). Relax fingers of left hand, drop thread from little finger of right hand and draw shuttle thread taut (e). Pass shuttle thread over little finger as before, slowly raise middle finger of left hand, slide loop into position close to first half of double stitch (g). This completes the second half of the double stitch (f).

172

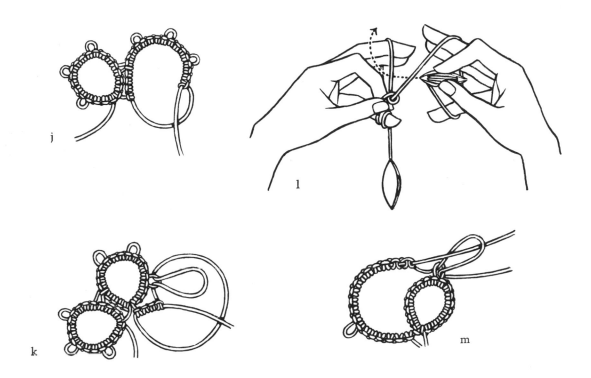

j

l

k

m

Tatted lace edges for handkerchiefs and place mats are made separately and sewn on when completed

After completing the double stitch work is continued with hands in position as shown in (g). Picots (loops) are formed between two double stitches (h, i). Work one double stitch then the first half of the next stitch, but as you slide it into position stop $\frac{1}{4}$-in. (6 mm) from preceding stitch, work the other half and draw the entire stitch close to the previous double stitch. The picot (loop) may be made larger or smaller by varying the length of the space left between the two stitches.

Note: it is important that the picots are of uniform size.

After working the required number of double stitches and picots, slip the circle thread from the fingers of the left hand and draw the shuttle thread tight (j) until the ring is closed. Work the next ring according to the pattern, either close to or the desired length from the previous ring.

To join two rings, insert the hook through the respective picot on the previous ring and pull the circle thread through to form a

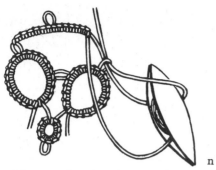

n

loop (k). Pass the shuttle thread through the loop from right to left. Draw up the loop. This stands for the first half of the next double stitch. Work second half to complete double stitch.

A new thread is always worked between two rings or between ring and chains and covered with double stitch.

When working with two shuttles the ends of the thread on both shuttles are tied together and the knots are held with the thumb and index finger of the left hand. A small loop is formed when pulled tight. The yarn on the left hand is wound twice around the little finger and the shuttle remains hanging. The second shuttle is worked in the usual way with the right hand (l). Rings and picots follow each other closely when working with two shuttles (m) without the connecting yarn which is formed between two rings when working with only one shuttle.

The turning of the work is carried out simultaneously with the changing of the shuttle from the left hand to the right hand or from the right to left hand. Joining a chain

Tatting is done with one or more shuttles and is made up of rings and loops of knotted thread. The tiny loops at the edges of the rings are called picots

to a ring: the thread coming from the left shuttle will be carried through the corresponding picot on the ring; the thread must not be twisted in doing this. The second shuttle will be guided through this loop (n).

Abbreviations

R: ring; sr: small ring; lr: large ring; ds: double stitch; p: picot; lp: large picot; cl: close; sep: separated; rw: reverse work; sp: space; in.: inch; ch: chain; rep: repeat.

Tatted doily, page 175

Materials: 1 ball Coats Chain Mercer-Crochet Cotton No. 40, Milward shuttle.

Measurements: $7\frac{1}{2}$ in. (19 cm) in diameter.

1st Row: ★ r of 8 ds, p, 8 ds, cl; rep from ★ 7 times more, working rings close tog. Tie ends, cut and oversew neatly on wrong side.

2nd Row: lr of 4 ds, p, 2 ds, 5 ps sep by 1 ds, 2 ds, p, 4 ds, cl, rw, leave sp of $\frac{1}{8}$ in. (3 mm), sr of 8 ds, join to p on 1st r of previous row, 8 ds, cl, rw, leave sp of $\frac{1}{8}$ in. (3 mm), lr of 4 ds, join to last p on previous lr, 2 ds, 5 ps sep by 1 ds, 2 ds, p, 4 ds, cl, rw, leave sp of $\frac{1}{8}$ in. (3 mm), sr of 8 ds, join to p on 1st r of previous row, 8 ds, cl. ★ Rw, leave sp of $\frac{1}{8}$ in. (3 mm), lr of 4 ds, join to last p on previous lr, 2 ds, 5 ps sep by 1 ds, 2 ds, p, 4 ds, cl, rw, leave sp of $\frac{1}{8}$ in. (3 mm), sr of 8 ds, join to p on next r in previous row, 8 ds, cl, rw, leave sp of $\frac{1}{8}$ in. (3 mm), lr of 4 ds, join to last p on previous lr, 2 ds, 5 ps sep by 1 ds, 2 ds, p, 4 ds, cl, rw, leave sp of $\frac{1}{8}$ in. (3 mm), sr of 8 ds, join to p of same r in previous row as last sr, 8 ds, cl; rep from ★ joining last lr to 1st lr to correspond. Tie ends, leaving sp of $\frac{1}{8}$ in.

Tatting needs considerable patience. The technique is not complicated when one is familiar with the few standard knots, but it requires nimble fingers and concentration. (Instructions overleaf, detail of pattern on the right)

(3 mm), cut and oversew neatly on wrong side.

3rd Row: lr of 5 ds, p, 3 ds, 5 ps sep by 1 ds, 3 ds, p, 5 ds, cl, rw, leave sp of $\frac{1}{5}$ in. (5 mm), sr of 8 ds, join to centre p on any lr of previous row, 8 ds, cl, rw, leave sp of $\frac{1}{5}$ in. (5 mm), lr of 5 ds, join to last p on previous lr, 3 ds, 5 ps sep by 1 ds, 3 ds, p, 5 ds, cl, rw, leave sp of $\frac{1}{5}$ in. (5 mm), sr of 8 ds, join to p on same r of previous row as last sr, 8 ds, cl. ★ Rw, leave sp of $\frac{1}{5}$ in. (5 mm), lr of 5 ds, join to last p on previous lr, 3 ds, 5 ps sep by 1 ds, 3 ds, p, 5 ds, cl, rw, leave sp of $\frac{1}{5}$ in. (5 mm), sr of 8 ds, join to p on next r of previous row, 8 ds, cl, rw, leave sp of $\frac{1}{5}$ in. (5 mm), lr of 5 ds, join to last p on previous lr, 3 ds, 5 ps sep by 1 ds, 3 ds, p, 5 ds, cl, rw, leave sp of $\frac{1}{5}$ in. (5 mm), sr of 8 ds, join to p of same r of previous row as last sr, 8 ds, cl; rep from ⋆ joining last lr to 1st lr to correspond. Tie ends, leaving sp of $\frac{1}{5}$ in. (5 mm), cut and oversew neatly on wrong side.

4th Row: lr as in 3rd row, sr of 4 ds, join to last p on lr, 4 ds, p, 4 ds, cl, rw, leave sp of $\frac{1}{5}$ in. (5 mm), r of 8 ds, join to any centre p on lr of previous row, 8 ds, cl. ⋆ Rw, leave sp of $\frac{1}{5}$ in. (5 mm), lr of 5 ds, join to p of sr, 3 ds, 5 ps sep by 1 ds, 3 ds, p, 5 ds, cl, sr of 4 ds, join to last p on lr, 4 ds, p, 4 ds, cl, rw, r of 8 ds, join to centre p on next lr of previous row, 8 ds, cl; rep from ⋆ joining last sr to 1st lr to correspond. Tie ends, leaving sp of $\frac{1}{5}$ in. (5 mm), cut and oversew on wrong side.

5th Row: tie ball and shuttle threads tog. R of 8 ds, join to centre p on any lr of previous row, 8 ds, cl, ⋆ rw, ch of 4 ds, rw, lr of 2 ds, 10 ps sep by 2 ds, 2 ds, cl, rw, ch of 3 ds, 3 ps sep by 2 ds, 3 ds, rw, sr of 4 ds, join to 9th p on lr, 4 ds, cl, rw, ch of 3 ds, 4 ps sep by 2 ds, 3 ds, rw, sr of 4 ds, join to 7th p on lr, 4 ds, cl, rw, ch of 3 ds, 3 ps sep by 2 ds, 3 ds, join by shuttle thread to 5th p on lr, ch of 4 ds, rw, r of 8 ds, join to centre p on next lr of previous row, 8 ds, cl; rep from ⋆ to end. Tie ends, cut and oversew neatly on wrong side.

Tatted place mat, page 177

Materials: 2 balls Coats Chain Mercer-Crochet Cotton No. 20, Milward Shuttle.
Measurements: approximately 15 in. × 11$\frac{3}{4}$ in. (38 cm × 30 cm).

First strip

1st Row: tie ball and shuttle threads tog. ⋆ R of 4 ds, 2 ps sep by 2 ds, 4 ds, cl, rw, ch of 6 ds, 2 ps sep by 6 ds, 3 ds, join by shuttle thread to last p of previous r, rw, ch of 6 ds, p, 6 ds, rw, r of 4 ds, join to adjacent p on previous ch, 2 ds, p, 4 ds, cl, ⋆⋆ rw, ch of 3 ds, rw; rep from ⋆ 17 times more, ending last rep at ⋆⋆. At end of this and every row: tie ends, cut and oversew on wrong side.

2nd Row: tie ball and shuttle threads tog. Attach thread to last p on last r of previous row, ch of 6 ds, join by shuttle thread to next p on previous row, ⋆ ch of 2 ds, 2 ps sep by 1 ds, 1 ds, 3 lps sep by 2 ds, 1 ds, 2 ps sep by 1 ds, 2 ds, join to next p on previous row, ch of 6 ds, join to next p on previous row; rep from ⋆ to end.

3rd Row: tie ball and shuttle threads tog. R of 4 ds, 2 ps sep by 2 ds, 4 ds, cl, rw, ch of 6 ds, join by ball thread to last p on last ch of 1st row, 6 ds, p, 3 ds, join by shuttle thread to adjacent p on last r, rw. ⋆ Ch of 6 ds, p, 6 ds, rw, r of 4 ds, join to adjacent p on ch, 2 ds, joint to p on next r of 1st row, 4 ds, cl, rw, ch of 3 ds, rw, r of 4 ds, join to next p on 1st row, 2 ds, p, 4 ds, cl, rw, ch of 6 ds, 2 ps sep by 6 ds, 3 ds, join to p on last r, rw, ch of 6 ds, join to next p on 1st row, ch of 6 ds, rw, r of 4 ds, join to adjacent p on ch, 2 ds, p, 4 ds, cl ⋆⋆, rw, ch of 3 ds, rw, r of 4 ds, 2 ps sep by 2 ds, 4 ds, cl, rw, ch of 6 ds, join to next p on 1st row, 6 ds, p, 3 ds, join to adjacent p on last r, rw. Rep from ⋆ ending last rep at ⋆⋆. **4th Row:** as 2nd row.

Second strip

Work 1st, 2nd and 3rd rows as 1st strip.

4th Row: tie ball and shuttle threads tog. Attach thread to last p on last r of previous row. Ch of 6 ds, join by shuttle thread to next p on previous row, ch of 2 ds, 2 ps sep by 1 ds, 1 ch, 1 ds, join by ball thread to 1st lp on 2nd row of last completed strip, (2 ds, join to next lp) twice, ⋆ 1 ds, 2 ps sep by 1 ds, 2 ds, join by shuttle thread to next p on previous row, ch of 6 ds, join to next p on previous row, 2 ds, 2 ps sep by 1 ds, 1 ds, (join by ball thread to next lp on 2nd row of last completed strip, 2 ds) 3 times; rep from ⋆ to end.

Work five more strips, joining 4th row of each strip to 2nd row of last strip, following instructions for 4th row of 2nd strip.

Weaving

American equivalent terms:
U.K. shaft = U.S. harness
U.K. ribbon weaving = U.S. band weaving

A simple weaving frame with a cross shaft (harness) is adequate for beginners. It offers wide scope and differs from larger frames only in its width. There is no need for later re-learning and the experience acquired on the small loom can be applied to work on a full-sized loom. If, however, it is intended to undertake weaving on an extensive scale, a larger frame should be obtained at the start. Later a stand can be added and equipped with shafts and treadles for multi-shaft weaving.

The most important parts of the weaving frame are the warp beam (upper cross beam) and the cloth beam (lower cross beam). The longitudinal threads of a weave, known as

Satisfactory woven fabrics can be produced on a small school weaving frame (below). For larger work a wider loom is used. This type of loom is available as a table or free-standing model

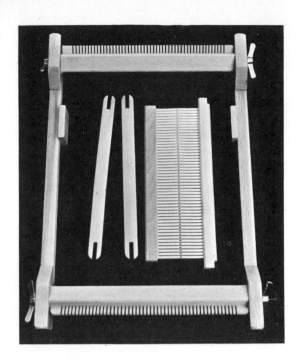

woollen yarns and synthetic yarns with wool characteristics (knitting and crochet yarns) are best for weaving. With the exception of thick wick wools or what are known as effect yarns, the yarns used for the warp are of the same thickness as the weft, or thinner. The weft yarns, however, must never be thinner than the warp. In carpet weaving, cotton, linen or hemp yarn, which is obtainable as carpet warp yarn, is used for the warp, and rug wool or synthetic yarn is used for the weft. Even unspun or slightly twisted wool (wick wool) can be used as weft yarn. Some practice is necessary in weaving these. The best way is to start with uniformly spun hand knitting yarn which is used for both warp and weft.

Preparation

The most important operation is the preparation and winding of the warp yarn on the beams. This is called warping the beam or threading the warp. For this purpose the length of the warp must first be calculated and the entire warp requirement worked out. This is carried out as follows: calculate the required size of the finished piece and add

warp threads, are stretched between these two beams. The thread which is woven across and between the warp threads is called the weft. In addition the weaving frame has a combined heddle, reed and beater, also called a shaft (harness), through which the warp threads are passed. The movement of this creates the gap, or shed, between the rows of warp threads and also serves to push each weft thread tight against the previous thread, to create a firmly woven cloth. The shaft is shown on the right of the photograph above, within the framework of the loom itself; the shuttle is on the left. The yarn used for weaving the weft is wound on to the shuttle, which is then passed through the gap, or shed, between the warp threads created by the movement of the shaft. Only one shuttle is necessary for work of one colour; for multi-coloured work a separate shuttle is required for each colour.

The material

Any yarn can be used for weaving: wool, cotton or synthetic fibre. Medium-thickness

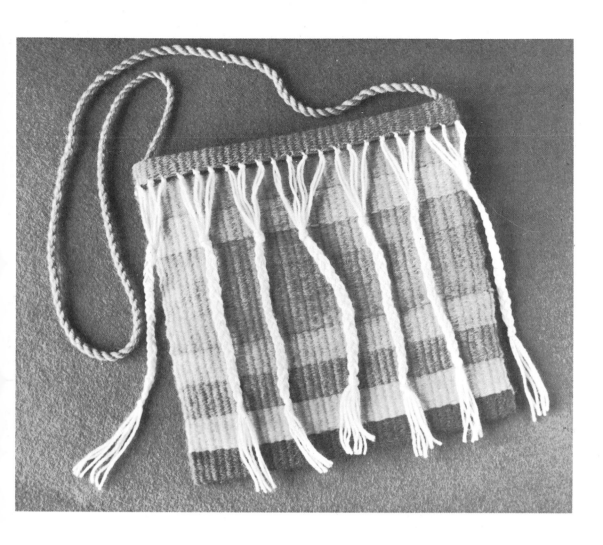

This bag was woven from wool scraps in raised weft pattern on the small frame

Holding clamps for the warp threads

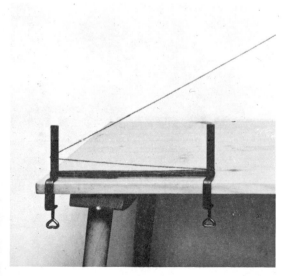

10 per cent for the reduction of length in the weaving. This is called take-up. To this total is added 12 in. (30 cm) or, for beginners, 16 in. (40 cm) for loom loss allowance. If the cover is 48 in. (120 cm) long, the calculation is therefore 48 in. (120 cm) + 10 per cent = 52 in. (132 cm) + 12 in. (30 cm) for loss = a total of 64 in. (162 cm). This is the length of the warp yarn to be fitted on the loom. Two clamps with spikes (screw clamps with a projecting arm – see photograph on the left)

are clamped on the table and these are used for warp preparation. The distance between them should be half of the finished warp length. The yarn will be wound between the spikes 10 times back and forth. Then the yarn is taken off and cut open at one end. This gives the required length. In order to ensure that the threads do not tangle they are twisted into a bundle, or a band is tied round the bundle. This process is repeated until the total number of threads has been obtained. This method is especially suitable for short warps not longer than $2\frac{1}{2}$ to $3\frac{1}{2}$ yards (2–3 m) and above all for beginners. If you have no clamps of this kind, find two fixed points at the required distance from each other (window handle and door handle, wardrobe hook and door handle, etc.) around which can be wound five lengths of yarn, tied together with one thread and cut open at both ends. Ten lengths of yarn can be wound around a 32 in. (80 cm) wide table top, and cut open only on one side. The thickness of the table top will add about $\frac{2}{5}$ in. (1 cm) at each end so that the final length of the 10 threads is 65 in. (162 cm). All threads are prepared in bundles of 10 threads each. This facilitates counting and prevents the threads from tangling. The number of necessary warp threads can be calculated as exactly as can their length. The weaving shaft in the modified weaving frame is arranged so that there will be four threads to ½ in. (1 cm). In the trade it is called a 40/10 shaft (40 threads per 10 cm or 4 in.). The most useful shafts in addition to 40/10 are 30/10 for thick materials and 20/10 for rugs. The width of the required woven fabric multiplied by four, in case of a 40/10 shaft, gives the number of warp threads. For a 7 in. (18 cm) wide scarf $18 \times 4 = 72$ warp threads are used, for example; that is six bundles of 10 and one bundle of 12 threads. When all warp threads have been cut to the right length they are then weighed on ordinary kitchen scales. About the same amount of yarn is needed for weft, as the warp and weft have equal density in plain weaving. The beginner should become thoroughly familiar with ordinary, plain weaving before experimenting. However, when the weft threads are woven at a higher density, a ridged fabric is formed. For the weft of this fabric one-and-a-half times, or even twice the weight of warp is required. The prepared lengths of warp yarn are picked out separately from the bundles and pulled into the shaft with a crochet hook, one going into each hole and each gap. For this purpose the shaft can be clamped upright between two books or clamped on the table so that the row of holes just reaches over the table edge. The weaving frame is placed on the table. The mounting blocks on the inside at the longitudinal

beams for the shaft, which are known as shaft supports, must be at a greater distance from the lower work beam than from the upper warp beam (see photograph, page 182). The dressed shaft is placed into the frame with the shaft frame extension, i.e. the broader cross beam, downwards. The warp threads will be placed in pairs (individually in more elaborate shafts) into a slot of the warp beam and wound around the next four teeth as shown in the diagram. The last threads will be looped back. When all threads are fastened the warp beam is covered with a strip of paper, the wing nuts are loosened slightly and the threads wound on to the warp beam by turning it outwards. When doing this the warp threads must be wound with as uniform spacing as possible. The inserted paper strip prevents the threads from slipping in the slots. The warp is wound until the ends are just long enough for fastening on the cloth beam; the wing nuts on the warp beam are tightened, then the threads are also placed in pairs into the slots of the cloth beam and wound round the next four teeth. Before this the shaft will have been placed on the shaft support. In doing this care must be taken that all threads run straight. No slot must be omitted. Correct beaming of warp is important for the uniformity of the woven fabric. The nuts on the cloth beam must be tight. After the warp has been beamed, the weft yarn is wound round the shuttle from slot to slot.

Weaving process

It is easier to work with the weaving frame clamped between the lap and the table edge. The slots at the upper ends of the longitudinal beams prevent slipping from the edge of the table. The weaving shaft will be placed on both shaft supports, or 'set up'. There will now be a gap between the warp yarns pulled through the slots and those pulled through the holes. This gap is called the shed. When the shaft is taken from the blocks and clamped under the shaft supports, a shed appears once again. Depending on the position of the shaft these gaps are called upper and lower shed. In fact these are only half sheds, which are adequate for all single-shaft weaving. In half-shed weaving, only the warp threads pulled through the holes will be moved with the shaft; the threads which have been pulled through the slots do not change their position. In full-shed weaving, which is carried out with a number of shafts, all the threads are guided by the shafts. The up and down movement of the shaft is called change of shed. The weft yarn is inserted with the shuttle across each shed, i.e. alternately into the upper and lower shed as they are made, and the weft yarn is beaten with the shaft against the cloth beam. The weft yarn should be inserted loosely in the form of an arc. The result of the work depends on the correct insertion of the weft and on uniform beating with the shaft. When the weft is too loosely inserted, the edges of the woven fabric become puckered. If however the weft is too tight, the woven fabric will become progressively narrower. When the weft is not beaten uniformly the

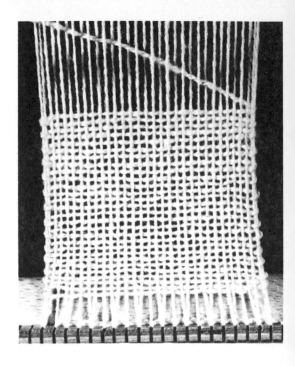

The weft yarn must be kept loose, otherwise the fabric will pull out of shape.

Rug in tabby. Warp: cotton yarn; weft: dark-blue wool

fabric will be of uneven firmness and what are known as roads are formed. The shed will be changed only after beating. It is important to observe these points rigorously in weaving; a freshly inserted weft thread must be immediately corrected or removed and re-inserted when an irregularity occurs. When the warp threads have been woven through up to the warp beam so that it is no longer possible to form an adequate shed, the work must be wound on the cloth beam. For this purpose the four wing nuts are loosened, but only until the warp and cloth beams can be just about rotated. The completed fabric will be wound on the cloth beam and simultaneously a corresponding length of warp is unrolled. After the fabric has been wound tight the wing nuts are tightened again and the work can continue. When the warp is finished, i.e. when no shed of adequate size can be formed, it will be cut off closely at the teeth of the warp beam and the threads knotted in pairs to form fringes. This is repeated with the warp threads at the cloth beam end. The cut-off weft thread is darned into the fabric.

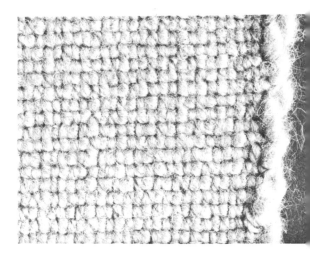

Extension of the weft yarn

If a weft thread is not long enough for the whole work, it can be extended without much trouble. Threads must never be knotted together in weaving. When the end of the thread has been reached it is cut off so that it will run out about in the middle of the woven fabric. The new weft thread is placed into the same shed so that the end of the old and the start of the new thread overlap by a width of a few warp threads. A weft

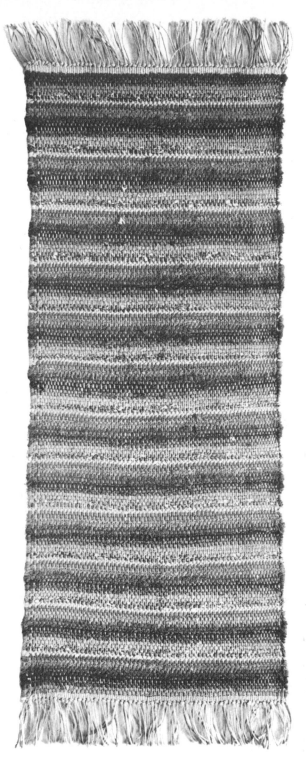

thread should not end, nor should a new one be inserted, at the edge.

Multi-colour weaving

Weaving with different colours is not difficult. Longitudinal stripes can be woven by beaming warp yarn in different colours. A woven fabric is given transverse stripes when the weft is inserted by several shuttles holding different colours. The woven fabric will have a rectangular pattern when worked with weft and warp in several different colours. In the case of multi-coloured weft some rules must be observed in forming the edge. When, for example, two wefts are to be woven in a bright colour and four wefts in a dark colour, the bright weft yarn must twist over the four dark wefts until the weaving is continued with the shuttle carrying the bright yarn. Where thick yarns are used, this gap between stripes can be quite wide and it would be unsightly to let

A rag rug. Warp: cotton yarn; weft: strips cut from textile scraps.

Chair cover in wool

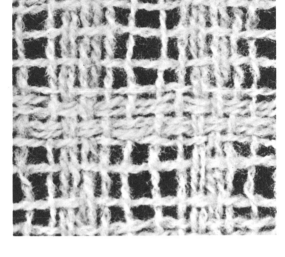

the unused weft thread form a large loop at the edge. For this reason it is woven in by taking the working yarn around the outer warp yarns and the unused weft yarn around the other colour (see photograph, above). When a colour is to be finished off, the weft yarn is cut off about 2–4 in. (5–10 cm) longer than the width of the fabric; this end is placed around the outer warp yarn, back into the still unchanged shed, and the weft is beaten only after the change of the shed with the shaft. In order to ensure that the woven fabric will remain straight the new yarn is started on the opposite side on the other edge of the weave.

Weaving samples in plain weave. Above: the gaps are made by omitting two warp threads at a time (missing a slot and a hole in the shaft). The weft is worked in the same way. Centre: the warp is partly double-ply; it is beamed by missing slots and holes. The weft follows this sequence. Below: the ribs are made by placing three warp threads each into two adjacent slots, the hole between remaining free. The six threads form a thick rib. Either the weft yarn is shot six times into one shed or a six-ply weft yarn is shot once into the shed

189

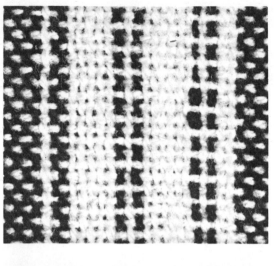

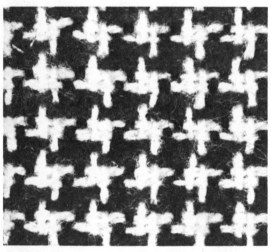

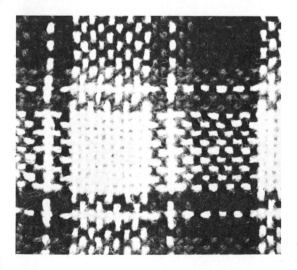

Weaving samples in plain weave. Formation of pattern by multi-coloured warp and multi-coloured weft

Fabric patterns

The weaving technique described in which warp and weft are woven from the same yarn in the same density is called tabby, taffeta or calico weave. Panama weave will result when double yarns are taken for warp and weft. A filling rib weave occurs when the weft yarns lie closer together than the warp. This occurs on the one hand when the woven yarns of each shed are quite firmly beaten in

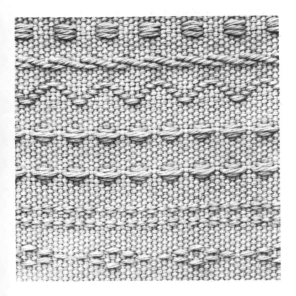

Fancy weave: background in plain weave, weft yarns inserted by hand for pattern formation.

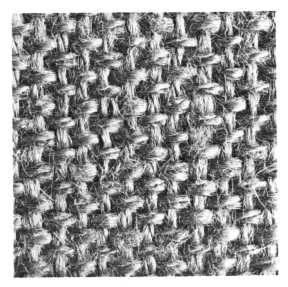

Fabric in classic tabby: warp and weft equally spaced.

Fabric in half panama: warp threaded singly, weft threads doubled

20/10 division is used, i.e. 30 or 20 warp yarns on a 4 in. (10 cm) width.

In the case of the warp repp this is reversed. Here the warp yarns are denser than the weft. Warp repp is produced industrially usually only on fully automatic weaving machines. Warp repp will be made in the ribbon (band) weaving described on page 195. Attractive effects are achieved when individual yarns are not pulled in for warp or weft or when on shooting the weft a gap is left. The basic rule is always to miss an even number of threads. The weft must always be woven continuously in the upper and lower shed sequence.

Weaving with a pick-up stick

A stick is provided with some frames. It is flat like a shuttle, but without notches at both ends, and is slightly longer; this is called a pick-up stick. When this pick-up stick is inserted into the yarns behind the shaft and placed into the lower shed edgeways, or pushed into the upper shed flat and close to the shaft, it is possible to form

the direction of the cloth beam, and on the other hand when the warp yarns can be beamed with wider spacing. For this a shaft with 30/10, or in the case of thick weft yarn,

191

another shed. This creates scope for a variety of patterns.

On inserting the stick the shaft must always be in the lower shed position. To make this easier, a strip of paper can be inserted into the shed formed behind the shaft. The pick-up stick can be inserted e.g.: 1 thread on top, 1 thread under the stick; or 1 thread on top, 2 threads under and so on. Not more than three threads should be placed under the stick.

Suggestion for a pattern

In a woollen warp, shaft 40/10, material thickness 8/2 with the basic weft from the same material the insertion order is: 2 high, 2 low, 1 high, 2 low etc. Weaving technique: 3 shots tabby as basic weave (high, low, high), 1 shot nubby wool; in doing this the stick is placed into the lower shed behind the shaft. One shot in upper shed of basic material, then again nubby wool in pattern lower shed, etc. This is, of course, only one of many possibilities on weaving with a stick (photograph, on the right).

Fancy weave formed by a pick-up stick. Instructions on the left.

The bands shown on the right can be used as ties, belts and decorative edgings and are woven simply, without a frame

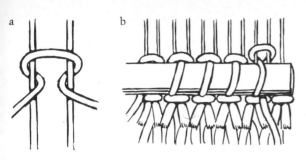

a   b

Knotted fabric

Knotted fabric is made by a combined technique which consists of knotting and weaving. Wool is knotted into a normally beamed 40/10 or 30/10 warp by Smyrna technique; each knotted row will be secured by weaving a weft yarn in the lower and upper shed before making the next knotted

Rug in knotted weaving. The yarn is shot in alternate rows and the cut threads are knotted into fabric. A thick but pliable material is produced. (Example made with Patons Turkey rug wool)

194

row. The Smyrna knots can be worked from cut wool or they can be worked over a wooden gauge with a blunt needle and long yarn. Both techniques are described on pages 208 to 214 in rug knotting.

The knotted fabric is particularly suitable for rugs and hangings. It gives an especially thick elastic woven fabric (photographs, pages 192 and 194).

Ribbon or band weaving

Ribbons, bands and ties can be woven with a small shaft or harness in warp repp.

The most suitable materials are cotton, pearl yarn or embroidery twist, i.e. a firm, smooth, not too thick material.

The warping and threading is carried out as on page 182. On ribbon weaving the pattern is formed by the warp. Cross stripes appear when the holes and slots are threaded in different colours. Different colours are threaded side by side for longitudinal stripes. In the case of squares the colour varies from hole to slot. For this, two yarns of the same colour are placed side by side. On combining these three possibilities, complemented by various colours and materials, a variety of pattern combinations is obtained (see photograph, page 193). The warp yarn is seen only at the edges. It must be thin and its colour must not be noticeable. On warping a generous end is allowed (about 20 in. or 50 cm). After threading all threads are aligned at one end and knotted. The knot is fastened to a fixed point such as a window frame or door handle. The warp is easily arranged by using the shaft. The other end will also be knotted and fastened to the body by a girdle. The shaft hangs freely between these within reach. The tension is regulated with the body.

On weaving, the shuttle in this case is again pushed through the upper and lower shed. The warp yarn is, however, not beaten with the shaft but with the shuttle. One hand holds the shaft in the correct position (raised and lowered shed) while the other one inserts the shuttle into the shed. Then the shaft is released, the shuttle is picked up with both hands and pressed against the weave. The warp threads are pulled together by the weft yarn to the width of the ribbon. The warp threads must lie closely and tightly side by side. When a length of fabric is completed it is wound around the girdle (in place of the cloth beam in the loom) and continued in the same way.

Tapestry weaving

Tapestry weaving is a very artistic technique. The basic weave is a ribbed weft, a fabric in which the warp is not visible. The motif is formed from the weft which does not run in one colour over the whole woven width but in smaller areas of colour as specified by the pattern. There are special frames for this kind of work, called Kelim frames, but the

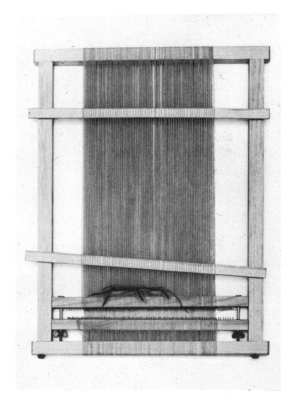

Kelim frame for weaving pictures. The weft is laid by hand

larger areas it is used for forming the shed. For small surfaces it is placed into the upper shed position and the opposite shed is formed by hand. The threads must not be twisted in doing this. The weft is pushed in with the fingers; a needle or a beating hook can also be used for this purpose.

The individual colours are woven now to the drawing below. One area after another will be woven, a step at a time. Care must be taken in doing this that the backward sloping areas are woven first of all (below). In the case of large areas the weft yarn must be inserted in large arcs. When the weft length of a colour is short, the arc must also be short. The weft yarn must be pulled tight over

Primitive loom from Guatemala. The toothed pattern of weft yarns which are taken around the same warp when the colour is changed, is clearly visible here and on the photograph on page 180.

work is equally well carried out on a normal weaving frame. The weft yarn is not wound on the shuttle since it is not going to travel across the whole fabric. Small bundles are made from weft yarns of different colours which can be unwound again from the start. For this the yarn is wound a few times around the hand; care must be taken that the start is not lost. The best way is to let a length of it hang over or take it between two fingers. Then it is all taken from the hand and the yarn end is wound a few times around the middle and looped. From a sketch, also called cartoon, a drawing is made in which the outlines are sharply delineated. The drawing must be the actual size of the tapestry. It is placed under the fabric. The shaft cannot be used for beating the weft, but in the case of

Picture weaving: the backward sloping areas must be worked first

196

Wall hanging in Kelim technique. The slits between colour changes typical of this work are clearly visible on the photograph on the left.

Picture rug in Gobelin technique, woven in handspun sheep's wool by Alen Müller-Hellwig, Lübeck

individual threads. If this rule is not observed the picture becomes puckered where there is a complicated change of pattern.

Slits appear between individual colour fields. If these are only short, they are left open (Kelim technique, above). Longer slits are sewn together later at the back. The formation of slits can, however, be avoided when, on changing the colour, the weft yarn is guided round the last warp thread of the adjacent colour area before turning (Gobelin technique, right). In any case, there is the danger that the pattern will become inaccurate because the weft yarns of two colour areas on the boundary warp yarns are doubled and correspondingly covered. In order to avoid this, change of colour can be

made by using two or more warp threads between two colour areas so that the colours will blend.

It is important to decide first of all between the Kelim or Gobelin techniques and to base the design on this. The pattern can be woven so that it appears between the two selvedges (horizontal); alternatively, it can be formed between the warp beam and cloth beam (vertically, i.e. standing on the side). Carpets woven across the design produce finer

Picture rug in Gobelin and Kelim technique. The slits between the different colours are closed by seams at the back of the work

outlines, but the figures appear stretched, because the warp will give after release and the fabric is subjected to take-up. On building up the design from top to bottom the figures and ornaments appear compressed. This must also be considered in the case of a design drawing with geometrical shapes.

Rug knotting

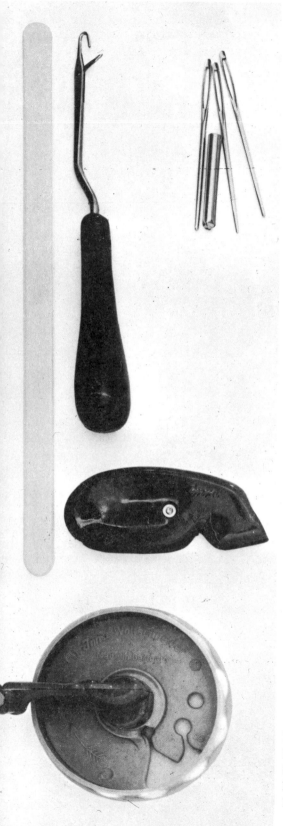

Large wall rug, knotted on Rya fabric in Finnen technique.

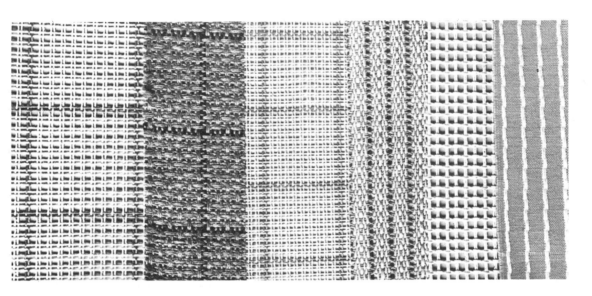

Materials and tools

The selection of the yarn depends on the knotting technique, on the foundation material and on the use of the rug. The following rug foundations are described below:

Smyrna canvas is a firm cotton material which is sold in widths from 32 in. (80 cm) to 80 in. (200 cm). Work can be carried out on this material with a knotting hook as well as with a crewel needle and gauge. The knotting follows the counted pattern (13 squares = 4 in. or 10 cm). As a guide, there is

Knotting foundation for rugs from left to right: Smyrna canvas, jute canvas, fine Smyrna canvas (Sudan canvas), Rya fabric, Dreher canvas, Smyrnafix foundation fabric

a blue cross marking at every 10 squares.

Sudan canvas for fine Smyrna work is closer than the normal Smyrna canvas: 18 squares to 4 in. (10 cm).

Dreher canvas is firmer still because the pairs of yarns which cross between the squares are twisted in one direction. Twisted canvas, which is 40 in. (100 cm) wide, is suitable only for Smyrna technique with knotting hook.

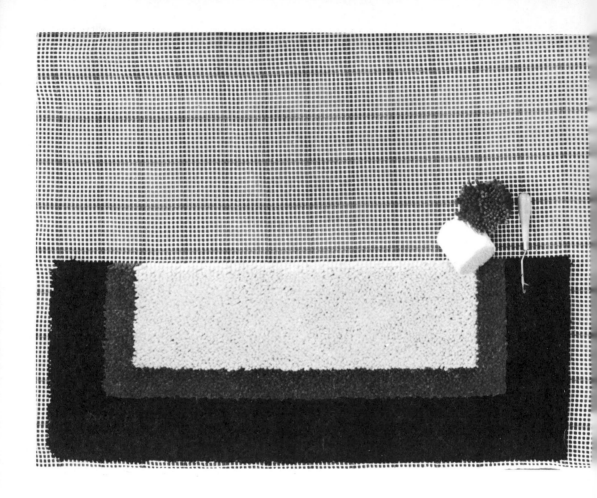

Smyrnafix foundation material is not knotted right through. Only the loop pairs are picked up with the knotting hook. There are 13 pairs of loops or knots to 4 in. (10 cm). *Smyrnafix backing* material is marketed in widths from 30 in. (75 cm) to 45 in. (115 cm) or in various sizes with pre-printed patterns. *Jute canvas.* On this flexible and hard-wearing fabric the pattern is worked with a crewel needle, using continuous yarn and a gauge. There are 11 knots to 4 in. (10 cm). A mark at each 10th knot facilitates the counting of the pattern.

Finnen material from jute is used for the Finnen knotting technique (page 215). The knotting is done with two lengths of Smyrna wool and one crewel needle, without gauge, at 10 knots to 4 in. (10 cm). The rows of knots

are $\frac{3}{4}$ in. (2 cm) apart. The fabric comes in widths of 20 in. (50 cm) to 58 in. (145 cm).
Rya fabric is somewhat closer than the Finnen fabric. Spacing of the knotted rows is $\frac{3}{5}$ in. (1·5 cm) giving 12 knots to 4 in. (10 cm). The work is carried out with fine Rya wool, crewel needle and gauge (technique, page 216). Rya fabric is sold in widths of 28 in. (70 cm) and 48 in. (120 cm).
Ryafix is worked with the knotting hook.
In the U.S., Bernat Rug Canvas carries a line of supplies imported from Britain.

Smyrna work with latch hook on Sudan canvas. Cut wool in beige and brown: Patons Turkey (above)
Knotted rug on the right by Alen Müller-Hellwig. Owner: Dr Heinrich Lubke

It is best to buy all the knotting wool you will need at once in order to avoid colour variations of different batches. Smyrna rug wool is used for Smyrna and Finnen knotting techniques, Sudan wool for the fine Smyrna technique, and fine twisted special Rya wool for Rya technique.

Smyrna knotting wool made from synthetic fibres can also be used for the Smyrna technique. This material is fully washable and does not felt.

The amount of wool you will need depends on the wool thickness, pile length, knot spacing and on the knotting technique. For 1 square yard or metre of Smyrna knots in embroidery technique (Ghiordes knots in embroidery technique) about $5\frac{1}{2}$–$6\frac{1}{2}$ lb (2·5 to 3 kg) of wool are used: for 1 square yard or metre of knotted Smyrna rug (ordinary Smyrna knot with knotting hook) about $7\frac{3}{4}$ lb (3·5 kg) are used, and for 1 square yard or metre of Finnen rug about $4\frac{1}{2}$–$5\frac{1}{2}$ lb (2 to 2·5 kg) of wool are used.

The choice of the various tools you will need depends on the kind of knotting. Special crewel needles with blunt, upturned points are used for embroidery technique, with a separate needle for each wool colour. In addition to a knotting stick (Smyrna gauge)

Knotted rugs, worked on patterned Smyrnafix foundation (above).

Below and on the right: Smyrna rugs, knotted to counted patterns with Patons Turkey rug wool

with or without groove, the range of tools can be extended by a cutter for cutting open the knotted loops. Knotting gauges have different widths which determine the length of the loops (which form the pile later).

A wool cutter is needed for cutting up wool from the hank when Ghiordes or ordinary Smyrna knots are made and if there is no ready-cut wool. These wool cutters are for wool lengths of 2–2¼ in. (5 to 5·5 cm) for Ghiordes knots and 2½–2¾ in. (6·5 to 7 cm) for ordinary Smyrna knots. Cut wool is

worked with a latch hook, a device which resembles a crochet hook with a swivelling latch. Latch hooks (also called knotting hooks) are made by several firms. Anyone making a large number of big rugs would find it worth investing in a knotting frame. This holds the rug foundation firmly on the table so that it does not slip down with the completed work. A wooden slat into which headless nails are driven at intervals of 2 in. (5 cm) is a good makeshift. It is fastened with two screw clamps on the edge of the table.

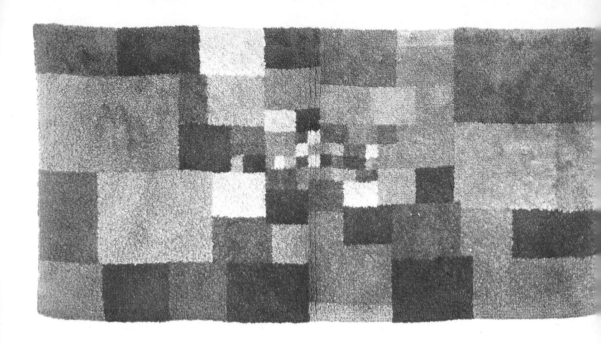

Smyrna rug, knotted with latch hook and cut wool. Material: Readicut.

Small Smyrna rug, knotted on patterned Smyrnafix foundation with hook

However, it is quite possible to work without one.

Square rug knotted in Smyrna technique with cut wool

Knotting pattern

The knotting pattern is a counted pattern in which the knots and their colours are given in detail. Each colour is represented by a different symbol. Counted patterns are read in rows from left to right and from the bottom upwards. Each square of the counted pattern means a knot. The wool is knotted into the foundation fabric exactly according to the pattern. When the counted pattern shows only half of the rug it is necessary to work from the centre in reverse (i.e. a mirror image is made). If only one quarter of the rug is shown then the rows are to be repeated from the centre (note the markings!) in the opposite manner – sideways and upwards. In the case of a partial section which is a repeating pattern the specified colour combinations are repeated continuously.

The rug foundation is prepared according to the counted pattern. The pattern of the design is counted out into fabric squares. The centre is established and the knots are counted from here in length and width and the boundary of the knotted area is marked. An extra six to eight squares must be allowed all round in addition to the knotted area. Hence the foundation must be larger than the counted pattern. Preparation work is not needed when one has a rug foundation with a printed colour pattern for layout of knots.

Smyrna knotting technique

The Smyrna technique can be carried out equally well with a latch hook or with the crewel needle. There is a difference between the ordinary Smyrna knot and the Ghiordes knot. Less wool is needed for the Ghiordes knot since it has a shorter pile.

Ordinary Smyrna knot: either a Smyrna or Dreher canvas can be used for the foundation.

a

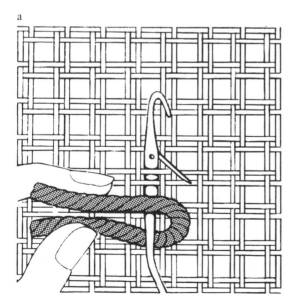

Smyrnafix foundation material is also suitable. The work is carried out with wool cut in lengths of $2\frac{1}{2}$–$2\frac{3}{4}$ in. (6·5 to 7 cm) and with the latch hook. Both ends of a length of wool are taken between the thumb and index finger of the left hand and the latch hook is pushed through the loop formed (a). The hook is pushed upwards through the canvas under two cross yarns which separate two boxes. Both ends of the wool are inserted into the hook (b) and these are pulled forward

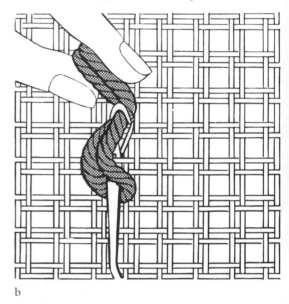

b

c

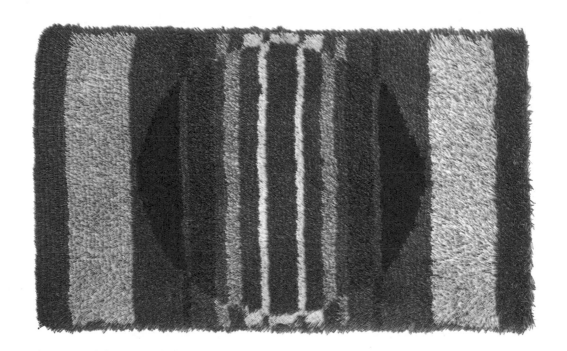

The rug above in the attractive brown shading is knotted with Rya wool and in Rya technique. It is called 'Equator'

The rug below, 'Nevada', is also worked in Rya technique. Both rugs were knotted to patterns by Leibfried

through the loop in the wool from behind the cross yarns of the canvas; the latch closes in the movement. The knot loop is pulled tight by pulling with the thumb and index finger on both ends of the wool (c).

There is another method for making the ordinary Smyrna knot: the latch hook is pushed upwards through the canvas and under two cross yarns. Then the loop in the wool is placed into the open hook, the hook is pulled downwards and the two ends of the wool are held tight with the thumb and index finger. The hook is now pushed upwards, the latch opens, both ends of the yarn are placed into the hook and they are pulled through the loop in the wool. This knot is made exactly the other way round from the knot (c). No matter which method is used the appearance of the rug is not affected. It is immaterial whether the hook is held with the opening to the right or to the left. What is important, however, is to learn to work right

a

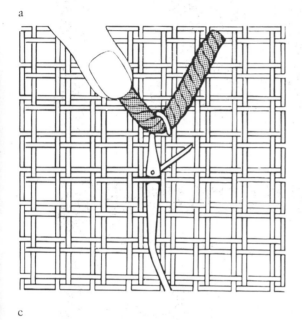

b

c

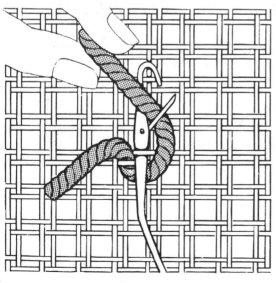

d

from the start without putting the knotting hook down so that there is a steady rhythm to the work. It will take a beginner about 45 hours to finish 1 square yard or metre of knotted work, experienced workers somewhat less.

Ghiordes knot: the Ghiordes knot is made on the Smyrna canvas with the latch hook. The cut wool must be $2-2\frac{1}{4}$ in. (5 to 5·5 cm) long. The latch hook is inserted under the lower yarn of the two cross yarns on the upward movement of the latch hook. The yarn is then placed in the hook (a) and the hook is pulled back and about two-thirds of the yarn is pulled downards to the right. The left (shorter) end of the yarn is held down (b) on second insertion. The hook is then inserted upwards beside the first insertion under the upper cross yarn of the canvas until the latch is free. The longer end

Heavy rug in pure wool (Patons Turkey). Ghiordes knots on Sudan canvas, worked with latch hook

of the yarn is placed from the right into the hook (c) and pulled back with the hook through the canvas downwards. The Ghiordes knot is now completed (d). The ends of the yarn are pulled tight with the left hand. The latch hook is kept in the hand to maintain the rhythm of the working. (This was also mentioned earlier for ordinary Smyrna knots.) Beginners sometimes find it difficult with the first knots to estimate the length of the yarn to be pulled through (two-thirds of the total length) however, it will soon be learnt. Irregular knots are best undone and reknotted. Above all, do not forget to pull uniformly tight.

Cushion, knotted on a pre-patterned foundation (above).

Chair cover in Smyrna technique, knotted to a pattern drawn directly on the foundation fabric.

The square rug on the right is in Smyrna technique. The pattern is woven into the foundation fabric and is worked with a latch hook. Pre-printed canvas can be obtained in many patterns

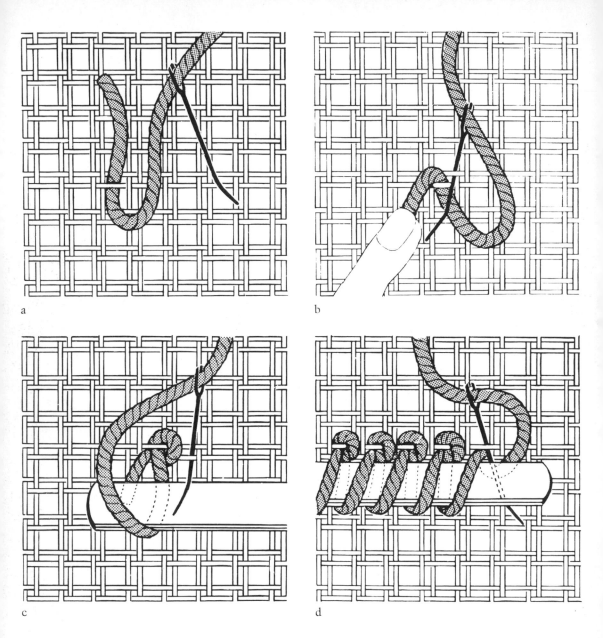

a

b

c

d

Smyrna knots with crewel needle and gauge: the formation of the knots in the gauge technique is carried out in the same manner as in making Ghiordes knots with the latch hook. However, in Smyrna embroidery the work is carried out with the crewel needle and continuous yarn by using a gauge $\frac{3}{10}-\frac{1}{2}$ in. (8–14 mm) wide, depending on the desired pile depth. A threaded needle is held ready for each colour of the pattern. The needle is inserted downwards under the lower of the two parallel cross threads of the foundation and the yarn is pulled through until one end is at the width of the gauge (a). The needle and yarn are then pulled through behind the upper of the two cross yarns of the canvas. The end of the yarn left standing previously is held down with the thumb of the left hand (b). The working yarn is pulled tight and the first knot is now complete. The gauge is placed for the next and all sub-sequent knots on both downwards pointing yarns of the first knot (c) and the work is continued as at the start. In this work the yarn will be guided from below over the gauge; the needle is inserted downwards through the lower of the two cross yarns in the canvas, then downwards through the upper cross yarn and under the gauge (d). It is important that the working yarn is always pulled tight so that the knots do not become loose and that the loops become uniform. When the gauge is covered with loops, it can either be placed on its edge and all the loops cut open along the groove with scissors or with the cutter, or, alternatively, the gauge can be pulled out and the loops cut individually with scissors. Smyrna embroidery can also be made on jute foundation fabric.

Finnen and Rya techniques

Finnen and Rya rugs have deeper pile than Smyrna rugs. The rows of knots on the foundation stand further apart. Finnen rugs are knotted with Smyrna wool with continuous double yarn and a crewel needle but without the gauge. For Rya technique a Rya gauge $1\frac{1}{2}$–$2\frac{1}{2}$ in. (2 to 6 cm) wide, depending

on the desired pile depth, is used with Rya special wool or Sudan wool. Both wools are of fine thickness and softer than Smyrna wool and three to four yarns are worked together. Finnen and Rya rugs are worked on a special foundation. It will take 25 to 30 hours of working to make 1 square yard or metre of rug in Finnen or Rya technique.

Finnen technique: each knot spans two foundation fabric crossings. The work can be carried out either horizontally from left

b

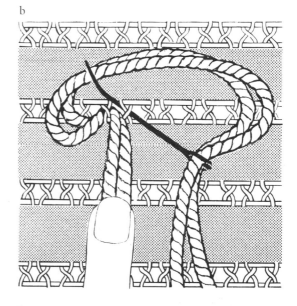

a

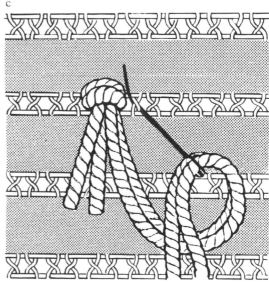

c

215

to right or vertically downwards. The horizontal method is the most usual. Knotting is carried out with double yarn. If the design specifies two colours then one yarn of each colour is threaded into the needle. The needle is inserted at the start from right to left through a yarn crossing (a) and the double yarn is left $1\frac{1}{2}$ in. (4 cm) long. The ends of the yarn are held down with the left thumb while the needle is pushed from right to left through the next crossing of the foundation fabric threads. The working yarns from which a large loop is formed stay on top (b). The first knot is formed on pulling the yarn through the foundation. The needle is then inserted from right to left under the next thread crossings. The threads of the first knot point downwards while this is done (c). The working yarn is pulled through to form a loop of about $1\frac{1}{2}$ in. (4 cm) long which is held firmly with the thumb of the left hand (d). After that the needle is again inserted from right to left through the next crossing of the foundation threads and the work is continued as described to the end of the row. The loops are cut individually and irregularly, i.e. not exactly at their crease.

Rya technique: in this case, exactly as for Finnen technique, there are always two yarn crossings enclosed from right to left (a). The broad gauge is used after the first knots. The working thread is guided upwards round the gauge. The needle is inserted from right to left through a crossing of the yarns. The working threads form a large loop at the top and then the needle is pushed through the adjacent crossing of the foundation yarns downwards to the right and to the left down-

b

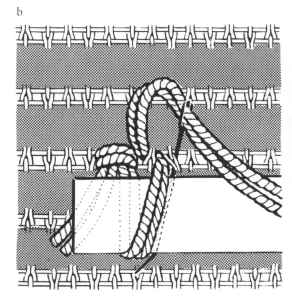

a

c

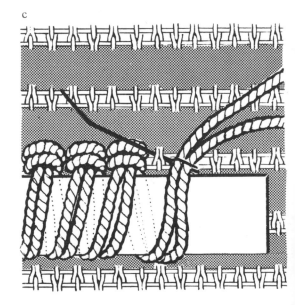

Shoulder bag in various colours: Rya technique with knotting needle and gauge.

Wall hanging from scraps, knotted on Rya foundation fabric in Finnen technique with double-ply wool

wards under the gauge (b). The work is continued in this manner to the end of the row. After that the gauge is turned on its edge and the loops are cut in alternate rows in the groove and on the side of the groove. This produces the characteristic irregular pile length of the Rya and Finnen rugs. The Rya technique can also be carried out without the gauge, over two or three fingers of the left hand.

Finishing the rug edges

After knotting the rug must be shaken out and loose wool fluff is removed with a fairly soft brush. After that the edges are trimmed. This can be done in various ways, depending on the knotting technique used, on the foundation and on the rug size.

Smyrna rugs are sewn round the edges. A row of squares is left standing next to the outer knots and the rest of the foundation folded on the wrong side. The folded-over material is creased at the back to make a mitred corner seam. The foundation fabric under this corner is cut off so that the corners will not be too thick. The folded-over edge is then fastened with herring-bone stitch. After that the edging stitch (ordinary overcast stitch) is made through the doubled row of squares. The edging will be thicker if a double length of wool yarn is placed on the right side of the canvas overhang, and oversewn.

After edging, carpet braid is sewn to the underside of the carpet edge. If the rug is to have a fringe on the two ends then only the two longitudinal edges are overcast. After that a tassel bundle is knotted, by means of a crochet hook, into each doubled edge square from four 14 in. (35 cm) lengths of woollen yarn (page 283). The knots must be pulled tight. The carpet braid is sewn on after that. Round rugs and cushions are best trimmed with a crochet edging. The foundation is cut off, leaving a border six squares wide. This foundation is folded over to the wrong side and is fastened at first with sticky tape so that it will not fray. Double crochets are crocheted into the foundation from the wrong side (page 68) directly along the edges of the knotted work, in order to hold the edge. To avoid puckering of the edge it is advisable to miss one square of the foundation every now and then. Carpet braid is not used on the underside of round rugs. Instead, broad bias strips of hessian (burlap), which conform to the shape better, are sewn into place. Round cushions must always be fully lined. Finnen and Rya rugs are edged in the following manner: a carpet braid is sewn on the right side of the rug, folded over to the wrong side and sewn on the wrong side on the foundation.

Appliqué

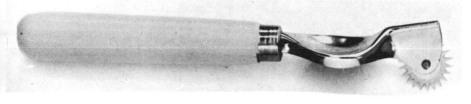

Patchwork
Decorative stitching

Design and cutting out
Appliqué work
Openwork appliqué
Appliqué in reserve technique
Layered appliqué
Appliqué in Cut work technique
Fabric inlay
Indian appliqué
Oriental appliqué
Split appliqué
Appliqué in filigree technique

Material and pattern forming
Technique
Patchwork with sewing machine
Patchwork in appliqué technique
Irish patchwork
French patchwork
Italian patchwork

Tucks
Fine cording
Bold corded piping
Stitching in appliqué
Monogramming
Quilting

Fabric appliqué is a decorative form of textile embroidery in which a variety of artistic effects is obtained by using different colours and shapes of fabric pieces sewn on to a background fabric. These pieces can be sewn on by sewing machine or by hand. On sewing with the machine either a close zig-zag stitch (buttonhole stitch) or a closely spaced decorative stitch is used. The best results are obtained with the traditional method of sewing by hand. A choice can be made between invisible stitches and visible decorative stitches. The decorative stitches bring additional character to the variety of forms in the appliqué work.

The background fabric for appliqué work must not be a material which is weaker and thinner than the applied pieces. A fabric which is too loosely woven can be reinforced on the wrong side with a bonded fibre interlining which can be ironed on. When this method is used the finished article will have to be lined. It is important that the appliqué work fabric pieces are cut and sewn on so that all their threads run in the same direction. If this is not so there is the danger that the work will distort owing to different tensions in the fabric and it may pucker in places. In cases where the diagonal run of the weave cannot be avoided because it is specified by the design (sloping stripes, diagonal pattern from squares) the pieces of fabric must be ironed on to Vilene or other bonded fibre interlining.

Designing and cutting out

Two methods can be used for designing appliqué work: (1) a rough sketch is made keeping the outlines as simple as possible. The pieces of fabric to be applied are then cut to the shapes of the outlines; alternatively all the fabric shapes are cut roughly, placed on the background fabric and moved around until the best effect is achieved. No matter which method is chosen the size and shape of the background must first be established accurately. If an area is to be geometrically divided then the individual areas can be marked with ironed creases or basting stitches.

When the appliqué design is not free but requires precision, do not attempt to cut the fabric pieces without a pattern. A template should be prepared from cardboard for each shape. The template is then placed on the fabric and the outline drawn with a soft pencil. This method ensures that the finished shapes are uniform, always assuming that they have not been distorted by the sewing. As already mentioned, distortion can be avoided by the use of a bonded fibre interlining ironed on to the wrong side of the fabric. This has the additional advantage that it will not fray readily on the cut edges and will form neat outlines.

Appliqué

By hand: the pieces of fabric are fastened to the background fabric with long stitches without turning in the edges. Fastening with pins is not recommended since the fabric puckers at the point of insertion and often does not allow a correct view of the appliqué arrangement. The size of the stitches is not as important as their uniformity. Fabrics which fray readily must be sewn with closer stitches than those with firm cut edges (e.g. felt, American cloth). In the case of pieces of material which are to be worked with the edges turned in, the patchwork principle (page 238) is used: a template is made for pieces of fabric to be appliquéd, a bonded interlining shape is made and this shape is basted with its adhesive side upwards on to

the wrong side of the fabric. The fabric is then cut $\frac{1}{4}$ in. (6 mm) larger, all round and the surplus fabric is folded back over the shape and secured with a hot iron. In the case of outlines with curves and arcs (hearts, circles, ovals) the hem allowance is snipped at regular intervals all round so that the folded over fabric can be ironed on without pulling or creasing. The shapes to be appliquéd are then arranged in the desired pattern on the background fabric and lightly ironed so that the bonded interlining and the background fabric are lightly joined to each other (do not iron on firmly, or the work will appear too stiff). The ironing on saves fastening by stitching. The pieces of fabric will be sewn subsequently to the background fabric with slip stitches. The sewn edges can be finished with decorative stitches.

With the sewing machine: the machine is set at the decorative or zig-zag stitching to produce a small, close stitch. Stitch with a multi-purpose thread such as Coats Drima which is suitable for all types of fabric. Machine appliqué is always done without a folded edge. The pieces placed on the background fabric are sewn on first close to the edge with ordinary stitches, stitch length

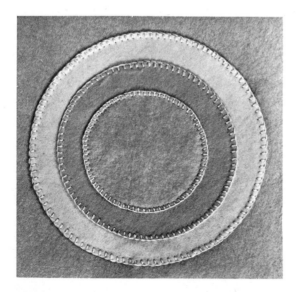

$\frac{1}{8}$ in. (3 mm), and then stitched over with zig-zag stitches. If the zig-zag stitch is used without first straight stitching there is a danger that the work will distort, especially on curved edges and corners.

When working with felt the pieces need be sewn only with blanket stitches (below left).

Openwork appliqué

Openwork appliqué is a simple technique which is worked to a pattern. For this a check pattern and a self-coloured fabric of the same type are used. If the fabrics are of different weave and the areas are large there is danger of distortion, especially after laundering. The self-coloured fabric forms the background and the appliqué is made in check pattern fabric. Square or rectangular cut-outs are made into the check pattern fabric and the background is visible through these openings. These parts are not completely removed, the size of the cut-outs are marked with pins and the fabric is cut along crossed

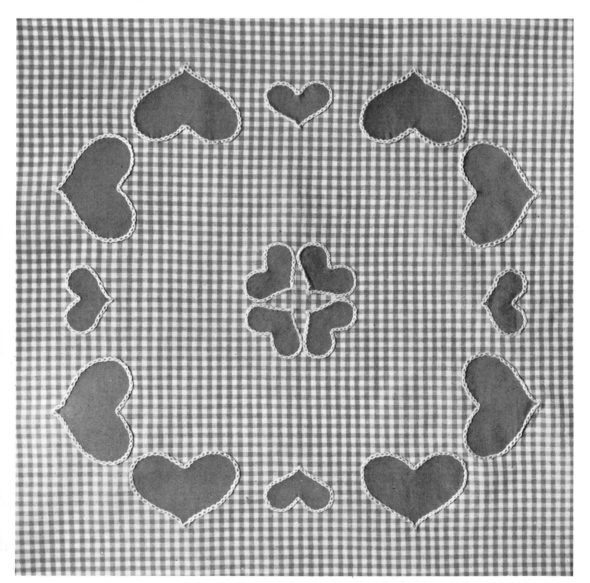

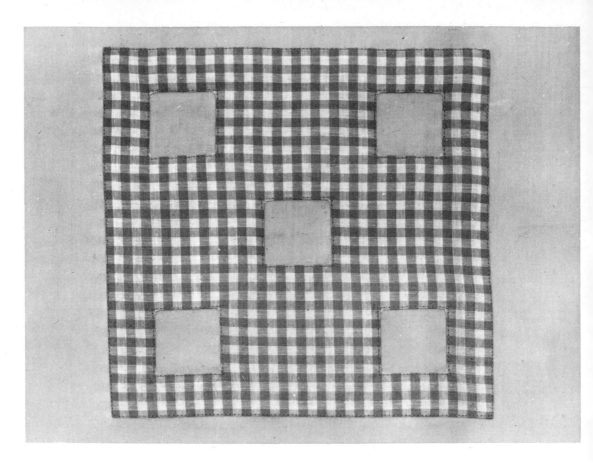

diagonals. Care must be taken in counting the diagonals; mistakes are easily made! The four wedges are turned over to the wrong side of the fabric and accurate edges are formed by ironing the creases. Then the check pattern fabric with cut-outs is placed on the background fabric. The work is started with the edges of the cut-outs which are furthest from the centre. All cut-outs must be fastened around the edges to the background and attention must always be paid to correct position of the fabric grain. Subsequently the cut-out edges are sewn with small stitches (by hand or by sewing machine) on the self-coloured background. The start and end of the thread must meet exactly at the same corner. The end will be pulled through to the wrong side of the work and darned in pairs (not knotted as that would result in ugly ridges). Only then

are the outer edges of the check pattern fabric folded over and sewn with fine stitches on the self-coloured background fabric (photograph, above).

Appliqué in reserve technique

In the reserve technique, fabric and crocheted parts are combined (on the right). The crocheted parts to be appliquéd are worked first in the required number (see Irish crochet, motif C, page 85). Cut a template from cardboard to correspond with the outline of the crocheted motif (in the case of crocheted parts of different sizes, cut one for each size). The template is placed on the wrong side of the fabric and the fabric is marked with soft pencil whenever crocheted parts are to be appliquéd. A second circle is drawn $\frac{1}{4}$ in. (6 mm) inside these markings (or to a shape corresponding to the form of the crocheted

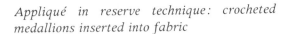

parts); this will subsequently be edged with closely spaced blanket stitch (page 51). In this work the blanket stitch loop edges are towards the inside of the circle and the fabric is cut out from within this stitched circle. The crocheted parts are then fastened on the right side and sewn by hand with Coats Drima in the matching colour into the stitches of the outer and inner edges (see photographs).

The edges of the circles can also be machine stitched (zig-zag stitch). The crocheted rosettes, however, must not be sewn on with the machine.

Layered appliqué

This technique is carried out by machine on thin materials (batiste, voile, organza, fine silk). Two layers of the same fabric are tacked on top of each other. The shapes to be appliquéd are then drawn with a soft pencil on the top fabric. The pencil lines are machine stitched so that the layers cannot move. The stitching is then covered with close zig-zag stitches. The surplus fabric is then cut neatly away from the outer edges. The appliqué can be further decorated with embroidery (photograph, page 226).

Appliqué in Cut work technique

In this work, which is similar to layered appliqué, two fabric layers are placed on top of each other and secured with basting stitches. The shapes to be appliquéd are cut from cardboard and the outlines drawn lightly with a sharp pencil on the fabric. These lines are embroidered with small close

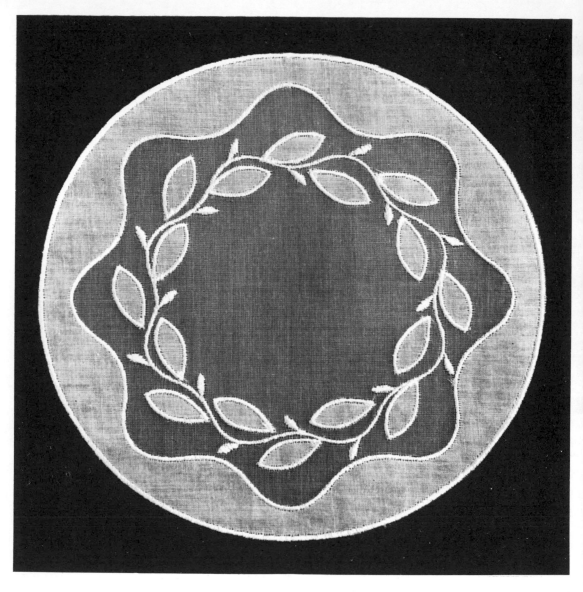

Layered appliqué: two fabric layers are sewn together by machine, one layer partly cut out (above)

chain stitches using two strands of Clarks' Anchor Stranded Cotton in the same colour as the fabric. In this work sections of both the fabric layers are cut away. Subsequently the basting stitches are removed and the upper and lower fabrics are cut outside the

embroidered outlines close to the chain stitches as in Cut work (pages 60 and 61) (photographs, page 227, above).

Fabric inlay

The attraction of this technique is the use of a motif reversed positive and negative: a self-coloured motif on a patterned background and the same patterned fabric used for motif on a self-coloured background (photograph, on the right). The individual motifs designed

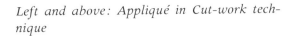
Left and above: Appliqué in Cut-work technique

in this manner are prepared as for patchwork (page 238). The work is carried out as follows: the motif (in this case a heart) is cut from cardboard and is placed on the right side of the fabric. The outlines of the template are drawn with pencil on to the fabric and the pencil lines are machine stitched (normal sewing stitch). The fabric to be appliquéd is fastened with the right side to the background fabric so that the stitched pattern is covered. Both the fabric layers are

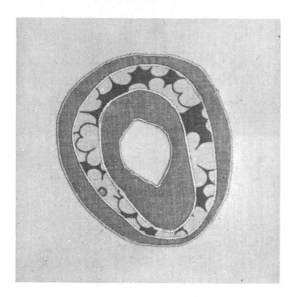

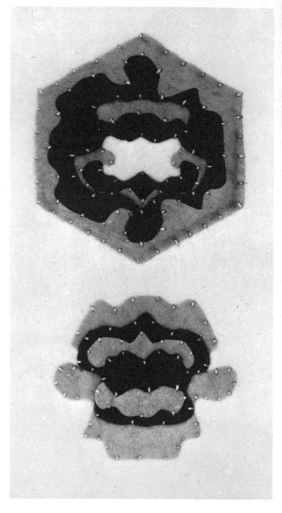

sewn with close zig-zag stitches along the already stitched outline of the motif. The work will be turned to the other side and the appliquéd fabric cut away close to the outer edges of the zig-zag seam. The cut edges on the right side are now once again sewn with a close stitch and the fabric cut away on the wrong side within the seam so that the motif is inserted as an inlay.

Indian appliqué

This technique can be carried out by hand or by machine. A number of fabric layers are tacked on a background fabric; these must all be the same size as the largest appliqué motif. At first the outline of the appliqué work is established and the covering fabric layers are cut to match. The lower fabric layers follow this outline, but are cut approximately $\frac{1}{4}$ in. (6 mm) smaller. The top fabric is then folded over at the edges and sewn to the background fabric. Now the top layer is cut out to a previously pencilled outline so that the layer below is exposed. A narrow hem is turned in and that layer sewn to fabric below. The fabric layer below

will then have a somewhat smaller cut-out and the layer which was covered will become partly visible. The work is continued in this manner through all the fabric layers until the background fabric becomes visible. The separate cut-outs are turned inwards at the edges and sewn against the fabric below. When stitching by machine the edges are stitched with zig-zag stitches through all the

Wall hanging: Appliqué in Filigree technique on pure silk. The appliquéd parts are crocheted or knitted from gold yarn. The lattice work between in embroidered

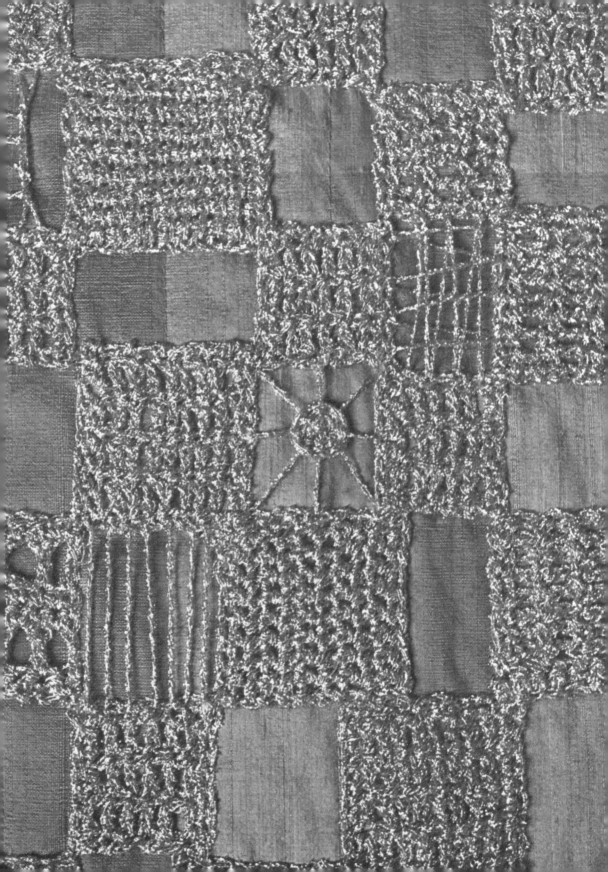

fabric layers. The classical Indian technique, however, is carried out by hand.

Oriental appliqué

In the classical method of this technique the work is carried out with native silk; this fabric, however, frays readily at the edges and the work rapidly becomes unsightly. Clear outlines are obtained by using felt. Oriental appliqué consists of a number of layers of fabric which are cut out in a rich variety of shapes and beginning with the background layer are appliquéd one on top of the other. These cut-outs differ in size and shape, the larger cut-out always providing a frame for the previous one. The fabric pieces are placed on top of each other in reverse order and sewn together under the frame motif. In doing this a straight stitch is made at regular intervals around the cut edge of individual motifs or cut-outs. The completed appliqué appears sculptured (see page 228).

Split appliqué

Split appliqué is very simple to work, but in spite of this is no less decorative, as shown in the photograph on page 220. For this work a large simple shape (circle, square, rectangle, triangle) is chosen first and is cut out from stiff paper. This basic form will be cut into pieces of different shape and size and placed on the background fabric (in the example, a woollen blanket). All the pieces are then pushed apart so that they are clearly separated but retain the basic shape – giving the split effect. Choose which fabrics are to be used for the individual shapes and plan the arrangement. Before cutting the fabric shapes place the pieces of fabric on the paper pattern. When the arrangement has been decided the fabric (in the example it is felt) is cut from paper patterns and placed in position on the background fabric. In order to avoid confusion, cut fabric sections one at a time and position on background fabric in place of the paper section. When all the parts

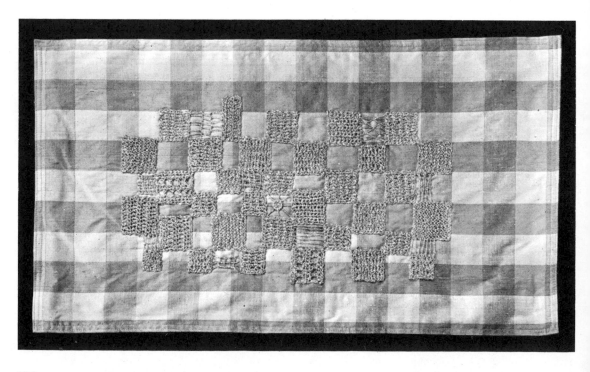

to be appliquéd are arranged in the correct order and position then they will be tacked to the background and carefully stitched all round. To achieve the best results it is important to keep the stitching accurate. The fabric appliqué is then sewn to the background fabric with overturned edge or directly on the edge of the cut, depending on the type of fabric used. Embroidery stitches can be used in this work (Chain stitch, Blanket stitch, Herringbone stitch) which provide an additional decorative effect, especially when only self-coloured fabrics are used.

Appliqué in filigree technique

This type of appliqué is purely decorative; it is suitable only for decorative wall hangings and not for articles in use. The background fabric is pure silk which is lined with bonded interlining and stitched through horizontally and vertically several times (in check pattern fabric following the colours). The motifs made from golden yarn should be knitted or crocheted in a variety of stitches, then sewn by hand to the background fabric. Some of the spaces between the appliquéd golden squares and rectangles are embroidered with Laid stitch, Weaving stitch, Herringbone stitch and Spider's web stitch (see pages 37, 51 and 52) so that the appliqué has the appearance of filigree work.

Patchwork

Patchwork consists of a number of small fabric pieces, usually of geometric shapes, artistically arranged to form colourful mosaic patterns and sewn together either by hand or machine. Hand sewing is the traditional method. All patchwork must be lined at the back in order to make it more durable and retain its shape. When used for quilts, a warm interlining is inserted between the patchwork and lining, then all three layers stitched through either with straight rows of machine stitching; or, if desired, a pattern may be formed by stitching in squares, curves or waves. One of the most suitable fabrics for patchwork is plain weave cotton. Fabrics in which the weft and warp yarns

Small rug: the fabric pieces are dyed using the 'tie and dye' method

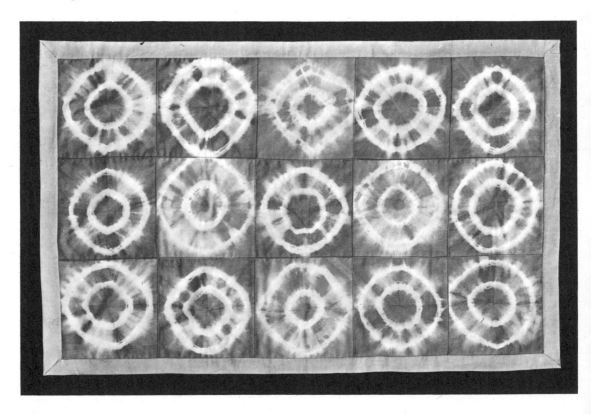

are of different thickness or have fancy weave may create distortion. The use of fabric with the same or similar weaves is necessary when a large surface area is to be made up from small geometric sections. The use of different fabric weave will produce an untidy result. Scraps of fabric may be used if these rules are followed. The patchwork technique originated of necessity, when scraps of fabric were too precious to discard and were stitched together, both economically and decoratively, into quilts and garments.

Material and pattern design

Patchwork can be made from any patterned fabric but small prints are the most suitable. Interesting new designs can be made from checked and especially from striped fabrics. It is not advisable to use small print fabrics exclusively for a large article; it would look too 'busy', especially as the seams between the fabric sections give an additional pattern. Bright and pleasing effects can be obtained by combining patterned and self-coloured fabrics, using either a colour or design as the dominant feature. When designing a piece of work it must be observed that self-coloured

Patches of various shapes are arranged on cardboard before sewing

fabrics appear flatter than multi-colours, which will tend to steal the limelight. Patchwork made exclusively from self-coloured material can look very attractive but it makes heavy demands on skill and patience; the patchwork sections must be cut out and sewn with great accuracy as

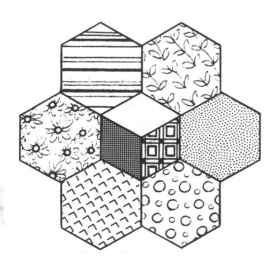

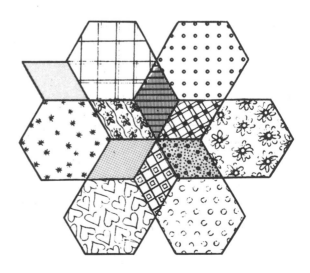

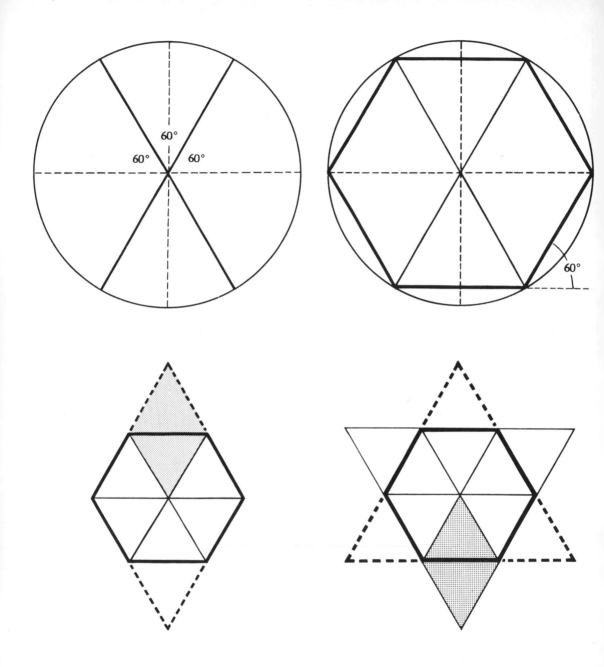

slight faults which may be concealed in multi-colour fabrics are immediately obvious in self-coloured patchwork. It is advisable in self-coloured patchwork to place the patches together first on a foundation (photograph, page 233) and to re-arrange them as necessary. Do not attempt to correct faulty patches by re-cutting. Such a correction will result in a whole series of further corrections to other patches and in the end nothing will fit together. It is better to discard them.

If patchwork is to be designed individually then self-coloured fabric sections can be dyed in the manner of 'tie and dye' and fitted together (photograph, page 232). Before beginning the work it is advisable to prepare a sketch which shows how the shapes and colours will be arranged. Squared

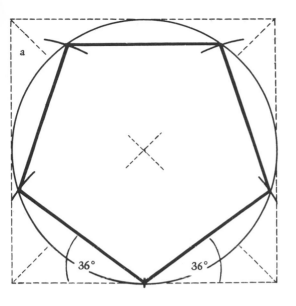

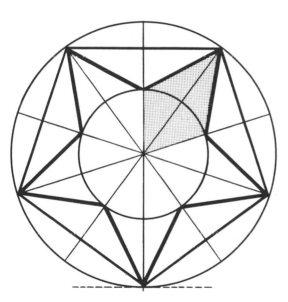

a trial basis. The most useful basic shapes for the fabric sections are: square, diamond, triangle, pentagon, hexagon and octagon (drawings, pages 234–237).

Technique

A template is prepared before the fabric is cut out. The desired shape is drawn on cardboard and around this another outline is made at a distance of $\frac{1}{2}$–$\frac{3}{4}$ in. (1·3–1·9 cm) depending on the size of the patch section. The template is cut from the cardboard on

Chair cover: made up from cotton fabrics, lined with bonded fabric and quilted through at the seams

(graph) paper can be coloured in to show the effect – it is a great help to have this visual aid. The colour composition is easily established in this way and it is possible, then, to calculate how many patches are needed of each colour. If, however, patterned fabrics are used it is better to prepare a number of sections from various colours and patterns in a basic shape and to put them together on

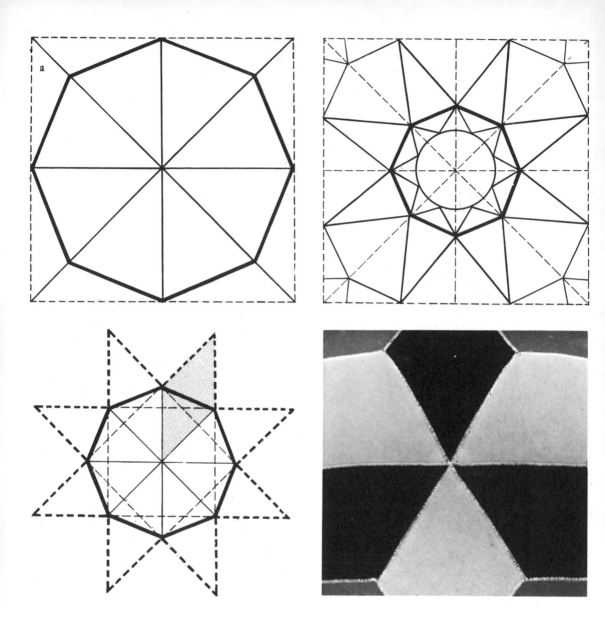

the outer line, the centre is removed by cutting on the inner line thus forming a 'window'. The frame is now placed on the fabric and moved about until the window shows the best section for cutting out. The outlines are then marked with a soft pencil. A corresponding paper section, to the dimensions of the window, must be cut for each fabric section. The paper sections are placed centrally on the wrong side of the fabric sections and pinned. (Page 238 a). The surplus fabric is then turned over the paper and secured with tacking (basting) stitches (b). When a number of patchwork sections are prepared, two are placed with their right sides together and joined along

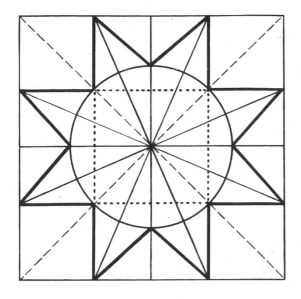 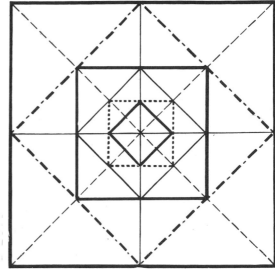

Photograph on the left: patchwork in appliqué technique.

Photograph below: patchwork, quilted through at the seams

one edge with short stitches (c). The individual sections are first joined into strips and the strips are then fitted together into a complete area. The basting stitches and the

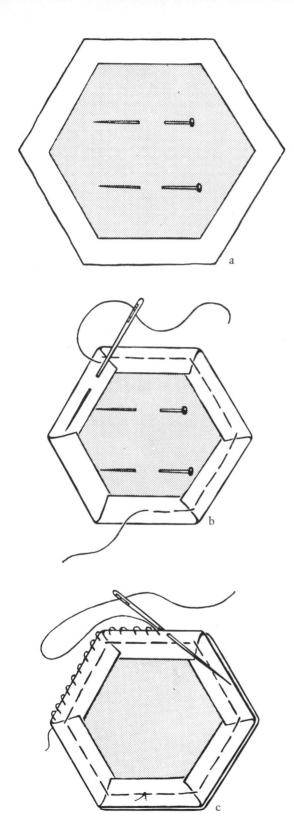

paper sections are removed and the work ironed lightly on the wrong side. Finally the work is lined with a suitable fabric.

Iron-on bonded interlining can be used instead of paper. To do this cut the interlining accurately by the template and place it with the coated (rough side) side upwards (that is with the right side downwards on the wrong side of the fabric). The surplus fabric is ironed all the way round on this insert. This saves laborious tacking and removal of threads and the work becomes firm but pliable; if interlining were placed with the coated side on the fabric and ironed firmly the finished work would be too stiff. To make patchwork from squares the cardboard frame is unnecessary. The paper or interlining squares are cut $\frac{3}{4}$ in. (1·9 cm) smaller than the fabric.

Patchwork with the machine

The patches can be sewn together by machine. This technique, however, is suitable only for simple basic shapes. Working with paper inserts is eliminated in this method and the individual fabric pieces are stitched after tacking together into strips.

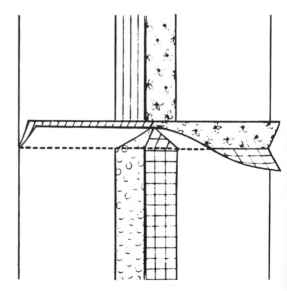

The patchwork method was used to join diagonally-cut jersey squares to make the toy snake.

the individual felt sections are crocheted to each other with double crochet (page 68) on the blanket stitched edges. The completed work is then spread out and the smaller felt sections of the same shape are placed on the individual patchwork sections. These sections are fastened in position with pins and then appliquéd with small but visible running stitches (page 52). The traditional Irish technique is always built up with similar shapes: hexagons with hexagons, diamonds with diamonds, squares with squares.

All the seams are then ironed flat. Subsequently the strips are fastened and stitched together into areas, and the seams ironed flat again. To avoid bulk, the corners of the seams are cut off at an angle.

Patchwork in appliqué technique

In this method the individual fabric sections (with raw edges turned in) are placed right sides upwards, in the final arrangement on a lightweight fabric base (cretonne, muslin) close together with all edges meeting. These section edges are sewn by machine with zig-zag or curved stitches until all sections are joined, then the foundation fabric is cut away on the wrong side close to the seams and the fabric sewn to an interlining base.

Irish patchwork

In Irish patchwork all separate sections are cut out from felt without seam allowance and edged with blanket stitch (page 51) then

Irish patchwork – hexagonal sections are crocheted together

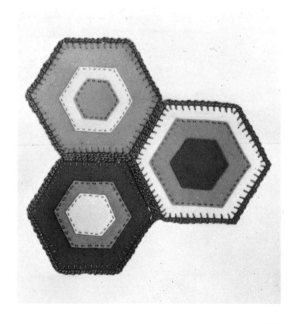

French patchwork

The patchwork technique practised in France is similar to the methods already described. The patchwork sections are cut from felt and fitted together without seam allowance, being sewn together with small Herringbone stitches (page 51) which must not be visible on the right side. The patchwork sections are decorated with embroidery.

Italian patchwork

As in the traditional technique the patchwork sections are cut with seam allowance and fastened around the paper insert. The fitting together, however, commences in the centre – usually starting from a square – and the sections are sewn together with narrow overlapping seams (as in appliqué) by hand or by machine.

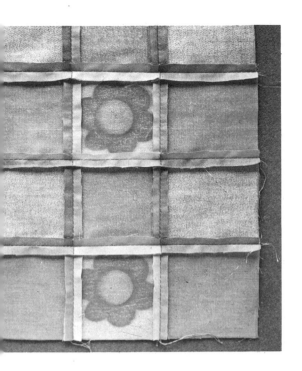

Tablecloth in self-coloured and printed cotton in bright green, yellow, orange and pink. Fabric squares are sewn by machine into strips and the strips joined together

Decorative stitching

The creation of a surface texture on a fabric with motifs raised in relief is achieved with decorative stitching. As is the case in patchwork, the technique originated in the Anglo-Saxon countries, where it is skilfully executed. The stitching of outlines without padding is frequently erroneously called quilting; it is, however, an embroidery technique. Decorative machine stitching can be carried out in many ways. Techniques used are cording, stitching in appliqué technique, monogramming, stitching to a motif and free stitching.

Tucks

Tucks are made before the final cutting out of the fabric since it is considerably pulled together in length and width depending on the spacing and width of the tucks. The amount of fabric required can be calculated accurately in advance; however, it is advisable to measure the fabric generously. When tucks are to be made, on check pattern fabric for example (see picture on the right), then it is adequate to indicate the tucks by an ironed-in crease. In other cases then the spacing of the tucks must be accurately

calculated and the creased edges (tuck edges) marked with basting stitches. The fabric is ironed along these threads and stitched $\frac{1}{8}$ in. (3 mm) from the markings. When the tucks are to be made in both the length and breadth of the material then they must all lie in the same direction at the intersections. This rule must also be observed on continuing work on the seams. After stitching, the tucks are ironed backwards so that they stand-up.

Fine cording

Geometrical fine cording is very simple to do. Two layers of fabric are placed on top of each other and stitched through with two parallel lines of stitching. The spacing must correspond to the thickness of the cord. A thin cord pulled into the channels formed by these parallel stitched lines is seen on top of the fabric as a raised ridge. You can twist the cord yourself from cotton yarn (Anchor Soft Embroidery). A small safety pin or a bodkin is used for inserting the cord in the channel formed by the two rows of stitching. When the cord is thicker than the eye of the bodkin, a cotton thread is sewn to it and threaded through the eye of the bodkin. When all cords have been pulled through, the fabric is pulled straight in the direction of the ridges so that the inserted cords will lie loosely without stretching the fabric. The ends of the cords are stitched through at their starting points or sewn by hand and cut off. Motifs, too, can be raised by cord piping. This is carried out as follows: first the motif is drawn with a soft pencil on a piece of fabric which is used as the lower layer (lining). Always use a strong, firm fabric for lining. The lining is now basted to the top fabric so that the motif is outside and it can be followed for stitching. This work is carried out by hand, using small stitches, or can be machine stitched. When machine stitching the needle and spool thread must be of the same colour and thickness. The outlines of the motif are stitched in two parallel lines, the spacing of which corresponds to the thickness of the cord to be inserted, the outside line follows the drawn line of the motif and the second line is sewn inside it. A small slit is then cut in the lining to allow the cord to be inserted. When the motif has a

number of corners and curves the lining will require a number of slits so that the needle can be brought out and reinserted. The slits are later closed with overcast stitches. The beginning and the end of the cord must be reduced in thickness after it has been pulled through before sewing together with a small overlap. To make a join, a length of cord is allowed to protrude from the insertion point; it is thinned while the remaining cord is pulled through but not yet threaded and the thinned cord is pulled into the channel. The needle with the still threaded cord end is then guided into the channel until the cords overlap approximately $\frac{1}{4}$ in. (6 mm). The needle is then inserted through a small cut into the lining and the emerging cord is held tight at this point and cut off, then a short length is pulled out (so that the fabric is slightly gathered), it is thinned and allowed to slide back into the channel. Both ends of the cord are sewn together through the lining.

Bold corded piping

Bold corded piping is used mostly for decorative edging of cushions and bedspreads. In contrast to fine cord piping the basically

In Bold Corded work the cords are placed between two fabric layers and stitched, in contrast to Fine Cording (pages 242, 243) in which the cords are inserted after stitching

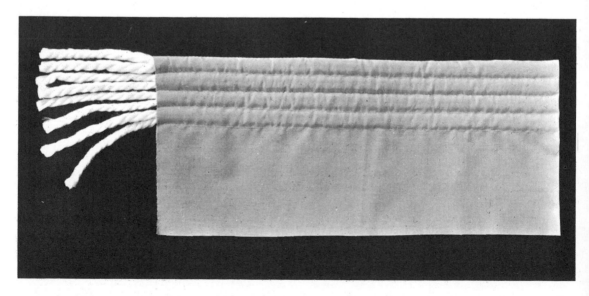

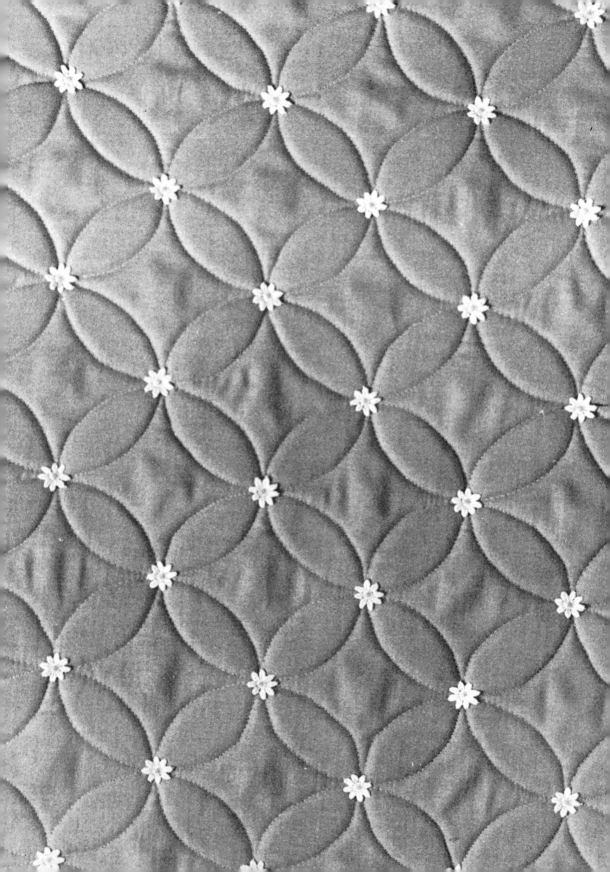

thicker cord cannot be pulled into the stitched channels because the ridges formed would be raised by an equal extent on both sides of the joined fabric which would reduce the raised effect. In bold corded piping the lower fabric must remain flat while the upper fabric will follow the contour of the cord (photograph, page 244). This is achieved in the following manner: the work is started with a simple stitch on the right side of the top fabric which is placed on the lining. The cord is now placed between the two layers of fabric close to the stitched line and the upper layer is pushed against the cord while the lower fabric is pulled tight. Both layers of fabric are secured with tacking (basting) stitches. The final stitching is made close to the cord with a cording foot attachment to the machine (if available). In this case the cord is to the left of the foot. The work is continued in this manner, for each subsequent row. The cords, which can also be inserted in pairs, can be drawn out of the channels far enough to avoid a double thickness when turning the hem. The ends of the cords are sewn through the lining.

Stitching in appliqué

In this technique, which is easy to carry out, the motif sections are appliquéd on a background fabric (see also page 222). These sections (flowers, leaves, figures) are padded with cotton wadding in the course of the work and are subsequently stitched over.

Monogramming

The monogram stitching technique is matched to the type and size of the article. The small monogram for a pillowcase requires a different method from the monogram covering an area on a large bedspread (photograph, on the right).

Small monogram: the position of the monogram is marked out with pins and should

Key:
Arrows denote – leave open for filling

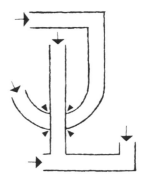

Triangles denote – end of stitching

not be smaller than $2\frac{1}{4} \times 2\frac{1}{4}$ in. (6×6 cm). The monogram is then drawn in block letters on to the fabric. When the letters are arranged to overlap and not side by side, it must be ensured that there are as few intersections as possible (this applies also to the ornamental stitching). When the pattern drawing is prepared a corresponding piece of taffeta, cotton or other firm fabric is placed under the marked part. The contours of the letters are then stitched by hand or by machine. Only the outlines of one letter (especially that of the surname) is stitched continuously; the crossing lines are interrupted at these points and must be freshly started (see the curve of the J on the drawing). The narrow ends (start and finish of the letters) must remain open so that the space between the outline stitches can be filled from the wrong side with cotton wadding rolls or cord. The basting stitches with which the lining was fastened are then removed and the ends of the letters stitched. The smaller the letters the more difficult it is to fill them. The cotton wadding is pushed in with a matchstick or a crochet hook. If it becomes trapped, it can be pushed through the lower layer with a darning needle.

Large monogram: it is advisable to measure the fabric generously since it will be reduced

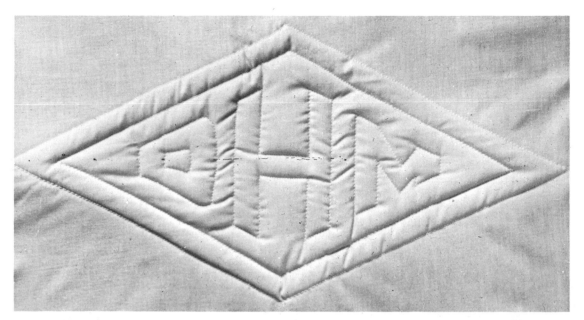

by the stitching in both length and width by about 1 in. (2·5 cm). Large running stitches are used for marking out the area for the monogram. The work is based on a design drawn to the required size on paper and positioned on the fabric, later being transferred on to bonded interlining or other light material. A piece of wadding is cut $\frac{1}{4}$ in. (6 mm) larger than the monogram surface. Upholstery material and lining (Vilene or other bonded fibre interlining) is fastened on the wrong side of the fabric in the marked position so that the monogram with the drawing is facing upwards and will not move out of position. The placing of the design must be accurate as the success of the work depends largely on this. The stitching of the letters is started in the middle of the vertical centre line and worked outwards. Do not start on the side as the work will move towards the centre and become puckered or it will no longer be in the centre. If the monogram is to be surrounded by a frame then this should be worked at the end starting from the inner line. The fabric must be held constantly tight with the hands, otherwise small folds will form. When this stage of the work has been completed the lower fabric is cut away on the outside stitched line. The padding below will be graduated so that a smooth edge is achieved.

Quilting

There is a difference between quilting following a pattern and free quilting. In the case of quilting following a pattern the top fabric has printed or woven designs, the outlines of which are traced with stitches (on the right). An interlining of $\frac{1}{8}$ in. (3 mm) thick wadding is placed between top and lining fabric. Before starting the stitching all three fabric layers must be secured with basting stiches over the whole surface lengthwise and widthwise, spaced 4 in. (10 cm) apart. If this basting is not done the quilting will not be successful as the fabric layers will slip during sewing and will stretch and pucker. The patterned fabric can be used as the lining and a self-coloured material used for the top. The outlines of the pattern are stitched on the lining side with thread such as Coats Drima to match the top fabric and an impression of a free quilting (photograph, above) pattern is obtained. Free quilting is the classical and also the most difficult technique chiefly because large areas are to be worked. Even if the

whole area is not to be quilted, it must be interlined with a padding.

The most important preparation in quilting is the tacking together of the lining, interlining and top fabrics. The softer and more pliable the top fabric the more marked is the raised design. If the lining fabric is too soft then the quilting appears more pronounced on the underside than on the decorative side. All fabric layers must be tacked together by lines of stitching, both up and down and across, which pass through all the layers. The narrower the spacing between individual tacking lines, the neater the completed work will appear. The stitching is commenced in the middle of the area or at the line nearest

Quilting to a pattern: two fabrics plain and patterned are placed wrong-sides together and the outlines of the pattern are stitched (right). The stitched outlines appear as free stitching on the plain fabric (top) which is then used as the top fabric, the patterned fabric forming the lining

250

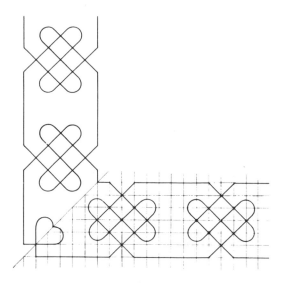

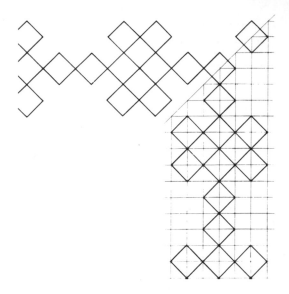

to the centre of a pattern and the work is carried on – as far as the pattern allows – towards the outer edge. When working with continuous lines (vertical, horizontal, diagonal, waves, zig-zag) special attention must be paid to uniform spacing of the lines of stitching. Any irregularities are very noticeable on a large surface. The work is simple if a sewing machine with a sliding stitching bracket is available, by means of which the spacings can be kept uniform.

The crowning glory of a quilting design is the interruption of a continuous pattern by ornamental quilting as a border or centre motif. The drawings on page 250 and above, give inspiration for rigidly stylised borders and for free designs. The motifs are transferred as described for embroidery on page 41.

These latter designs are stitched after the remaining quilting has been completed. This work is carried out as follows: the quilting stitching rows are stopped at the same level before the pattern, the work is pulled under the machine stitching foot (without cutting the yarn) and is continued under the intended motif, and similarly in rows at the same level. Subsequently the

sewing thread which runs over the motif is cut, pulled to the wrong side and firmly secured. A further improvement to the technique: the stitching of the motif outlines is stopped leaving a space of $\frac{1}{2}$ in. (1·3 cm) from the motif, and the work is continued under the motif in the same manner, so that a free space is created.

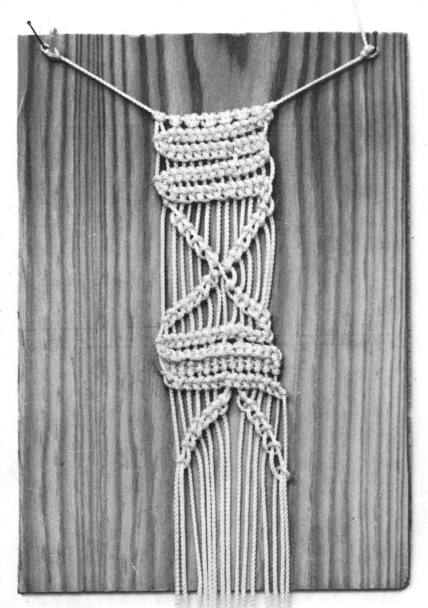

Macramé

Material
Technique

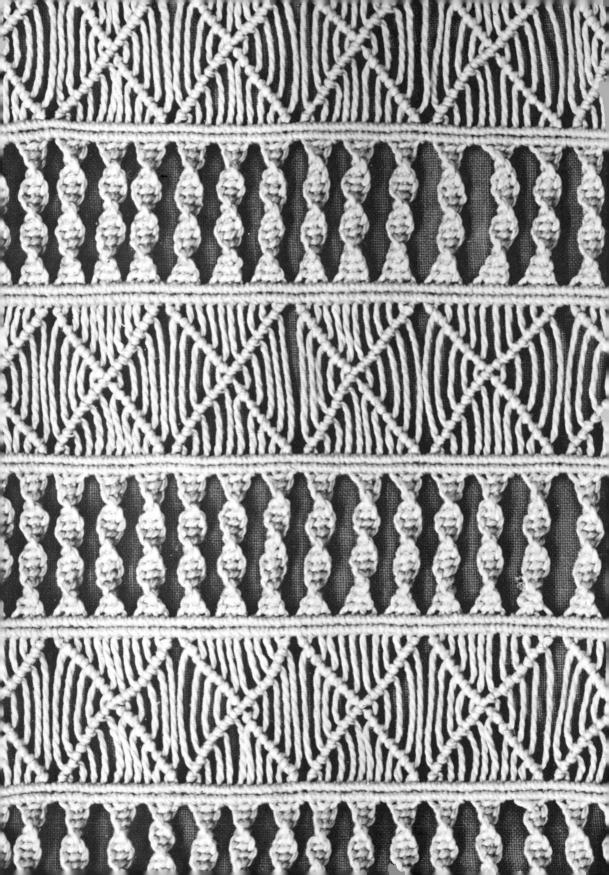

Macramé, derived from the Arabic 'mukharram' (trellis), is a relatively simple knotting technique, even though it appears complicated. It is based on a few knots which are repeated in various arrangements. The knots are: the half knot, the square knot (also called flat knot), and recognisable to most people as a simple reef knot, the horizontal, the vertical and the diagonal double half-hitches. The rib knots are all knotted around a single cord (called foundation cord), which can be mounted – independent of the position of the knots – either vertically, horizontally or diagonally. The plaited ring (page 264), called Turk's Head, and the cords made from a number of strings (page 261), known as plaiting technique, are grouped with macramé knots. The braided knots which were popular in Victorian times must also be included in this branch of handicrafts (page 261).

Various cord materials can be used for

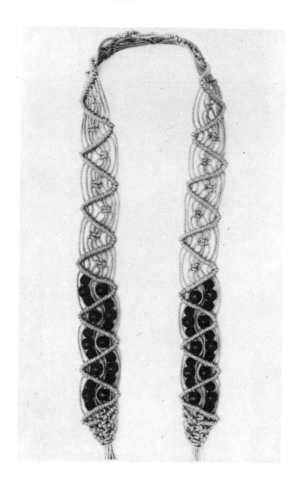

or knitting. The cords for knotting must be at least four times the length of the completed work. Since the work is based on a double cord, half the length is lost right away. The remaining excess length is more or less taken up by the knots, depending on the knotting method. The two outer cords on the right and left must have double the length of the cords which hang between them since they 'travel' across the centre ones (the knot bearers). The holding cord on which all the others are mounted must be 4 in. (10 cm) longer than the width of the completed work, and knotted at each end so that the working cords will not slip off. A holding cord is used where a flexible edging is required (belt, shopping bag); where a firm edge is needed (e.g. for a wall hanging) a cane or wooden dowel can be used. In this case the wooden strip must be $1\frac{1}{4}-2\frac{1}{2}$ in. (3–6 cm) wider than the completed work or design. Rubber bands twisted at each end prevent the cords slipping off during work.

Some kinds of knots require more cord than normal, for example the double half-hitches. The vertical double half-hitch needs twice the cord used in the horizontal double half-hitch. If such knots are to be worked, allowance must be made for this when cutting the outer cords. Extra long knotting cords can be added when doing vertical double half-hitches and the ends woven in later.

macramé. Any smooth, thick handicraft yarns are suitable. The material must be reasonably flexible, yet firm enough not to 'give' too much when the knots are tightened, otherwise the pattern will appear uneven. One of the most suitable materials is medium cotton cord (sash cord); the least suitable are cords made from synthetic materials. But any string – fillis (jute) garden twine, parcel twine or piping cord will do.

Material requirements

It is necessary to have clear idea about the size (and above all the length) of the work before you begin, because the cords cannot easily be joined to add length, as in crochet

Technique

The knotted work consists of a horizontal cord (holding cord) and vertical pairs of cords which hang from it. To start with, the holding cord can be fixed with two nails or pins on a piece of soft wall board or foam plastic. If large areas are to be worked, the

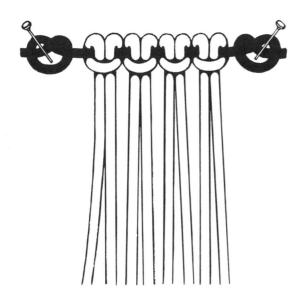

ends of the holding cord can, instead, be secured firmly by tying them around the upright struts of a chair back – extra length would need to be allowed for this, of course. It is important that this cord is kept taut throughout the work. To 'mount' a cord on the holding cord, it is first doubled, then the loop formed is passed behind the holding cord and both long ends pushed through the loop (as on knotting fringes). All the cords are lined up on the holding cord in this manner (drawing). This is called a 'lark's head' knot. The half knot is made from two neighbouring pairs of cords. The two central cords, around which the two outer ones are knotted from left and right, must be knotted at the ends and held by nails or pins. A small wooden strip can be tied horizontally to them and held down firmly with the feet. The outside right-hand cord is now taken over the central cords, the outside left-hand cord is guided over the right-hand cord, across behind the central cords and over the right-hand cord (drawing a). A row of half knots worked in this way results in a spiral (see key ring, photograph, page 261, above). The square knot consists of two half knots, one of which is knotted in the opposite direction (drawing b). In doing this the outside right-hand cord is taken behind the firmly held central cords, while the left-hand one is guided behind the end of the right-hand cord, which now hangs on the left, over the central cords, to be pushed backwards and to the right through the loop. Luckily the tying of the knot is much simpler than the description of the process, as you will find when you practice it.

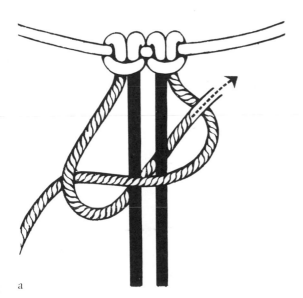

a

b

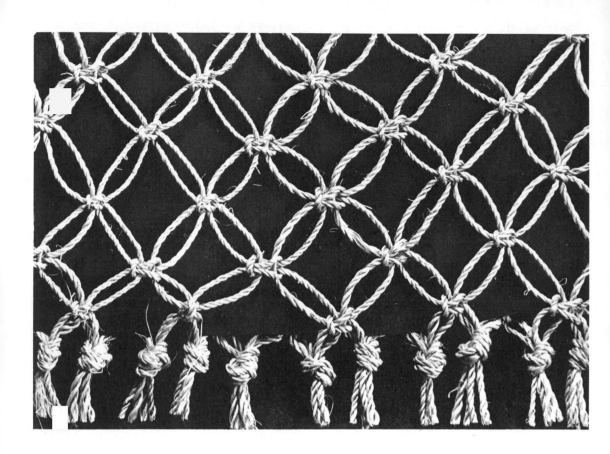

Alternating flat knot (square knot): the arrangement of the knots is clearly seen from the worked sample (left). The work is carried out as described for the square knot, with two stationary (knot-bearing) cords and two working cords. When one row is completed, the roles of each pair of cords are reversed; the knot-bearing cords are knotted while the working cords become stationary. The third row is worked as the first one, the fourth as the second, and so on. For the shopping bag (on the right), two rings are first covered with half knots and then used as the base for the knots. Slits have been left open at each side for the bag. These are formed when each half of the bag is started in forward and return rows and the cords of both halves are then knotted together and worked around with a block of foam or piece of cardboard inside as a working base. The pairs of cords are knotted together at the bottom of the net in fours with a looped knot.

The horizontal double half-hitch. The designation horizontal refers to a form of knots, not to the arrangement of the knots within a row. The double half-hitch can be arranged horizontally, vertically or diagonally; the horizontal double half-hitch will be knotted at an interval of a cord thickness to the upper row of knots (starting row). The work is carried on at the start from right to left and the outside right-hand cord is used as the knot-bearer. This cord will be placed from right to left over all other cords and held taut with a pin or nail. Then the second cord is taken from the right and guided clockwise around the horizontally held cord (c). The whole row is worked in this manner: loop next to loop. The working cord must always be pulled uniformly tight. When the row is completed, the process is repeated in the

Hammock of twisted cotton cord with ordinary flat knots, cord ends knotted and subsequently glued

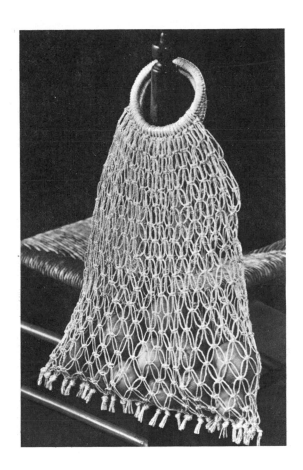

Shopping net of sisal cord in flat knot technique. The round handles form a base for knots

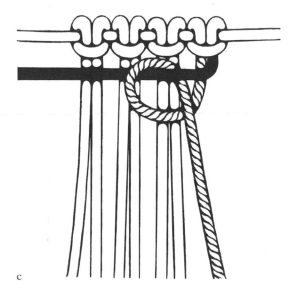

c

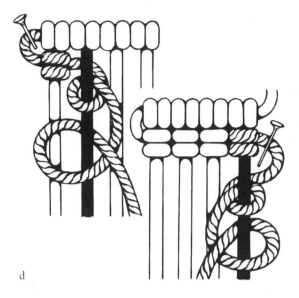

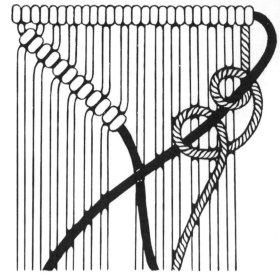

d

e

reverse direction: the outside left-hand cord now becomes the knot-bearer on which the loops of the hanging cords are arranged in anti-clockwise direction.

The vertical double half-hitch. The outermost left-hand cord is fastened under the previous row with a pin or nail. Then the cord is pulled under the next one and looped around clockwise. This knot is repeated once again (d). Each vertical ribbed knot consists of two identical loops. When the row is completed, the process is repeated in the reverse direction: the outside right-hand cord is fastened with a pin before it is looped twice around the next cord in anti-clockwise direction.

The diagonal double half-hitch. The cords are divided into two groups. The outside right-hand and the outside left-hand cord in this case are the knot-bearers. These cords will be guided from outside to the middle at an angle so that they meet there (e). They are fastened with pins so that they are pulled tight during the work. The looped knots are made in exactly the same way as for vertical double half-hitches, with the right-hand group of cords clockwise and the left-hand

group in the opposite direction.

When both groups reach the middle, the diagonal cords of the base of knots are released and a double half-hitch is made with the left cord over the right-hand cord so that an X is formed. After that these cords are fastened again in a diagonal direction and knotted around from the centre outwards to the right or to the left. The loops of both cord groups must be made in the opposite direction to those above the crossing point. The knots described up to now can be arranged in any manner, so there is a wide range of application. For example, the cords can be divided into a number of groups and knotted vertically in order to continue in a horizontal direction; they can then be divided again into other groups (from a different number of cords) and braided around. A further possibility of introducing variety is provided by the position of the knot-bearing cord. Besides being held horizontally or diagonally, it can be held in a pattern (it is not absolutely necessary to carry out working from right to left up to the outer edges of the work). A group of cords can equally well be knotted in the middle of the work in

Key holders of sisal cord. Technique: round plaiting, star knots and half knot helix (above). Below: braided knot

diagonal double half-hitches technique, while half knots in spiral form, or alternating half knots, are arranged on both the left and right-hand side of it. A ring instead of a straight cord can be worked in as a base

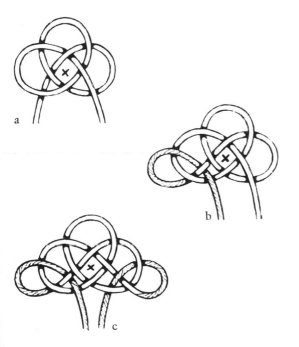

for knots when sufficient experience has been gained.

Decorative braided knots are very easy to make. The work is carried out with only one cord or string which is looped according to the drawings (a) to (c), page 261. A large loop is formed with the end which is sewn together with the start; this is covered with a small wound ring.

Circular plaiting (see keyholder) is worked with two cords which are knotted together at one end; the work is hung up before commencing. A loop is made with the left cord close behind the starting knots, the right-hand yarn is brought through, another loop is formed from this and the first loop is pulled tight. Then the first yarn is brought as a loop through the second one and this is now pulled tight. Then comes the next loop again and the work is continued as in crocheting. The two cords will have a decorative knot at the ends, for example a star knot (see photograph). On first sight the star knot appears very complicated, but it is easily learned when worked step by step. It is made from four cords, on the assumption that the previously made plaited chain was made from doubled cords (two pairs of cords).

The four cords are separately formed into a twisted loop. After that a half knot is knotted in the opposite direction with each cord around the end of the one on the left-hand side of it (page 257). The whole round is once again knotted in the same manner in the direction of the arrow on the drawing. The cord ends are guided through the middle of the knot, pulled tight and cut off short. If the knotting is to be continued with it then it is pulled through the subsequent loop upwards and left there.

The Turk's-Head is plaited with only one cord. The drawings (a) and (b) show the separate windings. The end of the cord is held between the thumb and index finger of the left hand; the cord is then placed around the three middle fingers of this hand so that the first winding points to the finger-tips and the other points to the base of the

a

b

Napkin ring in twisted hemp string. Technique:
Turk's-Head plaited with single string

fingers. It must be guided over the start held by the thumb. The cord will now be guided over the cord of the second round, under the cord of the first round and again over the cord of the second round. After that the bight (bight = bulged arc made by the cord in plaiting) of the first round is lifted over the second round and plaited on as described. The bight is now pushed under the second round and plaited as described.

The end of the cord will be pushed through under the first bight of the second round at the end of the plaiting round. The two ends of the cord are sewn together so that the sewing point vanishes under a crossing point of the plaiting, which now looks like a cable. In order to extend the cable the cords are plaited a number of times parallel to the first cycle.

Various handicraft techniques

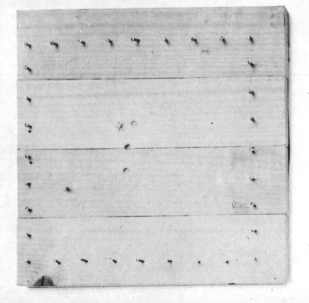

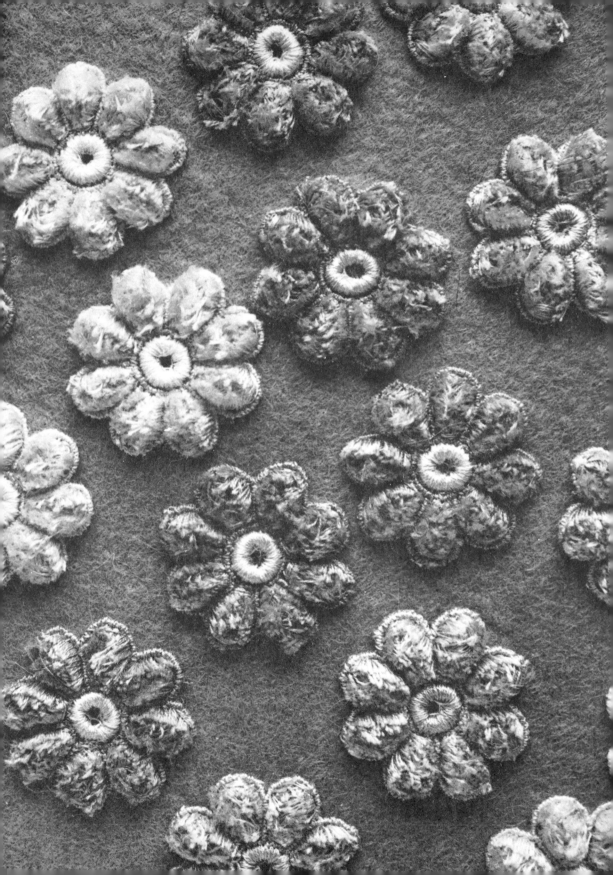

Knitting with accessories

A knitting bobbin – a small wooden cylinder – is a very simple device to use. It can be made at home or purchased from wool and handicraft shops.

To make one you will need a large empty cotton reel made of wood, a pencil and four or six brass nails with rounded heads.

Using the pencil, mark points equal distances apart round one end of the reel. With a medium-weight hammer tap the nails into place ensuring that they are quite straight.

To begin the work, pull wool or yarn through the hole at the centre of the reel and loop round the nails, going from right to left. The

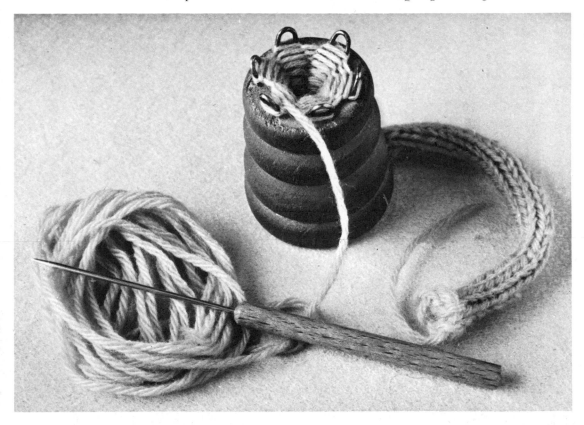

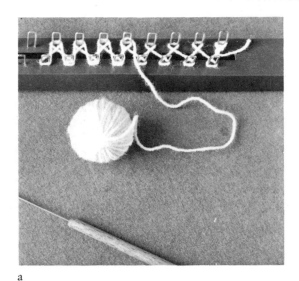

a

b

yarn is then pulled across the outside of the first looped nail and with a cable needle, knitting pin or wooden-handled pin supplied with a purchased bobbin, the looped yarn is pulled over the straight yarn and over the head of the nail. So, the first stitch is made.

Then, hold the bobbin in the left hand and let the wool flow gently through the curved fingers looping the under loop with the needle, over the new yarn and turning the bobbin round from left to right. Gradually a small tube of knitting will appear and this increases in length as the process is repeated. When the tube of circular knitting is long enough, break the working yarn, making sure to leave enough to thread into a darning needle. Pull this thread through the remaining stitches on the bobbin nails and sew securely in to the tube.

The knitting frame (above) is used exactly like the well-known knitting spool. It can be made at home from strips of wood and staples. The scarf and bag (right) were made on this frame

The same principle can be used to knit forward and return rows thus giving a flat length of knitting. The frame for this work is made from wood and 'U' staples or small nails with rounded heads fixed as in the photographs, an odd number of nails or staples facing each other in staggered rows. The frame is taken in the left hand and the beginning of the working yarn is firmly held by the index finger. With the right hand, wind the yarn round the staples or nails in a herringbone pattern as shown clearly in the

268

photograph far left. When the yarn has been wound round the last staple, it is then passed from left to right around the staples in a simple snaking movement. The working yarn is held at the end of the row with the small finger of the left hand. To begin knitting, the lower loops are lifted in the same order as they were made over the upper loops and over the staples or nail heads. That completes the first row. Work

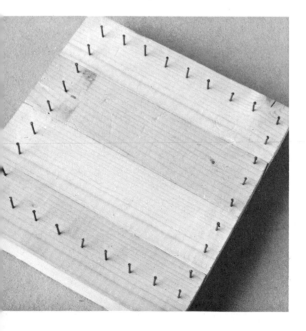

subsequent rows the same way. The complete, loosely knitted fabric will eventually emerge from the lower edge of the slot in the wood. When the required length has been produced, the last row is taken from the frame stitch by stitch, on to a knitting needle and cast off by the method shown on page 147 or with a crochet hook.

Braiding on a nail board

Mats and place mats of wool or cotton are very attractive and easily made in this way. For this a frame with nails (page 36) or a nailed board such as the one photographed on the left, is used. This can easily be made at home and like the bobbin, the nails should have smooth, rounded heads. Small brass nails are best.

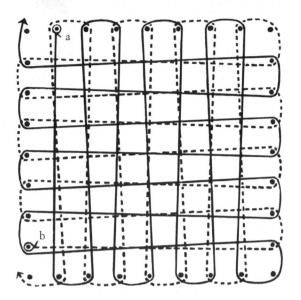

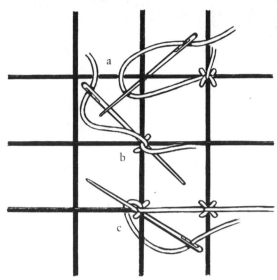

Attractive work can be made by winding yarns on a wooden board along the edge of which nails are inserted at regular intervals (photographs, below and right)

The board should be larger than the article to be made and the nails placed evenly in a square the size of the mat required. Arrange the nails as in the photograph. They

should be approximately $\frac{3}{4}$ in. (2 cm) apart and there must be an odd number of nails on each side – nine nails are shown here.

The work is carried out with two separate lengths of yarn which are wound round the nails as follows: make a loop at the end of the 'a' yarn and place over the second nail from the left in the upper horizontal row; then take the yarn straight downwards around the second and third nail of the horizontal row, then upwards around the third and fourth nails of the upper row, downwards around the fourth and fifth nails, upwards around the fifth and sixth nails, downwards around the sixth and seventh nails, upwards around the seventh and eighth nails and downwards around the eighth and ninth nails and the eighth nail of the right vertical row. The yarn is now wound in the same manner, but in a horizontal forward and return movement upwards and right and left around a pair of nails. The winding finishes at the upper left-hand corner nail, having been guided round the nail from right to left and is then left there. The 'b' working yarn is also started with a loop and this is hooked over the eighth nail of the left-hand vertical row (marked in the diagram). The yarn is wound from left to right and then upwards from right to left. For example, the yarn comes from the eighth nail at the left-hand side to the eighth nail at the right-hand side, around the seventh nail and back to the seventh and sixth nails on the left-hand side. Continue in this manner as with the 'a' yarn and the yarns will be crossing in layers.

Each yarn should be wound about ten times so that twenty layers of yarn lie on top of each other. If thicker yarn is being used, fewer layers will be needed, whereas with a fine cotton, more layers are required. The yarns are then cut off, leaving an end.

The crossing points of the yarns are now stitched with a contrasting colour and the stitching should be started at the outer edge and continue inwards around the work. A small cross stitch is made at each crossing point to the next one, shown clearly in the diagram above. The completed mat is then unhooked from the board.

A large cover can be made from four or six mats like these by crocheting the edge loops into each other by frame crochet as described on page 110, or sewn together with small cross stitches. An attractive variation can be made by cutting the top three layers of yarn between the crossing stitches after these have been made and fluffing them up to make small tufts (photograph, page 271).

Rosettes

Winding on a small circular loom will produce rosettes. These looms are called Flower Looms and are produced in the United Kingdom by H. J. Twilley Ltd. In America they are known as Daisy Winders. Soft light wool such as Twilley's Afghan wool, cotton yarn, fluffy synthetic yarns such as Patons Double Plus, or fancy luxury yarns such as Emu Candlelite or Twilley's Goldfingering are all suitable.

The circular loom as 12 pins on the outer edge and 12 on the inner edge and the outer pins are numbered. Double rosettes of one or two colours can be made up to $3\frac{1}{2}$ in. (9 cm)

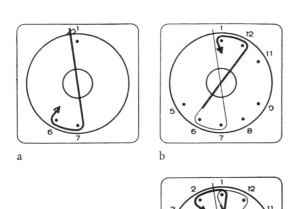

a   b

c

Crocheting over rings and cords

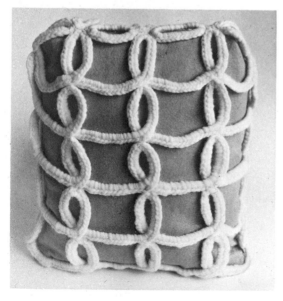

diameter or single rosettes can also be made with a diameter of $3\frac{1}{2}$ in. (9 cm) or smaller if the inner pegs are used. Fewer or more petal loops can be made according to the type and thickness of the yarn.

To wind a rosette, work with the loom on a flat surface and the first peg at the top. Begin with the outer petals and place the end of the yarn in the slit at the top. Guide the yarn downwards from peg 1 at the top and from right to left around pegs 7 and 6 (a). After that it is taken upwards at an angle around pegs 12 and 1, also from right to left (b). The work is continued in this anti-clockwise manner, with the yarn guided each time around one peg which is still free and one peg carrying a loop of yarn, i.e., first around 8, then 7, then around pegs 1 and 2 (c). Any number of rounds can be worked: the more rounds worked, the thicker the rosette. The white rosettes on the light blue christening shawl in the photograph on page 273 were made in 10 rounds of the small, inside circle of pegs. The rosette is then sewn together. To do this, leave a length of yarn about 16 in. long and thread through a tapestry needle. Take the needle to the back of the work, being careful not to split the wool, and then bring to the front. Backstitch every petal so that the backstitching makes a circle. Gently remove the rosette from the loom, pushing from the back, and neatly darn in, on the wrong side, the centre and the beginning ends. Square rosettes can also be made on Twilley's square looms.

Some unusual crochet techniques

Articles of crochet work need not be made entirely of wool, cotton or other yarns; they can be formed over core materials such as curtain rings, piping or curtain cords. In addition crochet stitches can be worked on to a backing of coarse fabric such as canvas, to achieve a completely new effect.

Crocheting over curtain rings
Small roundels which can be joined together

to form mats, curtain holders or napkin rings, or which can be sewn on as decorations, are simple to make. Each roundel requires a curtain ring of $\frac{3}{4}$ in. (18 mm) diameter and approximately $2\frac{1}{2}$ yards (2 m) of crochet yarn (cotton, wool or raffia) and a crochet hook. The curtain ring is enclosed with a ring of 18 double crochets and the round is closed with a slip stitch (see also page 68). Then make nine loops, each of three chain stitches, working one double crochet between each three chain stitches into every second stitch

of the previous round – that is, missing one stitch for every loop. Leave the end of the yarn long enough to use later for finishing.

Crocheting over cord

The most suitable core material is cotton curtain cord of medium thickness. The working process is simple. It is started with a ring of chain stitches and continued round the cord; the hook is inserted into the two

Crocheting into rug canvas (below and over page)

loops of the stitch of the previous round, the yarn is picked up and the stitches on the hook are completed over the cord. When the work is completed, the cord runs between the double crochet stitches and is completely covered (photograph, page 274). A very strong and solid circle is produced, which can be used in many ways, the individual crocheted circles being joined together to make various articles. It is, of course, also possible to work in this manner in forward and return rows, the cord being covered with crochet, and articles such as the coffee pot cosy on page 274 can be made in this way.

Crochet on canvas

Two methods are used in crocheting on to canvas. In one of them the work is carried out straight through the canvas. The working yarn is brought upwards with the crochet hook from the underside of the canvas through the fabric. The hook is re-inserted through the next square of the canvas, the yarn is brought upwards and is pulled through the stitch on the hook. Then the hook is inserted again, downwards, the yarn is brought up and the stitch on the hook is worked. The work is continued in the same manner. The thickness of the yarn and the

size of the hook used must be suitable for the weight of the canvas. The stitches must cover the foundation fabric completely. In the photograph above on the right a thinner yarn was used in order to show the method

Below and opposite: combined knitting and crochet work

of working. The correct relationship between foundation fabric and wool is seen in the photograph on the left. To achieve a fabric which can be used very well for hangings and rugs, being made up from smaller squares, the hook is not inserted straight downwards, but the fabric is bent over along the longitudinal or transverse yarn which is to be crocheted and each cross thread between two holes is counted as one stitch. The work is done in double crochet with an additional chain stitch at each corner, and is carried out in a square starting from the centre. The work acquires a slight right-hand twist which can be eliminated by damping and stretching the work (page 275).

Knitting/crochet

A special needle can be obtained for knitting and crochet without having to change over. The needle has a sharp tip at one end and a hook at the other end, while the middle section is flexible. The crochet hook can also be used for casting off stitches. The stitches must not be slipped off on changing over from crochet to knitting and, as in Tunisian crochet, they must all be held on the crochet hook. On changing from knitting to crochet, the stitches are worked off separately as is done when crocheting the last row of a piece of knitting. The two work samples above and left show a few possible patterns.

Woollen tie: seven lengths of chain stitch are placed side by side and joined together at the back with needle and yarn using weaving technique

Interwoven chain stitches

The tie on page 278 is partly crocheted and partly woven. It is made from seven rows of chain stitch which are joined to each other by forward and return rows of darning or weaving stitches. First four chain stitch chains, each 40 in. (100 cm) long are worked in dark wool and two chain stitch chains of the same length are worked in a lighter-coloured wool. After that another chain stitch chain 20 in. (50 cm) long is crocheted in dark wool. The completed chain stitch chains are placed side by side around the index finger of the left hand, so that the flat surface, showing the V stitches, is underneath and the vertical loops can be picked up separately with the needle. The colours are arranged side by side in the following order: 2 rows dark; 1 row light; 1 row short dark; 1 row light; 2 rows dark. A length of wool is then threaded through a thick darning needle and its end is invisibly darned into the chain stitch chains. No knot should be made. The adjacent horizontal loops of the chain stitch rows are now picked up with the needle, row after row. The work is carried out forwards and backwards, as in weaving or darning. When the end of the shorter chain stitch chain has been reached, the remaining chains are pushed together and the work is continued, thus making the tie narrower at one end. Care must be taken to pull the weaving thread uniformly tight, so that an even edge is obtained. The end of the yarn is fastened tightly as at the beginning, and cut off. Belts and strips for covers can be made in this way.

Raised appliqué

To make the large star-shaped wall decoration opposite, you will need an assortment of fabric scraps, preferably cotton, a piece of dark fabric roughly 14 in. (35 cm) square, a square of cardboard about $\frac{3}{4}$ in. (2 cm) smaller all round, wallpaper paste and sewing thread. The cardboard is cut into a circle, using a long-playing record as a pattern.

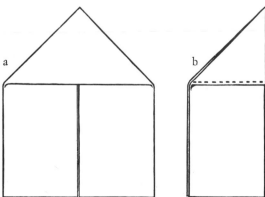

Star rosette is made up from fabric scraps on a fabric-covered cardboard base

The dark fabric is also cut into a circular shape, but $\frac{3}{4}$ in. (2 cm) wider all round, and is pasted on to the cardboard. The overhanging edge is then snipped all round, turned over to the wrong side and also pasted down. Three hundred small strips, $6 \times 1\frac{1}{2}$ in. (15 × 3 cm) are then cut from the fabric scraps and folded as shown in drawings a and b.

The small points so formed are ironed, and pinned to the cardboard in separate rounds, starting from the outer edge. Each round is stitched down by machine before the next one is pinned on. Before starting, arrange the fabric pieces in their right order on a paper disc of the same size as the finished work; this makes the final arrangement much easier.

Pile embroidery

In pile embroidery, the embroidered motifs are raised from the background fabric by cutting or looping the threads. The cut-pile effect is obtained by using a certain kind of embroidery technique which entails working over matchsticks to make small flowers or over strips of paper to make larger flowers. In the case of looped pile (shown opposite) the effect is obtained by using a special needle.

Flowers made by embroidering in close Herringbone stitch over matchsticks. The threads over the sticks are then cut open

Cut pile

The photograph on the left below shows a detail of the embroidery from the cushion next to it. The small flowers are made as follows: first the exact arrangement of the flowers is marked on the background fabric (which in this case was felt), using crossed pins pushed through the material. The work is then pierced at each crossing with a punch such as is used for cutwork embroidery (an example is shown on page 7). The holes are embroidered round with small Buttonhole stitches and a circle of stem stitch (page 51) is worked round the embroidered circle. Four crossed matchsticks are then placed over the hole in star formation. The sticks are held together in the centre by a thread, and each stick is fastened to the background material with a stitch at each end. Each stick is then over-embroidered from the edge of the hole to the tip of the stick, using closely spaced Herringbone stitches (see Shadow embroidery, page 58). Use the same number of stitches for each matchstick. Embroider over all the sticks, then start again, in the same way, embroidering closely over the first stitches but missing one stitch at the start and one at the finish of each stick (thus

if the first round gave eight stitches, the second would give six). A third round is completed in the same way, leaving off one stitch at each end, and finally a fourth round is worked. In our example only two stitches will be worked for each stick in this last round. The centre is therefore the thickest part of the embroidery. When all the embroidery has been completed, the stitches are cut through longitudinally exactly over the sticks, using sharp pointed scissors or a razor blade. The holding threads are also cut and the sticks removed. The pile thus produced is trimmed with scissors and ruffled with the needle. Finally the petal edges are outlined with closely spaced Stem stitches. In order to prevent the pile from being pulled out, the

Cushion with felt appliqué and pile embroidery in Bouclé technique

completed embroidery is placed on a soft base and a bonded fabric interlining is ironed on to the wrong side. If the pile is pressed flat, it should be covered with a damp cloth and a hot iron passed over the cloth without touching the embroidery in order to lift it again.

Boucle pile

A rug needle is used for this technique, which is best worked with a fine, soft wool (see photograph, below). The work is carried out on canvas mounted on an embroidery frame. One of the three small tubes of the rug needle, which are interchangeable, depending on the thickness of the yarn, is pushed into the hole in the handle and screwed tight. The depth of the pile depends on the length by which the tube projects from the handle of the needle, and this length can of course be varied according to the work in hand. The working yarn is pulled through the tube and out through the eye at the tip of the needle by means of the wire loop provided, until about 3–4 in. (8–10 cm) of yarn is showing. The needle is held vertically in the right hand and the sloping tip is turned towards the body. The working yarn runs outwards, away from the body. The needle is inserted into the fabric up to the stop (brass ring)

and it is pulled out again but not lifted off the fabric, otherwise the loop which has been formed on the underside will be pulled out. The embroidery follows the design drawn on to the canvas, and attention must be paid to the uniform spacing of the stitches. When the embroidery is completed, it is ironed on to a bonded fabric interlining, so that the loops cannot be pulled through. When some experience has been gained, then it is possible to use this technique on fabrics with a close weave, such as felt. However, in this case each loop must be held tight to the underside at every stitch.

Bead embroidery

Special embroidery beads are sold in small tins or tubes or by weight and the basic method of bead embroidery uses the Half Cross stitch (page 10). The work is carried out with embroidery silk. The beads are embroidered by a different method when beading initials or monograms. The initial is first drawn on to the material with a pencil and the beads are sewn on in the same direction as the letter is written. At the start of the first stroke, the needle is inserted upwards from the wrong side of the fabric, a bead is picked up and the needle is inserted

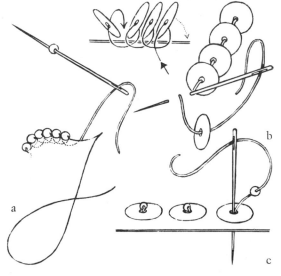

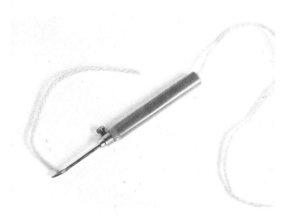

The Bouclé loops are embroidered with a special needle. The work is done from the wrong side of the work

282

again at a point the width of the bead from where it was brought out. On the underside of the work a gap, also the width of a bead, is left before the needle is brought through again. Another bead is picked up and the needle inserted directly beside the first bead. Two spaces are now left on the underside before the needle is brought through and the work continues in this way, which resembles back stitch with a bead on each stitch.

Sequins in rows or groups are embroidered in a downwards direction in individual rows, working from left to right. The drawing b shows how the sequins are taken on to the thread and how the stitches are made. Individual sequins are fastened by using an embroidery bead as a stopping device. To do this the needle is inserted from the wrong side of the fabric upwards, a sequin and a bead are picked up and the needle is inserted downwards into the same hole.

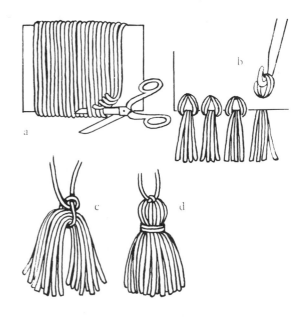

Fringes, tassels and pompons

Fringes can be made in various ways. A strip of fabric can be fringed at both ends or on all four sides by pulling out threads from each edge. Such fringes must be stitched (see page 30) so that the rest of the threads will not work loose. In handwoven fabrics the warp threads can be knotted in pairs or in small bundles. Separate fringes can be attached to machine-woven fabrics as well as to knitted and crocheted articles. To make these the yarn is wound around a board, a book or a piece of cardboard of the required width and the wound yarn is cut open on one side (a). After that, depending on the desired thickness of the fringe, the wound threads are made in bundles of two or four each, doubled and pulled through with a crochet hook as shown in the drawing b. In the case of closely woven fabrics, the fringes must be pulled through the fabric separately with a darning or embroidery needle. They can then either be knotted as in drawing b, or one half of the fringe pulled through the fabric and both ends knotted with a large loop knot. If desired the fringes can be divided and knotted to the adjacent half of the next group of fringe, as is shown in the christening shawl on page 273.

Tassels are prepared in exactly the same way as the fringes (drawing a). The cut bundle of yarn is wound in the middle with a thread; a knot is made and the long ends are left attached for sewing on the tassel (c). The bundle of yarn is then doubled over and a thread is wound around several times, as shown in drawing d. The ends of this winding thread are double-knotted and pushed into the top of the tassel.

Pompons are made in the following manner: two discs, having fair-sized holes in the centre, are cut from cardboard. The discs must be exactly the same size and the eventual size of the pompon is determined by the diameter of the discs. Wool or other yarn is wound round both discs together, until the hole in the middle is completely filled and no more yarn can be pushed through. The yarn is then cut through with sharp pointed scissors which are guided between the

Weaving with textile materials

When making rag rugs, whether by crocheting, knitting or weaving, the material used is obtained from cut up textiles. The strips can be made in two ways.

1. On the longitudinal side of a piece of fabric, a strip of $\frac{1}{2}-\frac{3}{4}$ in. (1–2 cm) wide is cut, the cut being stopped before it reaches the opposite edge of the material. The width of material left between the end of the cut and the edge of the fabric should be equal to the width of the strip. A second cut is made, starting at the opposite edge from the first one, to produce another strip of the same width parallel to the first. At the end of this second cut another piece of uncut fabric is left in exactly the same manner (see drawing, below). The work is continued in this way, cutting from alternate edges, and thus a continuous strip of fabric is obtained. The

outside edges of the two cardboard discs. The discs, which are now free, are pushed slightly apart and a length of yarn is wound tightly round the cut threads between the discs and securely tied. The long ends of the tie-thread are left hanging, so that the pompon can be attached to the finished article. The cardboard is removed and the pompon is trimmed until it is uniformly round.

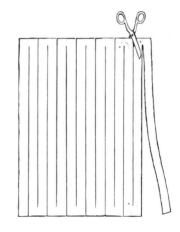

corners are rounded off afterwards.

2. The material is cut into two broad bias strips, which are joined to form a ring. This fabric ring is cut spirally to make a strip of constant width. This method has the advantage that the yarn obtained, being cut on the bias, does not fray easily and is more elastic than that produced by the first method.

Material for weaving can be made by the first method, but the bias method gives a material which is more suitable for crochet and knitting.

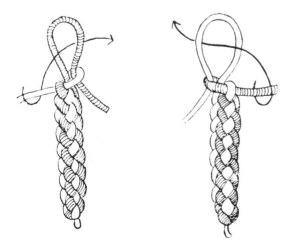

Finishing

Finishing, ironing, making up, practical hints

Embroidery

When ironing embroidery, the work is placed right side down on a very soft under-lay or folded blanket. It is covered with a damp cloth and ironed with moderate pressure on the wrong side. Cotton fabric worked with embroidery twist or pearl yarn can take heavier pressure than wool embroidery, especially when the latter is worked on woollen foundation fabric. If the embroidery has been flattened by too heavy pressure, place the work face upwards, cover it with a damp cloth and pass the hot iron to and fro just above the surface of the cloth, without actually touching it. A steam iron is also useful for this, as the flattened embroidery is lifted by steam. Do not iron canvas embroidery, Bargello or Flat Cross stitch. Instead stretch and pin the work in shape over a wet cloth, cover with another wet cloth and leave undisturbed until all three fabric layers are dry. Filet and Tulle embroidery are treated in the same way as tatting (see below).

Knitted and crochet work

When completed, knitted or crocheted articles are pinned out to shape, wrong side up, using non-rusting pins. Cover the pieces with a damp cloth and steam with a hot iron. Ribbed knitted sleeve bands, necks or edgings should not be either pinned or steamed.

Raised knitting and crochet patterns are not ironed. The pinned-out parts are covered with a damp cloth and the pins are removed only when both fabrics are dry.

Do not try to enlarge knitted or crocheted articles by excessive stretching and steaming. The attempt may be temporarily success-ful but the stitches soon shrink back to their original size.

Knitted and crocheted sections are joined after stretching and steaming. Sew them together with small back stitches, running stitches or zig-zag stitches according to the kind of work and its purpose. They can also be crocheted together. When a seam is required not to stretch, as the shoulder seam of knitted garments, it should be backed by a fabric strip. Buttonholes in knitted and crocheted articles must be finished exactly as those in fabric.

Knotted work

Knotted articles can be lined or, alternatively, they can be edged or trimmed with braid. The choice depends entirely on the purpose and on the foundation fabric used. Rugs, cushions and bags which are knotted on Smyrnafix foundation (with pairs of loops fastened on the surface, not knotted right through) do not have to be lined. Decorative wall hangings need not be lined either – regardless of which foundation fabric has been used. A hessian, burlap or cotton lining is useful for floor rugs on canvas foundation. A backing of lightweight foam material can be used to prevent rugs from slipping.
Knotted articles are shaken out after completion. Any loose fluff should be removed with a damp sponge, not with a brush.
The canvas foundation used for smaller articles (bags, cushions, chair covers) may be washed before working to make it more pliable.

Woven work

After completion woven fabrics are ironed under a damp cloth without pressure. Synthetic yarns are covered with a damp cloth and the cloth and fabric are allowed to dry out. In order to prevent the fabric from fraying at the warp ends (usually the narrower side) the warp yarns are either knotted or secured by sewing with hemming stitches (page 30). The edges can also be sewn by machine. Whichever method is used, care must be taken that the seams are not visible. If the fabric is not to be made up but used as a whole piece, for instance as a runner or cover, then the warp yarns are darned in separately

on both sides of the fabric so that they are not visible on either side. This, however, is possible only where the yarns are not too thick. It is better to use thinner weft yarns at the start and end of the weaving and to use these for seams. Knotting of the warp yarns is more of an emergency solution for beginners and should not be used except in rugs.
Handwoven fabrics made from fine yarns are treated in the same way as those made industrially. Fabrics woven from thick yarns are calculated in advance so that the selvedges can be sewn edge against edge, i.e. without folding over. Zig-zag stitches are used for this and insertions are made into the turnings of the weft yarns. Handwoven furnishing fabrics are always lined with muslin. This applies also to covers for chairs and armchairs.

Patchwork

Patchwork is ironed without pressure on the wrong side after it has been sewn together. Articles made from cotton or linen are thoroughly dampened and ironed directly onto the fabric.
All other fabrics are ironed under a damp cloth. The seams must be slightly stretched while ironing so that the whole work has a uniform tension and does not show any small puckers.
Irish patchwork is ironed on the wrong side under a damp cloth after it has been crocheted together but before the smaller patches have been appliquéd.

Appliqué

Both the appliqué sections and the background fabric are ironed before working. The completed article should not be ironed, but if the background fabric is creased then it is placed with the decorative side downwards on a very soft cloth and it is ironed lightly on the wrong side. In no circumstances must the appliqué work be ironed so heavily that its outlines show through on the wrong side, as the typical raised effect of the work will be spoiled. If this has happened in spite of all precautions then the article must be steamed as described for embroidery work.

Decorative stitching

Decorative stitching work must never be ironed and therefore great care must be taken to avoid creases during the working. In the case of quilting in which a soft interlining rests between the top and lining fabric the hot iron is clamped sole-plate upwards between two heavy objects such as bricks; or somebody can be asked to hold it firm. The work is then held taut and pulled to and fro over the surface of the iron, only the lining fabric coming into contact with the iron. When the work consists only of the top fabric and a soft lining it must be lined before it can be pulled over a hot iron as described.

Tatting

After knotting all the hanging ends the work is wetted and rolled up. For covers, cut a paper template of the outline of the finished work and place it on an ironing blanket. The tatting work is stretched and pinned with non-rusting pins to the template. The heads of the pins are inserted inwards from outside so that they lie relatively flat and are not in the way when ironing. The pins are removed after the work has cooled, when all the bows and picots on the outer edge and any waves formed by the pins are ironed out. Filet embroidery is treated in the same manner. Tatted lace for cover and handkerchief edging is secured in a longitudinal direction and ironed crossways, picot by picot, bow by

bow. The length of the edges for which the tatted lace is designed should have been accurately measured beforehand and the work must be stretched so that it will fit exactly when sewing on.

Macramé

Smaller macramé articles do not need to be treated. Larger items, such as belts, wall hangings, or mats are held over steam and stretched to shape by fastening with brass nails on a wooden board, where they are left until dry. They can also be hung up and weighted at the lower edges, but avoid this method in the case of garments, which would become mis-shapen.

Sewing methods

Hems on a table cloth are made as shown on drawings a to c. First a narrow turning is made all-round the cloth and ironed down. Then the corners are turned over and they are cut off at an angle and turned down. Make

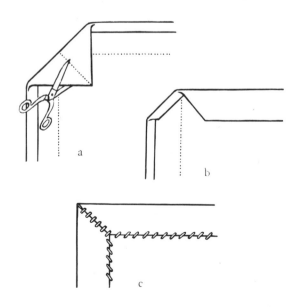

sure that the edges of the turned-over corners are parallel with the edges of the cloth, and that all corners are turned over equally.

Finally all the edges are turned over to the required hem width, so that they meet diagonally at the corners and are basted into place and hemmed. If the hem is hand-sewn only a few fabric threads should be picked up so that the stitches are not visible on the right side.

Spectacle cases: cut out the shape of the case twice from light card. These paper shapes, which serve as reinforcing inserts, are placed on the wrong side of the embroidered panels (see page 18) and tacked to them using large Herringbone or zig-zag stitches, once from top to bottom and once across. Pull the fabric tight but do not bend the paper insert. Cut a lightweight lining the same size as the embroidered fabric and slightly larger than the paper leaving a few millimetres of the seam turnover free all the way round, (otherwise the seams will be too thick). Subsequently the two halves of the case are placed with the insides together and joined from the right side, beginning at the lower short edge and using very small zig-zag stitches. The open ends are finished off with small loop stitch darning.

In principle bags are worked in the same way as spectacle cases. The interlining should be a fabric (muslin, non-woven lining material, buckram or canvas) instead of cardboard. The hems are not overcast with large stitches but they are sewn to the interlining with Herringbone stitches and the sections then sewn together to form the bag. The lining is cut out to the same pattern as the bag and the seams are joined. The lining is then inserted into the bag with the raw seam-edges to the interlining, turned in and pinned along the upper edge so that it cannot be seen from the outside of the bag, and stitched into place. The lining is then fastened at the bottom and lower corners of the bag with a few light stitches.

Cushion covers should be cut with an allowance of $\frac{3}{4}$ in. (2 cm) on all edges. The cushion covers can be made from a single, folded piece with the fold on the top or can be made from two pieces with four seamed edges. Cushion covers should always be cut out on the straight of the fabric or the diagonals will pull into folds.

A lightly hand-overcast seam at the bottom edge of the cushion makes the most unobtrusive closing. A zip fastener is more practical and it can be inserted into the seam before the other seams are made. Sew up the bottom seam and press it open. Baste the zip fastener under the seam, sew it in and carefully cut the stitches of the seam where it covers the fastener. The zip fastener is left open while the other edges are sewn up. In the case of round cushions the zip fastener is inserted across the middle of the wrong side before the fabric is cut out.

Coffee and teapot cosies consist of three layers: the top fabric, the lining and the insulating interlining of plastic foam or wadding. The fabric for the outside is cut with a seam allowance of $\frac{3}{4}$ in. (2 cm) and the interlining and lining are cut out to the same pattern but without seam allowances. Sew up the outside sections right sides together, and turn right side outwards. Sew the interlining sections together with large overcast stitches, edge to edge. Insert the interlining into the outside cover. Sew up the lining and insert with the raw edges of the interlining. Fasten all the fabric layers together in the middle at the top. Turn the lower edge of the outer cover inwards and sew neatly to the lining all round.

Dividing an area

Before starting to transfer a pattern for appliqué, quilting or embroidery the available area must be calculated exactly. In the case of a cushion cover with three seamed edges and one folded edge the allowances must be calculated only on three seams while a cushion cover made from two sections must have allowances for four seams. When the free area for the decoration has been worked out, the edges are marked with tacking stitches. It is also a help in making an exact layout to iron creases into the fabric, dividing it vertically, horizontally or diagonally.

When transferring a sketch or a design, start at the centre, matching the centre point of the design to the centre point of the fabric.

A circular decoration is marked out as shown in the drawing on the right. Join a thumb tack and a pencil with a piece of thread half the diameter of the required

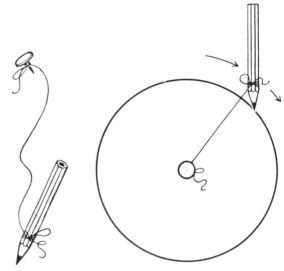

circle. The drawing pin is stuck in the middle of the fabric, which rests on a wooden board. Hold the pencil vertically and draw a circle, holding the thread taut.

Comparison of sizes of crochet hooks and numbering systems

mm.	steel (U.S.)	steel (U.K.)	aluminum or plastic (U.S.)	aluminum (U.K.)	New International numbering
0·60	14	$6\frac{1}{2}$			0·60
0·75	13	5			0·75
	12	$4\frac{1}{2}$			
1·00	11	4			1
		$3\frac{1}{2}$			
1·25	7	3			1·25
1·50	6	$2\frac{1}{2}$			1·50
1·75		2			1·75
		$1\frac{1}{2}$			
2·00	5	1		14	2
	4	1/0			
2·50	2	2/0		12	2·5
3·00	00	3/0	D or 3	11	3
3·50			E or 4	9	3·5
4·00			F or 5	8	4
4·50			G or 6	7	4·5
5·00			7	6	5
5·50			H or 8	5	5·5
6·00			I or 9	4	6
7·00			J or 10	2	7
			K or $10\frac{1}{2}$		

BRITISH	AMERICAN
single crochet	slip stitch
double crochet	single crochet
half-treble crochet	half-double crochet
treble crochet	double crochet
double-treble crochet	triple crochet
triple-treble crochet	double-triple crochet
quadruple-treble crochet	triple-triple crochet
long treble	long triple

British brandname	Description	U.S. substitute
Paton's Limelight	crepe yarn (cabled ply) of Courtelle (100% acrylic)	available in many brands
Paton's Baby QK	2-ply loosely spun nylon	Pic Yarn is polypropylene
Paton's Doublet	4-ply bulky sport yarn	widely available in wool and orlan acrylic
Paton's Double Knitting	4-ply knitting worsted	widely available in wool and orlan acrylic
Jaeger's Celtic spun	2-ply loosely spun yarn	imported to U.S. from Ireland and elsewhere (Reynolds)
Twilley's Afghan wool	2-ply rough-textured, loosely spun yarn	"Afghan wool" (Bernhard Ulmann) "rya wool" in imports from Scandinavia
Twilley's silver fingering	metallic fingering yarn	Spinnerin Entice, also other manufacturers make metallic yarns with harder texture
Twilley's mohair	thin 2-ply mohair	Spinnerin Frostlon Petite
Coat's tapisserie wool	tapestry wool; needle-point wool (4-ply)	widely available
Anchor stranded cotton	6-strand embroidery thread	widely available. Peri-Lusta from England. DMC
Anchor coton à broder	single ply, 4-strand embroidery thread (size 18)	————
Anchor soft embroidery	4-ply unmercerized cord (cotton)	not available as embroidery cotton, but is very similar to 4-ply crochet cotton (unmercerized)
Twilley's Knitcot	4-ply unmercerized crochet cotton	available. Lily Tru-tone carpet warp; Woolworth's 4-cord crochet thread
Twilley's Stalite	thick unmercerized pearl cotton (2 ply)	Lily Sugar-n-Cream cotton yarn
Anchor Pearl cotton	pearl cotton, size 5 (2-ply)	DMC coton perle, Coats and Clark, Star
Anchor Pearl cotton size 8	pearl cotton, size 8 (2-ply)	the thinner size not readily available; DMC
Twilley's Lysbet	8-cord cable mercerized crochet	Coats and Clark Speed-Cro-Sheen, Lily Double Quick
Coats Mercer Crochet (20) Paton's Mercer Crochet (10)	mercerized "big ball" crochet, size 20	widely available
Coats Chain Mercer Crochet (40)	mercerized "big ball" crochet or mercerized crochet 40	sizes 30, 40, 45 in available brands will approximate
Coats Chain Mercer Crochet (60, 80)	mercerized tatting-crochet	Coats and Clarks Tatting Crochet, size 70
Coats Drima	superspun polyester sewing thread	widely available
Emu Candlelight Paton's Turkey		

Other Supplies:

Milward Tatting Shuttles	widely available tatting shuttles Susan Bates (brandname)—metal with removable bobbin Boye (brandname)—plastic
Rug-Hooking Canvas	Emile Bernat Rug Canvas in U.S. This is brand which sells imported U.K. materials.

Large, blunt-ended needles with eyes big enough for yarn are Susan Bates: Yarn needle: Yarn End Weaver. Boye Needle Company: Stole-Weaving Needle.

Index

294

We thank the undermentioned publishers for their permission to use the following illustrations:

The Bonniers Magazine Group, Stockholm, for the coloured pictures on pages 14, 15, 42, 43, 44, 45, 48 and 49

The Jahreszeiten Verlag, Hamburg, for the photograph on page 90 from Für Sie (No. 110/70, page 80)

ICA förlaget AB, Stockholm, for 30 photographs on pages 41, 54, 55, 56, 59 and 227

We acknowledge with thanks the technical help and advice received from J. and P. Coats Limited of Glasgow, Patons and Baldwins Limited of London and Mrs H. M. McKeown of Hamilton during the compilation of this edition